# READING ECCLESIASTES
# FROM ASIA AND PASIFIKA

# INTERNATIONAL VOICES IN BIBLICAL STUDIES

General Editor
Jione Havea

Editorial Board
Jin Young Choi
Emily Colgan
Musa Dube
Julián Andrés González
David Joy
Gerald O. West

Number 10

# READING ECCLESIASTES FROM ASIA AND PASIFIKA

Edited by
Jione Havea and Peter H. W. Lau

Atlanta

Copyright © 2020 by SBL Press

All rights reserved. No part of this work may be reproduced or transmitted in any form or by any means, electronic or mechanical, including photocopying and recording, or by means of any information storage or retrieval system, except as may be expressly permitted by the 1976 Copyright Act or in writing from the publisher. Requests for permission should be addressed in writing to the Rights and Permissions Office, SBL Press, 825 Houston Mill Road, Atlanta, GA 30329 USA.

Library of Congress Control Number: 2020935135

## Contents

Preface .................................................................................................. vii

Abbreviations ........................................................................................ ix

Context Matters: Reading from Asia and Pasifika
    Jione Havea and Peter H. W. Lau ............................................................ 1

Wisdom of Waiz: Rereading Ecclesiastes 1:17–18 in Pakistan
    Sarah W. Ayub ................................................................................... 13

Toil(ing) in Two Cultures: An Australian-Samoan Reading of
    Ecclesiastes 2:18–23
    Brian Fiu Kolia ................................................................................. 29

Qoheleth Silences Women: Rereading Ecclesiastes 2:25–26, 4:1, 7:26, and 28
    from India
    Laila Vijayan ................................................................................... 43

Toiling with Qoheleth for Pasifika, Papua, and Palestine: Reading Eccl 3:9–13
    with 7:13–18
    Jione Havea ..................................................................................... 53

Justice in Ecclesiastes (3:16–4:3 and 8:10–17): A Missional Reading from and
    for Palestine
    Anton Deik ...................................................................................... 69

Sophia, Untameable like Moana: An Oceanic Reading of Sirach 24 with Ecclesiastes 7:10–12
    Mariana Waqa ................................................................................... 85

Understanding Ecclesiastes 7:15–18 through the Lens of Zhuangzi's Perspectivism
Clement Tsz Ming Tong ..............................................................................99

"She Is More Bitter Than Death": Reading Ecclesiastes 7:23–8:1 as an Asian Chinese
Elaine W. F. Goh ......................................................................................115

A Reading of Ecclesiastes 8:1–9 in Malaysia
Peter H. W. Lau .......................................................................................127

Fishing / Exile for Meaning: A *Fakahē* Reading of Ecclesiastes 8:1–17
Tauʻalofa Angaʻaelangi ............................................................................141

A Time to Judge: Seeking Justice with Qoheleth and Ancient Tamil Wisdom
D. Gnanaraj .............................................................................................153

Reading Ecclesiastes in the Light of Tamil Sangam Literature
M. Alroy Mascrenghe ..............................................................................171

A Comparative Analysis of the Philosophies of Qoheleth and Chuang-tzu: Shared Themes in Wisdom Literature and Taoist Philosophy
Sehee Kim ................................................................................................185

Contributors .................................................................................................199

Scripture Index ............................................................................................201

# PREFACE

The life of this collection began under trees and in corridors during the breaks of the 2015 meeting of the Oceania Biblical Studies Association (OBSA) at Piula, Samoa, and the 2016 joint meeting of the Society of Asian Biblical Studies (SABS) with the Society of Biblical Literature (International SBL) at Seoul, South Korea. Several of the contributors were at those gatherings and others joined as we began the long journey of submission, revision, and editing.

After an opening chapter on contextual biblical interpretation, the essays follow the order of the Ecclesiastes texts under study, with the last three essays reading the whole book crosstextually with Asian scriptures and philosophies. Unless noted otherwise, *Qoheleth* is used in the following essays to refer to the author or speaker, and *Ecclesiastes* to the text or book.

This collection follows upon another IVBS collection, *Reading Ruth in Asia* (2015), with new twists: other scriptures are engaged; Asia opens up to Palestine and Pakistan; and Pasifika comes not as the ignored tail of the Asia-Pacific region. In this collection, Asia and Pasifika are collectives in the *Moana* (a native Pasifika name for the sea that links us all).

This collection, also, is an invitation for more readings and more twists from within and beyond Asia and Pasifika.

# ABBREVIATIONS

| | |
|---|---|
| AB | Anchor Bible |
| BDB | Brown, Francis, with S. R. Driver and Charles A. Briggs. 1996. *The Brown, Driver, Briggs Hebrew and English Lexicon: With an Appendix Containing the Biblical Aramaic; Coded with the Numbering System from Strong's Exhaustive Concordance of the Bible*. Peabody, MA: Hendrickson Publishers. |
| BECNT | Baker Exegetical Commentary on the New Testament |
| BHS | *Biblia Hebraica Stuttgartensia*. 2012. Edited by Karl Elliger. Stuttgart: Deutsche Bibelgesellschaft. |
| *Bib* | *Biblica* |
| *BibInt* | *Biblical Interpretation* |
| *CBQ* | *Catholic Biblical Quarterly* |
| CC | Continental Commentary |
| ESV | English Standard Version |
| *HUCA* | *Hebrew Union College Annual* |
| IBC | Interpretation: A Bible Commentary for Teaching and Preaching |
| ICC | International Critical Commentary |
| ITC | International Theological Commentary |
| *JBL* | *Journal of Biblical Literature* |
| JESHO | Journal of the Economic and Social History of the Orient |
| *JSOT* | *Journal for the Study of the Old Testament* |
| JSOTSup | Journal for the Study of the Old Testament Supplement Series |
| *JTI* | *Journal of Theological Interpretation* |
| KJV | King James Version |
| LHBOTS | Library of Hebrew Bible/Old Testament Studies |
| MT | Masoretic Text |
| NAB | New American Bible |
| NEB | New English Bible |
| NICOT | New International Commentary on the Old Testament |
| NIV | New International Version |
| NJPS | New Jewish Publication Society Tanakh |

## Abbreviations

| | |
|---|---|
| NRSV | New Revised Standard Version |
| OBSA | Oceania Biblical Studies Association |
| SABS | Society of Asian Biblical Studies |
| SCS | Septuagint and Cognate Studies Series |
| SemeiaSt | Semeia Studies |
| SR | Studies in Religion |
| *TDOT* | Botterweck, G. Johannes, Helmer Ringgren, and Heinz-Josef Fabry, eds. 1974–2006. *Theological Dictionary of the Old Testament*. Translated by John T. Willis et al. 15 vols. Grand Rapids: Eerdmans. |
| WBC | Word Biblical Commentary |

# CONTEXT MATTERS:
## READING FROM ASIA AND PASIFIKA

Jione Havea and Peter H. W. Lau

We extend Qoheleth's question in Eccl 3:9 to the toils of biblical critics: is there gain in reading? We (hereafter, our "we" includes those who come along without needing to agree with all of our reasoning) respond in the affirmative: yes, biblical critics have something to gain from reading. Some readings (including some of our own) are more vain than others, but the task of reading is not total vanity. What we gain varies—we gain joy, pleasure, enlightenment, pain, frustration, confusion, and even despair—but gain we certainly achieve. Our affirmative response is therefore not only with respect to the (utilitarian) fruits of reading, but also with (optimistic) respect to the process of reading. By design as well as by accident, the process of reading is gainful. In this affirmation we take the process of reading as an intentional (there is something to gain) rather than a revelational (there is something to receive) exercise. Reading is political.

Under the sun, reading is unending for though "words are wearisome ... the eye [of readers] is not satisfied with seeing or the ear filled with hearing" (Eccl 1:8). Reading that rises out of dissatisfaction is restless. A generation comes, and round and round go the wind of change, pushing streams of consciousness into, without filling, the sea of readings (cf. Eccl 1:4–7). As such, the toil of readers is ongoing and unending. In fact, reading needs to be restless because no one is "like the wise person and who knows the interpretation of a matter/word" (Eccl 8:1). Like "the sun [which] rises and ... goes down, and hurries to the place where it [will again] rise" (Eccl 1:5), readers from different parts of the world return, again and again, to the same texts because we have something to gain from our toils. Indeed, we return to the texts that others have read before because we are not satisfied, we are restless, and we expect to gain something from reading (toiling) for ourselves.

To give a sense of what one might gain from this collection of essays, bearing in mind that gaining or losing is a matter of judgment (what is seen as gain by one reader may be seen as loss by another), we reflect on three assumptions that shape our toil with biblical texts and in the process locate the essays in this collection as well as past readings of Ecclesiastes in the linked region of Asia and Pasifika:[1]

- Texts are responses;
- Interpretations are contextual;
- Contextual interpretations hold texts open.

## Texts Are Responses

We read texts as *responses to something*—such as other texts, stories, events, episodes, dreams, revelations, conversations, and so forth. Texts are both evidences of and instruments for being connected or for violating connections (as fake news does in the so-called posttruth age), and so it is difficult to conceive of a text that started as prime mover or original. We here again borrow the words of Qoheleth, "there is nothing new under the sun" (Eccl 1:9c). We do not deny that there are prime, foundational, and original movers, but we maintain that texts, especially scriptural texts, are not among those. Texts are responses (or n+1) rather than originals.[2] In this respect, texts are transition-points between something (n or ground zero) and the next-something. Therefore, to revoke a theological illusion, no text is *ex nihilo* (out of nothing).

Responses come in many shapes and temperaments. Some responses affirm and endorse, some challenge and resist, some ridicule and reject, some rewrite and unravel, some sidestep and ignore, and some offer a different mix of the abovementioned responses. To again appropriate Qoheleth, there is a response for everything under the heavens, and a time for every text (cf. Eccl 3:1). Add interpreters and interpretations to this range, and we have a ripple (or spiral): texts are responses to something, and interpretations are responses to texts (see the next section) and to lived joys and anxieties.

We acknowledge, we must confess, that our views are influenced by the relational cultures of (but not unique to) Asia and Pasifika. We live because of and for relations (which involves responsibilities or *tautua*, see Brian Fiu Kolia, in this collection), and so we imagine texts and interpretations to be drifts in the ripple of relations between individuals, creatures, and nations (see Sarah W. Ayub, in this collection). We conceive this ripple in relation to "talanoa," a word in several native Pasifika languages that refers to the (three in one) triad of *story, telling*, and

---

[1] We refer to our region as "Asia and Pasifika" instead of the hyphenated "Asia-Pacific" out of respect to the many differences within as well as between Asia and Pasifika and also because Pasifika is often disregarded and belittled in conversations about Asia-Pasifika. While there are more Asian contributors in this collection, we have some restless Pasifika contributors as well.

[2] Shifting to a related platform, it is unfair to expect what we sometimes demand of students—to be original, as if there is something new under the sun.

*conversation* (see Havea 2013). In the world of talanoa, a *story* (talanoa) dies without someone *telling* (talanoa) it and holding *conversation* (talanoa) around it; a *telling* (talanoa) is an occasion for taking control (or telling off) when the teller does not respect the *story* (talanoa) or give room for *conversation* (talanoa); and a *conversation* (talanoa) is empty without a *story* (talanoa) and someone *telling* (talanoa) it. In talanoa cultures, there is no separation between story, telling, and conversation. Our invitation to read texts as responses comes with the vibes of talanoa; we treat texts as (at once) story, telling, conversation. We also invite readers to treat this collection of essays as talanoa, with proper respect due to Qoheleth for bringing many insights—as "goads" and "nails"—from different wisdom settings into one collection (cf. Eccl 12:9–11).

Texts are not like the Niua Fo'ou (an island at the north of the Tonga islands) native grub *'ofato*, which live in and bore through decomposed logs but do not cross each other's path.[3] Compared to the *'ofato*, texts (responses, talanoa) step into the paths of other texts, other stories, other events, and other somethings. We may not know exactly to what texts are responding, but seeing texts as responses is inviting—it invites readers to enter the text's ripple of relations and to even make the text jump through the covers of the book. Indeed, reading involves making texts jump out of (in most cases) the black marks on white leaves and screens.

Reading texts as responses affirms that texts are purposeful and contextual, silently waiting to tell something to querying eyes. We take texts that reveal something about distant beings (divine or otherwise) or future events as responses as well. They are responses to the need of the transcendent or distant to be known and/or the need of humans to know someone or something that is hidden, absent and/or yet to arrive.[4] But texts do not speak on their own (cf. Spivak 1988). Interpreters make texts speak in different contexts, and being able to do so is part of the gain in reading (toiling). Put another way, interpreters put texts upon the waters and expect that after many days they will get the texts back with much *interests* (in the ideological, "fruit of labor" or investment senses; cf. Eccl 11:1).

---

[3] Natives say that if a grub is visible to other grubs, it will die. The *'ofato* has thus become a figure for neighbors who do not get along or who do not help one another.

[4] Texts could be responses to fleeting memories, irritating customs, life situations, material representations, imagined realities, and even to business narratives (see, e.g., Denning 2005). Some intertextual and contrapuntal critics justify their reading habits with the assertion that "no text is an island," which makes sense to readers who romanticize what it means to be islanders and who do not know what it means to live and survive on islands. Out of respect to islands and islanders, we prefer some other expression like "no text is unoccupied," "no text is network free," "no text is self-satisfying," or something along those lines.

## Interpretations are Contextual

Claiming that *all interpretations are contextual* is common and even unchallenged nowadays, as the members of the "Crossing Borders: Biblical Studies from the Four Corners of the World" panel at the opening event of the 2016 international meeting of the Society of Biblical Literature at Seoul (South Korea) showed. Contextual biblical interpretation is alive and well both in the global north and in the global south; contextual biblical interpretation is not limited to only one or two, but to all four, corners of the world. One finds similar affirmation in two publications that review the past, present, and future of biblical studies (see Boer and Segovia 2012; Liew 2018). Contextual biblical interpretation is here to stay, notwithstanding that there is no consensus on what it involves and what it entails.

Interpretations are the fruits of reading (toiling), and they are unavoidably ideological and political. Interpretations are conditioned by the roots, agendas, orientations, and insecurities of the interpreters, and consequently no interpretation is free of subjectivity. No interpretation is free of context or is innocent; no reading is free of adding meaning to the text. As Rudolf Bultmann and many others have concluded, no interpreter is free of presuppositions, and we add, to paraphrase José S. Croatto, exegesis is always already eisegesis (Croatto 1981, 1–4). Put simply, all interpretations are contexted (rooted in particular contexts; see Havea 2013).

Because interpretations are contexted, no interpretation has universal relevance. This is a motivating conviction for this collection: many western and northern readings do not speak to us in Asia and Pasifika, so we need to read Ecclesiastes for ourselves. And we share our readings beyond the borders of Asia and Pasifika because we expect that they will make sense to others beyond our shores. Yet, the fact that our readings are contexted means that they will not make sense to everyone. So the underside of the motivation for this collection is humbling: like the dominant and the orientalist readings, our readings from Asia and Pasifika do not have universal relevance. And to be fair, there are more to Asia and Pasifika than are presented in this collection of essays. We do not pretend to be universal or to be totalizing of our region. The fruits of our reading (toiling) will not appeal to all readers (workers), near and far, in the field of biblical interpretation.

Our claim is simple, in three steps: interpreters are all contexted, and all interpretations are contextual but in different ways. As we indicated above, there are various ways of doing contextual biblical interpretation. Evident in this collection of essays are three general approaches to doing contextual biblical interpretation.

## Approaches

First, the dominant approach to contextual biblical interpretation is where the interpreter explains what a biblical text means for and/or how it applies to a context. The interpreter may use a word, concept, practice, or text from the local context to enable the explanation and application to happen. All of the contributors to this collection show some evidence of this approach, but they differ with respect to context and agenda. And when different contributors reflect on the same text, they reach different interpretations. This is expected, for context matters in the toiling of interpreters *and* interpreters read from and for different contexts.

A few scholars have used this approach previously to read Ecclesiastes. Emanuel Gerrit Singgih (2001) published a commentary on Ecclesiastes in Indonesian (English translation: "Living under the Shadows of Death: An Interpretation of the Book of Ecclesiastes") using a combination of Western interpretive methods (historical- and literary-critical) and applied it to the Indonesian context. K. Jesurathnam (2011) summarized elements of social justice in the wisdom books, then applied them to God's mission among the marginalized Dalit community in India. Elaine Goh has presented three readings of passages from Ecclesiastes from an Asian perspective. Goh (2016a) read Ecclesiastes (3:16–17; 4:1–3; and 10:16–20) from a political perspective, keeping in mind the original ancient Near Eastern context as well as the Malaysian context. Peter H. W. Lau's chapter in this collection can be viewed as a complement to Goh's reading, since it focuses on another passage in Ecclesiastes with political overtones (8:1–9). Goh (2017) also read Ecclesiastes (3:1–15; 7:15–22; and 11:1–6) within the context of salvation history from the Old Testament through to the New Testament. She also suggested some implications of Ecclesiastes' view of time, righteousness, and human ignorance for a Christian audience in an Asian Chinese context. Finally, Goh (2016b) applied Eccl 3:16–17 to the Malaysian court ruling that banned the use of the name "Allah" in Christian publications.

We make special mention here of the contribution by Anton Deik in this collection because it brings attention to the occupied and overlooked context of Palestine, the homeland of the Bible, as well as gives us an opportunity (in the ripple of the late Palestinian thinker Edward Said's critique of orientalism [see Said 2003], coined from a label associated with our region—the Orient) to welcome Palestine as a part of Asia. Because Palestine continues to suffer under the politics of orientalism, we see Palestine in the shadows of the Orient (extended in this work to Asia and Pasifika) where many lands are still under occupation (see Jione Havea in this collection).

One of the challenges with this approach to biblical contextual interpretation is that it permits interpreters to privilege the (foreign) biblical text over against the (local, native, indigenous) context, so that one's interpretation (toiling) could become a colonizing exercise. As in the missionary era, cultural (mis)appropriation is a potential: the contextual biblical interpreter is tempted to submit the context (and whatever local concept and wisdom one uses to contextualize the text) to the authority of the text. This is a challenge for all biblical interpreters (see also Havea 2011), and it helps to be reminded that the fruits of interpretation could constrain (see Laila Vijayan in this collection), suppress (see Peter H. W. Lau in this collection), exile (see Tauʻalofa Angaʻaelangi in this collection) and colonize (see Anton Deik in this collection).

A second approach to contextual biblical interpretation involves intertextual, contrapuntal, and cross-scriptural reading. This has been a relatively popular approach to interpreting Ecclesiastes. For instance, Peter K. H. Lee (1987) read Ecclesiastes in light of the eleventh century CE poetry of Su Ting-P'o, and R. Christopher Heard (1996) read Ecclesiastes intertextually with the popular Chinese classic text *Dao de Jing* (ca. sixth century BCE). John Jarick (2000) used concepts from the Chinese "Book of Changes," the *I Ching*, to read Ecclesiastes, and Graham S. Ogden (2007) discussed the intersections between Chinese wisdom literature and Ecclesiastes, although he did not apply this approach in the body of his commentary. A more sustained cross-textual reading was provided by Jayādvaita Swami (2015), who placed Ecclesiastes in dialogue with the Bhagavad-gītā (from the Hindu epic poem the Mahābhārata). Finally, Seree Lorgunpai (2016) used categories from Thai Buddhism, Wei Huang (2009) interpreted *hʻlm* through a Chinese Buddhist perspective, Huang (2018) provided a cross-textual reading of Ecclesiastes with the Chinese Buddhist text *Heart Sutra* (ca. seventh century CE), and Goh (2019) read Ecclesiastes cross-textually with the *Analects*.

While intertextual and contrapuntal readings are common in the worldwide web of biblical studies, given the advances in literary and postcolonial criticisms, cross-scriptural reading is a significant contribution of this collection especially with respect to Chinese (see Clement Tsz Ming Tong, Elaine W. F. Goh, and Sehee Kim in this collection) and Tamil (see D. Gnanaraj and M. Alroy Mascrenghe, in this collection) literature. Asia is a hotspot for cross-scriptural reading, and these authors avoid submitting the Asian literature under the authority of the biblical text (even though one could argue that the Bible too is Asian scripture). In general, the leaning of these authors is to read Ecclesiastes in the lights of Asian literature (as opposed to using Asian literature as illustrations for the biblical text).

The attention of the contributors is not confined to written texts. There are engagements with oral cultures as well (see Brian Fiu Kolia and Mariana Waqa, in this collection). As a collective, the contributors do not parade the ghosts of nativism (e.g., that only Chinese scholars could write on Chinese literature) or fall into the trap of exoticization. There are sharp criticisms of cultural (e.g., Kolia), ecclesial (e.g., Angaʻaelangi) and scriptural (e.g., Vijayan) heritages and bearings.

A third approach to contextual biblical interpretation involves affirming *by* unraveling, talking or pushing back at, the biblical text(s). For instance, Choan-Seng Song (1999) read Eccl 3:1–8 from the perspective of the marginalized *burakumin* in Japan. Instead of resignation as the response, he follows a 1922 *burakumin* manifesto in calling for change in Japan, to right previous wrongs, and to "build a society of justice and love" (92).

In this volume this approach is used differently by Kolia (from a diasporic situation) as compared to Havea (who problematizes the so-called final form of the text). Both readers push back at the biblical text(s), but neither one rejects or walks away from the bible.

To push back at the biblical text(s) or biblical tradition(s) is not encouraged in scholarships that discuss the reception of the bible or among readers who toil within scholarly or faith communities. In light of the latter, it is noteworthy that while several of the contributors write from within faith communities and commitments, including Kolia and Havea, they do not shy away from making critical observations (on gender discrimination, see Vijayan, and on the government, see Lau, Ayub, and Anga'aelangi) relating to Ecclesiastes. Reading within academic or faith communities is not an excuse to be uncritical about both the Bible and one's context.

Biases

Contextual biblical interpretation has received unfair (unwritten) critiques, in our humble opinion, around the issues of methodology and politics. At this juncture, we offer two observations on how this collection may respond to such critiques.

First, on methodology. No matter how one approaches or does contextual biblical interpretation, it is not appreciated alongside the two clusters of mainline methods of biblical criticism—literary and historical criticisms. The preference (read: bias) for the mainline methods is alive and strong in, for example, the operations of the Society of Biblical Literature, the foremost international association of biblical scholars. When the gatekeepers of the mainline methods serve on steering committees and editorial boards and they are rigid about proper (i.e., mainline, traditional) methodology, the inspirations among self-proclaimed contextual critics are quickly extinguished. The upshots are, on the one hand, that the number of underrepresented and minoritized biblical scholars grows, and, on the other hand, that the number of minority biblical scholars who put on, love, and defend Franz Fanon's metaphorical white mask increases even more. In these scenarios, the general assumption is that contextual biblical scholars do not (know how to) do the mainline or proper methods of biblical criticism.

To the contrary, all of the essays in this openly contextual collection use some version of the mainline or proper methods to biblical criticism (see esp. Lau and Kim). In our experience, we find contextual biblical critics using mainline methods (to look *behind* and *into* the text) whereas mainline biblical critics do not wander into the fields of contextual interpretation (to look *in front of* the text). The problem therefore is not with contextual biblical critics but with the strictly mainline biblical critics. We offer this observation as our push back at critics who assume that if one does contextual reading then one does not use the traditional and scholarly methods. In fact, all of the essays in this collection make use of historical, literary, and cultural criticisms, but not in a rigid manner.

Taking a step back, we admit that the reverse is also true: Society of Biblical Literature groups and publication ventures that are intentional about experimental and contextual works hesitate to consider proposals that exhibit full-fledged mainline methodologies, or, at the other extreme, they are selective about which contexts to engage. So proposals relating to Palestine or Pakistan (see Ayub and Deik in this collection), for example, are refused more easily as compared to proposals relating to less controversial contexts. Unfortunately, cultural and academic politics play a role in the decisions which committees and boards that are supposed to be contextual and experimental make.

There are two facets we wish to stress here with respect to methodology: the first facet is that pitting historical and literary criticisms over against contextual biblical interpretation is unfair because these are not blockaded from each other. One does not defile the discipline by adding contextual interpretation to one's literary and/or historical reading. And one's contextual interpretation is shallow without literary and historical readings as well. The second facet is that methodology has been used to erect a political arena so that, in other words, what happens in the reading room overflows into the board room. In this regard, what's important in Qoheleth's question "Who knows the interpretation of a matter?" (Eccl 8:1) is not the interpretation reached (whether it is valid or not, sound or otherwise) but *who* knows the interpretation, which is determined by *how* (method) one knows. This is the main reason why readers from alternative reading rooms do not get a proper hearing in the board room (the world of *who's who*).

The foregoing brings us to our second observation, on the upshot of interpretation. There is a strong element of advocacy in this collection, for example, for the migrants and exiled (Kolia, Anga'aelangi), women (Vijayan, Waqa, Goh), climate victims (Havea), Palestine and Palestinians (Deik), Pakistan and its diverse people (Ayub), West Papua (Havea), the wisdom cultures of Oceania (Waqa), China (Tong, Goh, Kim) and Tamil (Gnanaraj, Mascrenghe), and the operations of governments (Lau, Anga'aelangi). In the lights of this collection, we are therefore inclined to portray contextual biblical interpretation as *naturally* leading to advocacy. Readers who sit on the sideline are not contextual enough.

In addition to the proverbial reading and board rooms, the contextual biblical interpreter is also concerned with what happens outside the gates of the academy and of the faith communities. Because this is one of the reasons why contextual biblical interpretation is not considered to be academic enough (in terms of Antonio Gramsci's understanding of "traditional intellectual"), the cost of advocacy (which Gramsci's "organic intellectuals" do) to one's academic career should be taken seriously (see further Gramsci 1971, 9). But also, the place of advocacy and organic approaches to biblical criticism need also to be highlighted, as foundations upon which contextual biblical interpretation stands. We are thinking of the advocacy undertaken in the works of traditioned scholars like Julius Wellhausen (for the later priestly agenda), Martin Noth (for traditions that shape scripture), Norman Gottwald (for the Canaanites), Phyllis Trible (for victims of texts of terror), Elisabeth Schüssler Fiorenza (for the feminist cause), and several others. Each of these examples need further explaining, but the point we want to make here is straightforward: advocacy and organic intellectuals are not an abomination in the history of biblical criticism.

So What?

We accept that we will not all agree on *how* to do contextual reading, in part because so much is (pre)determined by what we bring to the text as readers. We are thinking especially of how we view the Bible text, especially its authority in relation to context, and other written texts. But we can all still learn from each other's readings, the different insights that we bring into the text, and how we might live in response. We do not seek in this reflection to give a blueprint on how to do, or what passes as, contextual biblical interpretation. We leave that for the masters.

Our affirmation is straightforward: we all do contextual biblical interpretation but differently, and we need to learn from one another. And we bow out to the caution of Qoheleth: "Of making many books there is no end, and much study is a weariness of the flesh" (Eccl 12:12b).

## Interpretations Hold Texts Open

Even though the scriptures of Jewish and Christian communities are closed, so no new texts could be added, we argue that *interpretations open the canon up*. This is not such a controversial claim because we find several attempts within the canons to open things up, for example, the legal revisions in Exodus-Deuteronomy; the rewriting of history in Samuel-Kings and 1–2 Chronicles; the addition to and movement of books between the covers of the Hebrew, Catholic, and Orthodox canons; the multiple accounting in the gospels; and the multiplying teachings in the epistles. That is, the energy to pop open is within the compositions of canons (see also Adams 2019). The number and wording of the books in the canons may be closed, but intratextual references, appeals, and contestings bubble within to pop the lids of the canons, and the toiling of interpreters open canons up by adding layers of meanings as well as by shifting and (re)situating meanings from and into new contexts.

Contextual readings open texts up and shift meanings from and toward new contexts, the kinds of move expected of faithful exegetes. One might consequently argue that the reader who opens the text up and shifts meanings around is *reading properly* and is at once *appropriately contextual*. We bring this assumption to Eccl 3:9–13.[5]

Three popular and traditional readings of Ecclesiastes lurk behind the reading of Eccl 3:9–13 that we propose here: (1) everything is vanity; (2) there is a time for gaining and a time for losing, for pulling down and for building up, (3) so the best thing to do is to enjoy (the gains of) life under the sun. The lot of humans is to enjoy and be at leisure, for we have no control over life which is in fact fleeting. In the eyes of these mainline readings, humans ought to relax, lay back, and accept what happens; in other words, in the romanticizing eyes of tourist minds, humans should seek to be like islanders.

Pete Seeger's 1965 song "turn, turn, turn" performed by *The Byrds* extends Ecclesiastes to the preference for love and peace. Seeger was an activist and his song drew upon Ecclesiastes to make his call for ecological responsibility and for peace. The chorus comes out as a call for repentance and transformation with the repeated call to *turn, turn, turn*. There is a season for everything—*turn, turn, turn*; and there is a time for every purpose under the sun—*turn, turn, turn*. The third verse opens and pushes the texts of Ecclesiastes to the war-ridden days of the 60s:

> A time of love, a time of hate
> A time of war, a time of peace

Seeger opens Ecclesiastes up and shifts it toward one of the struggles of his time—to end war and to embrace peace. Opening the text up through interpretation is not a privilege of biblical scholars only. Like trained biblical scholars, Seeger too gained a lot from his reading.

## Works Cited

Adams, Graham J. 2019. "*Ephphatha*! DARE to Be Opened! Scripture, Its Civil War and Shakenness." Pages 17–29 in *Scripture and Resistance*. Edited by Jione Havea. Lanham: Lexington Books; Fortress Academic.

Boer, Roland, and Fernando F. Segovia, eds. 2012. *The Future of the Biblical Past: Envisioning Biblical Studies on a Global Key*. Atlanta: Society of Biblical Literature.

Croatto, Severino J. 1981. *Exodus: A Hermeneutics of Freedom*. Maryknoll: Orbis.

Denning, Stephen. 2005. *The Leader's Guide to Storytelling: Mastering the Art and Discipline of Business Narrative*. San Francisco: Wiley.

---

[5] Contextual readings add variety and richness to the reading of the Bible. Owing to our specific contexts and circumstances, we all have reading blind spots. It takes readers from other contexts to enlighten us. We need readers from around the world to give us a fuller, global reading of the Bible.

Goh, Elaine W. F. 2016a. "Political Wisdom in the Book of Ecclesiastes." *The Asia Journal of Theology* 30:30–47.

———. 2016b. "Wickedness in the Place of Justice and Righteousness: A Reading of Ecclesiastes 3:16–17 in Response to Court's Ban for Malaysian Christians Publications to Use the Word *Allah*." Pages 227–32 in *Voices from the Margin: Interpreting the Bible in the Third World*. Edited by Rasiah S. Sugirtharajah. 20th anniv. ed. Maryknoll: Orbis.

———. 2017. "Qohelet's Gospel in Ecclesiastes: Ecclesiastes 3:1–15, 7:15–22, and 11:1–6." Pages 159–83 in *So Great a Salvation: Soteriology in the Majority World*. Edited by Gene L. Green, Stephen T. Pardue, and K. K. Yeo. Grand Rapids: Eerdmans.

———. 2019. *Cross-Textual Reading of Ecclesiastes with the Analects: In Search of Political Wisdom in a Disordered World*. Eugene, OR: Pickwick.

Gramsci, Antonio. 1971. *Selections from the Prison Books*. New York: International Publishers.

Havea, Jione. 2011. "Cons of Contextuality … Kontextuality." Pages 38–52 *Contextual Theology for the Twenty-First Century*. Edited by Stephen Bevans and Katalina Tahaafe-Williams. Eugene, OR: Pickwick.

———. 2013. "Diaspora Contexted: Talanoa, Reading, and Theologizing, as Migrants." *Black Theology* 11.2:185–200.

Heard, R. Christopher. 1996. "The Dao of Qoheleth: An Intertextual Reading of the *Dao de Jing* and the Book of Ecclesiastes." *Jian Dao* 5:65–93.

Huang, Wei. 2009. "The Meaning of *h'lm* in Qoheleth 3:11: From a Chinese Perspective." Pages 103–10 in *Mapping and Engaging the Bible in Asian Cultures: Congress of the Society of Asian Biblical Studies 2008 Seoul Conference*. Edited by Yeong Mee Lee and Yoon Jong Yoo. Korea: Christian Literature Society of Korea.

———. 2018. "*Hebel and Kong*: A Cross-Textual Reading between Qoheleth and the *Heart Sūtra*." Pages 134–44 in *The Five Scrolls*. Edited by Athalya Brenner-Idan, Gale A. Yee, and Archie C. C. Lee. London: T&T Clark.

Jarick, John. 2000. "The Hebrew Book of Changes: Reflections on Hakkōl Hebel and Lakkōl Zemān in Ecclesiastes." *JSOT* 25:79–99.

Jesurathnam, K. 2011. "A Dalit Interpretation of Wisdom Literature with Special Reference to the Underprivileged Groups in the Hebrew Society: A Mission Perspective." *The Asia Journal of Theology* 25:334–57.

Lee, Peter K. H. 1987. "Re-reading Ecclesiastes in the Light of Su Tung-P'o's Poetry." *Ching Feng* 30:214–36.

Liew, Tat-Siong Benny, ed. 2018. *Present and Future of Biblical Studies: Celebrating Twenty-Five Years of Brill's Biblical Interpretation*. Leiden: Brill.

Lorgunpai, Seree. 2016. "The Book of Ecclesiastes and Thai Buddhism." Pages 437–44 in *Voices from the Margin: Interpreting the Bible in the Third World*. Edited by Rasiah S. Sugirtharajah. 20th anniv. ed. Maryknoll: Orbis.

Ogden, Graham S. 2007. *Qoheleth*. 2nd ed. Sheffield: Sheffield Phoenix.

Said, Edward W. 2003. *Orientalism*. New York: Random House.
Singgih, Emanuel Gerrit. 2001. *Hidup Di Bawah Bayang-bayang Maut, Sebuah Tafsir Kitab Pengkhotbah*. Jakarta: BPK Gunung Mulia.
Song, Choan-Seng. 1999. "Ecclesiastes 3:1–8: An Asian Perspective." Pages 87–92 in *Return to Babel: Global Perspectives on the Bible*. Edited by Priscilla Pope-Levison and John R. Levison. Louisville: Westminster John Knox.
Spivak, Gayatri Chakravorty. 1988. "Can the Subaltern Speak?" Pages 21–78 in *Can the Subaltern Speak? Reflections on the History of an Idea*. Urbana: University of Illinois Press.
Swami, Jayādvaita. 2015. *Vanity Karma: Ecclesiastes, the Bhagavad-Gītā, and the Meaning of Life—A Cross-Cultural Commentary on the Book of Ecclesiastes*. Los Angeles: The Bhaktivedanta Book Trust International.

# WISDOM OF WAIZ:
# REREADING ECCLESIASTES 1:17–18 IN PAKISTAN

Sarah W. Ayub

<sup>17</sup> لیکن جب مَیں نے حِکمت کے جاننے اور حماقت و جہالت کے سمجھنے پر دِل لگایا تو معلُوم کِیا کہ یہ بھی ہوا کی چران ہے۔

<sup>18</sup> کیونکہ بُہت حِکمت میں بُہت غم ہے اور عِلم میں ترقّی دُکھ کی فراوانی ہے۔

واعظ 18–1:17 مُقدّس کِتاب

<sup>17</sup> But when I put my heart to knowing wisdom and understanding folly and ignorance, I came to know that this too is chasing after the wind.

<sup>18</sup> For in too much wisdom, there is too much sorrow and in promoting knowledge there is abundance of sadness. (Author's translation of Eccl 1:17–18 from the Bible in Urdu, Pakistan Bible Society 2010)

The age-old wisdoms in the book of Ecclesiastes (واعظ *Waiz* in the Urdu language) can shed light on contemporary problems in modern Pakistan (and India). The Hebrew name *Qoheleth* refers to someone who "gathers people together," while in Urdu واعظ (*Waiz*) refers to "one who teaches morals" (a moralizer) or "one who expresses opinions about something in terms of right and wrong." For Urdu readers, the book shares Waiz's ideas of right and wrong (but Waiz himself was not the author). The author introduces Waiz in the first chapter and then appeals to his wisdom to summarize, evaluate, and conclude the book at the end. Waiz has experienced life and developed his ideas on themes like emptiness, work, death, and wisdom. The book exhibits Waiz's conviction and confidence in life and what it offers.

## Fog of War

Human wisdom has brought about massive developments in the world. The industrial age heralded a new era of science and technology along with innovations in the fields of medicine, transportation, manufacturing, and construction. But the same technological advancement has enabled two developing countries like Pakistan and India (along with a few others) to acquire weapons of mass destruction and be among countries at most risk of climate change.

Pakistan and India marked their seventy-third Independence Day from British rule on 14 and 15 August 2019 respectively.[1] In the era of Indus Valley Civilization (3300–1700 BCE, the Bronze Age) this region was at the pinnacle of human wisdom. But in terms of today's measurement of progress and modernity, it is nowhere near the developed first world.

The word *archrivals* does not encapsulate all that these two sibling nations are to each other. They have shared a common history, the Indus Basin,[2] a large part of culture, similar economic and cultural challenges, love for cricket and Bollywood, along with existential threats from climate change and nuclear war.

February–March 2019 saw increased tensions between the two nations after a suicide attack by a young Kashmiri man in the disputed area of Kashmir.[3] Leaders on both sides, vowing to defend and defeat, augmented the risk of a nuclear war (Steer 2019). In control of the Indus river water supply, India also threatened its foe and neighbor Pakistan, an already water-stressed agricultural nation, with a new weapon—water![4]

---

[1] Throughout the centuries, the inhabitants of the subcontinent were introduced to Hinduism, Buddhism, and Sikhism, which greatly influenced the social fabric and way of life. Later on, Islam spread across the Indian subcontinent. The subcontinent also experienced several dynasties including the Turks, Afghans, and Mughal Empires. The Indian subcontinent with all its natural resources and wealth, known as the "Jewel in its Crown," remained under Britain through the East India Company and then as a colony until 1947, when Pakistan and India gained independence.

[2] The Indus is one of Asia's mightiest rivers. From its source in the northwestern foothills of the Himalayas, it flows through the Indian state of Jammu and Kashmir and along the length of Pakistan to the Arabian Sea. The river and its five tributaries together make up the Indus Basin, which spans four countries and supports 215 million people. Yet fast-growing populations and increasing demand for hydropower and irrigation means the Indus is under intense pressure (Nabeel 2017).

[3] Kashmir conflict is a territorial conflict between India and Pakistan. The conflict started (after the partition of Indian subcontinent in 1947) as a dispute over the former princely state of Jammu and Kashmir and since then has escalated into three wars between India and Pakistan. It is a continued source of tensions between the two nuclear armed nations.

[4] A water war could be catastrophic to the hundreds of millions of people in India and Pakistan who depend on river water. India has control over Baglihar Dam, for example, on the Chenab River, which flows from Indian controlled Kashmir into Pakistan. By stopping

More recently, on 5 August 2019, the government of India revoked the autonomy granted to disputed region of Jammu and Kashmir by article 370 of the Indian constitution, declaring it an internal matter and disregarding the wishes of Kashmiri people. In anticipation of unrest, the Indian government also sent thousands of additional troops, again causing heightened tensions in the region (Singh, Cookman, and Olson 2019). Article 370 allowed the Muslim majority state to have its own constitution, a separate flag, and independence over all matters except foreign affairs, defense, and communications (Peerzada 2019). As a response Pakistan downgraded diplomatic ties with New Delhi (Singh, Cookman, and Olson 2019). Confronted by Indian Prime Minister Narendra Modi's attempt to eliminate Kashmir's identity and autonomy; the people of occupied Jammu and Kashmir have no choice but to resist (Akram 2019).

Since partition, Kashmir has been the bone of contention between India and Pakistan. Both nations have been in control of different parts of the area and have fought three wars seeking to claim the entire region. The streets of Kashmir have become a battlefield since the 2000s when the Kashmiris turned to protests against the occupation of half a million Indian troops. The protest by Kashmiris sometimes armed with nothing more than stones was met with brutal force by Indian troops with bullets and pellet guns that has led to blinding hundreds of protesters (Peer 2019).

As the demonstrations have gained momentum over the years, so has the repression. On 14 February 2019, Indian elections were just around the corner when Indian Military forces in Kashmir were targeted by a suicide bombing attack. This attack reportedly killed forty Indian soldiers. India blamed Pakistan for providing moral and material support to terrorist organization Jaish-e-Muhammad (JeM), a militant group with links to Al Qaeda claiming responsibility for the blast.[5] The absence of a meaningful response from Pakistan, the brutality and repression by the Indian forces, and the invasive house searches and curfews has led numerous young Kashmiris to join such militant groups (Hoodbhoy 2019).

Political subjugation by the Indian state and structural violence prevalent in this conflicted region were also potent factors that led Adil Ahmad Dar (the 14 February suicide bomber) to pursue the path of death and destruction. The misconduct and atrocities of the Indian policemen towards Dar and his family led him

---

the flow of this river, India can turn hundreds of acres of farms into barren land (Gettleman 2019).

[5] Jaish-e-Mohammed is a Pakistan-based Deobandi jihadist terrorist group active in Kashmir. The group's primary motive is to separate Kashmir from India and merge it into Pakistan. Since its inception in 2000, the terror outfit has carried out several attacks in the state of Jammu and Kashmir. Al-Qaeda is a militant Sunni Islamist multi-national organization founded in 1988 by Osama bin Laden and several other Arab volunteers during the Soviet invasion of Afghanistan. Al-Qaeda operates as a network of Islamic extremists and Salafist jihadists.

to join the militants and cause bloodshed. According to his father, he was a hard-working son who took on multiple jobs to support his family, despite the humiliation and hardships brought on him by the Indian officials. His father disclosed an agonizing incident to reporters: Dar was mistreated by the Indian officials and forced to rub his nose on the ground while he circled their vehicles. Another cruel incident was when the Indian troops locked his family inside their own house and set it on fire. The same fire could just have engulfed not just Kashmir, but through mutually assured destruction (MAD),[6] Pakistan and India as well.

On 26 February, India launched air strikes on the Pakistani side of Kashmir claiming to have hit JeM's training camps. Pakistan retaliated, and an Indian pilot was taken hostage. Pakistan released the pilot, deescalating the tensions for the time (Zutshi 2019).

India's decision to revoke Jammu and Kashmir's special status rattled the foundations of status quo over Kashmir. With the area in a state of lockdown, curfew-like conditions were imposed; all communication lines blocked including internet and orders preventing the assembly of more than four people were introduced (Peerzada 2019).

Pakistan condemned India's decision to revoke the special status of its part of Kashmir as illegal, saying it would "exercise all possible options" to counter it (Peerzada 2019).

## Wisdom of This World

Once lauded, many of the inventions during and after the Industrial Revolution have brought mass destruction along with mass production. Arguably, the standard of living improved. Mass-produced goods became cheaper and accessible to masses and ultimately literacy and mass political participation increased with publication of newspapers and books (Hills 2015; Misa 1998, 243). But at the same time mechanized factories had to lay off many craft workers from their jobs (Levine 1985). In America, large scale cloth manufacturing led to increase in cotton demand causing (unskilled) labor shortages and high-priced labor, which made slavery attractive (Beckert 2014).

The emergence of these industrial units and the resultant increase in coal consumption gave rise to an unprecedented level of air pollution in industrial centers. Large volume of industrial chemical discharges added to the growing load of untreated human waste (Fleming and Knorr 2002). The irony is, the nations that have

---

[6] Mutually assured destruction (MAD) is a doctrine of military strategy and national security policy in which a full-scale use of nuclear weapons by two or more opposing sides would cause the complete annihilation of both the attacker and the defender (de Castella 2012).

borne less or no fruit from industrialization are the most afflicted by its byproduct, climate change.

Scientific advances also led to the advent of nuclear weapons, which has put human existence at perpetual risk. This threat feels even closer when a suicide blast or simply annulling of a constitutional article brings India and Pakistan head to head in a confrontation over Kashmir.

Pakistan ranked 150 among 189 countries in the United Nation's 2018 Human Development Index (HDI) ranking, which is measured according to indicators of life expectancy, educational attainment, and income (United Nations 2018). It is ironic that in Pakistan, resources are still being invested to attain and maintain nuclear technology. This too is in order to develop deterrence against a neighboring nation where people are facing similar challenges of poverty, illiteracy, and disease and where the government is investing in similar weapons of mass destruction. So basically, the human wisdom that has ultimately reached the people of this land holds the capacity to inflict sorrow and sadness through death and destruction, without granting many rewards.

Why is humanity in such a vulnerable position, despite all its efforts to achieve superior existence (that includes some level of peace) through its wisdom and knowledge? Humanity faces an existential crisis and endures a constant state of agony due to the awareness of this self-inflicted threat.

## Waiz and His Wisdom

Waiz's confidence is evident in Eccl 1:17–18. In these verses Waiz expresses how his inquiry is of somewhat empirical nature. Before declaring wisdom and knowledge to be *hebel*,[7] "a chasing after the wind," he first proclaims that he has "put his heart to knowing." After gaining the confidence of his audience he presents his argument in verse 18. As in Proverbs, Waiz uses the Hebrew word *hokma* for "wisdom" (حکمت *hikmat* in Urdu). The book of Proverbs declares "fear of the Lord" to be the foundation of wisdom and knowledge (Prov 9:10). Such wisdom (arguably) cannot be bad. But in contrast to Proverbs, Waiz states that حکمت *hikmat* leads to غم *gham*—*sorrow* or *grief*. And in Eccl 1:18b Waiz declares that promoting "knowledge" (علم *ilm* in Urdu) leads to فراوانی *farawani* "abundance" of دکھ *dukh* "sadness."

Scholars have studied and discussed Waiz's views and methodology in relation to the ideas of wisdom and knowledge. In Eccl 1, Waiz views wisdom as a prism through which reality can be observed. Waiz finds all that this world has to offer, including all its activities, to be vain. Then he reflects on wisdom in itself, separating wisdom from "madness and folly" in order to shed some light on life, its meaning, and the way ahead for human beings (Provan 2001, 240). Waiz uses

---

[7] The Hebrew word *hebel* has been translated in English bibles as "meaningless," but it could also be translated as "vapor." Alter 2010 uses "absolutely futile" and "mere breath."

empirical methodology to obtain knowledge from experience and to validate ideas experientially, as well as to discuss its powers and limitations. This knowledge, along with the reasoning ability to apply it, is wisdom (Fox 1987).

Benjamin Lyle Berger (2001) argues that it is Waiz's quest to figure out "why God does, what he does" and "what is the right path for the human being in life through the narrow framework of life" that leads him towards crucial accusations against wisdom and knowledge (see also Vogel 1997, 146). In Pakistan's scenario Waiz's quest would be to figure out why God lets humans use knowledge for destruction and what are the right paths in life while dealing with technology that can be used for good as well as bad. In search of answers to these questions, Waiz finds that worldly accomplishments and development are futile:

> Time soaks away the marks of history, rendering human action, perhaps even religious aspirations, wholly futile. Justice is nowhere to be found in this universe where predictability and rules do not exist. Even the pursuit of wisdom and knowledge has no lasting significance for the individual. And this whole perplexing system is suffused with enigma, and frustration, of an inscrutable God. (Berger 2001, 153–54)

Time, along with the reality of death, make human ambition and actions meaningless. At least to the extent that no matter how much or how less a wo/man toils, life's end is the same for all. Honesty, impartiality, and integrity are seldom found in day to day dealings. The system that God created for humans to live in is somehow broken. Even searching for answers through wisdom leads humans deeper into the abyss.

So how does this worldly wisdom and knowledge perpetuate misery and enigma? Old Testament scholar Craig G. Bartholomew argues:

> Modernity presented its Grand narrative of human anatomy, reason, science and progress as wise par excellence. However, after two world wars, the holocaust, the nuclear threat and the ecological crisis, postmodernism has helped us to see that much of that wisdom was folly. (Bartholomew 2009, 125)

Bartholomew's statement blames modernity for adorning all its factors with the crown of flawless wisdom, while it also perpetuated war, genocide, and environmental degradation. Although humans have held the tendency to perpetuate war and destruction even before the advent of the modern age, modernity with its so-called wisdom has augmented the frequency, force, and affliction of war and its derivatives along with accelerated degradation of natural resources. Thus, in agreement with Waiz, Bartholomew declares this wisdom to be folly.

Contrary to the above arguments, Prov 8 declares wisdom as a work of God's hand and discusses its relationship to humanity, along with its nature, powers, and effects. Waiz also speaks of wisdom and knowledge being given by God to a favored man in Eccl 2:26, along with happiness. So why is there contradiction?

Michael Fox argues that the wisdom that Proverb talks about and Waiz briefly discusses in chapter 2 refers to a "sense of a morality," to do what is judicious, in other words, to "wisdom as reason." It is more than just a statement about worldly knowledge. Whereas wisdom as knowledge, as a deeper understanding of life such as Waiz sought, can be increased through study and observation, that type of wisdom (without reason) brings misery (Eccl 1:16–18), not exactly an expression of divine favor (Fox 1987).

## A Sorrowful Wisdom

God created woman and man and gave them directions to lead their life according to certain rules. C. S. Lewis in *Mere Christianity* calls these "moral rules" and defines them as directions for running the human machine. These rules when followed are meant to prevent a breakdown, a strain or a friction, in the running of the machine (Lewis 2001, 40–44). Lewis talks about humanity and its morality as a fleet of ships sailing in formation. The voyage can be successful only if, firstly, the ships do not collide and secondly, if each ship is seaworthy and all its equipment is in good order. As a matter of fact, one thing cannot work without the other. If the ships keep on colliding, they will not remain seaworthy very long. And if their steering gears are out of order, they will not be able to evade collision. But there is a third thing that is extremely important, he states, in fact essential for a successful voyage: one has to take into account where the fleet is headed, its destination (Lewis 2001, 40–44).

Morality for Lewis has to do with three things, "firstly, with fair play and harmony between individuals. Secondly, with what might be called tidying up or harmonizing the things inside each individual. Thirdly, with the general purpose of human life as a whole: what man was made for: what course the whole fleet ought to be on" (Lewis 2001, 42).

When the modern man or woman puts his or her heart to knowing wisdom and separating it from ignorance (Eccl 1:17), he or she came up with ways to mass produce, rid humanity of several deadly ailments, achieve fast transportation, invent convenient materials like plastic, and even harnessing atomic power. All these inventions have good and bad sides to them, bringing numerous benefits for humanity but also causing immense sorrow.

Alfred Nobel's most famous invention dynamite facilitated the construction of canals, tunnels, and other infrastructure projects and proved to be extremely beneficial for humans (Braswell 2015). But in his April 1888 mistaken obituary a French newspaper called Nobel "the merchant of death," an inventor and arms manufacturer who "became rich by finding ways to kill more people faster than ever before." Harsh words for an obituary, especially since its subject was still alive and could read it himself. It was in this moment that he realized how his invention caused hurt to humanity and gave himself negative fame. This may have caused disharmony inside him and led him to ensure that his name would be tied to humankind's highest achievements and not its destructive potential. As per his will, the Nobel Prize was established in 1895 as a set of annual international awards presented in several categories in recognition of academic, cultural, or scientific advances (Nordlinger 2012; Braswell 2015). His efforts to encourage science working for the good of humankind may indicate an intention to encourage harmony between humans, and it may have endowed him with some kind of inner peace. But the third thing remains. If his invention, and the inventions thereafter encouraged by his prize, are not supporting the general purpose of human life, in other words not guiding the fleet towards ultimate destination, these are meaningless.

Thus worldly wisdom and the resultant technological advancement are means, not ends in themselves. Worldly wisdom in any of its forms seen as an end and used only for attaining and maintaining power (like for example nuclear weapons) would only lead to disaster and to "sorrow" (Eccl 1:18).

So what are the right paths for human beings in life in the age of technology? In Lewis's words, what is the general purpose of human life as a whole? What course the fleet ought to be on?

In the Bible, God created humans for life in his presence, and this worldly life is temporary. God created humanity in God's image (Gen 1:27) and put "eternity" in human hearts (Eccl 3:11). Humans cannot find real purpose anywhere else besides God.

The fruits of modern wisdom are used and aimed at acquiring worldly utilities, comforts, and power. These are aimed at ruling the world, conserving ideologies, propagating (false) narratives, and safeguarding the nation states. But to a person who believes in God and the doctrine of an afterlife, all those are transient. And if a human is everlasting than he is infinitely more important than a nation state. Thus, one could argue that all the weapons created and used, including the nuclear bomb, are in opposition of the moral law.

In a perfect world, wisdom would exist in the form of vaccines and MRI machines, but weapons of mass destruction would cease to exist. What about self-defense, defending the weak, or as in Kashmir's case, seeking self-determination? The sorrow of the Kashmiri people accumulated over the years. Basharat Peer attributes this suffering to a painful past, anguish over an oppressive present, and an uncertain future. He observes that "India and Pakistan blame each other, each country obsessed with proving itself better than the other, but they share the responsibility for reducing Kashmir to a ruin and destroying generations of Kashmiri lives" (Peer 2019). Some in Kashmir despair of the future, saying "better than the last 30 years is to have a seven-day war and finish this issue for once and all" (Farooq and Safi 2019).

The blast that triggered the February standoff between Pakistan and its neighbor (not exactly nuclear in nature) was perhaps a technological derivative of Nobel's dynamite. A suicide blast carried by a young man with his whole life ahead of him, his wish to kill as many fellow beings as possible seems to defy logic, including the first level of morality. The argument of oppression faced by him and his family stands, but what he did translated into injustice and oppression for many others. A way of delivering justice in his own eyes, but as Berger puts it, in the long run it is all *futile*. True justice does not exist in this world, "predictability and rules do not exist" (Berger 2001, 153). In this perplexing scheme of things, immersed in enigma and frustration, it seems like "knowledge and reason" (Fox 1987, 139), the wisdom that comes from God, does not exist.

Lewis distinguishes between *moral law* and *natural instinct* by mentioning the instincts of patriotism along with instincts of mother love, sexual instinct, fighting instinct, and instinct for food. These instincts urge us to act in a certain way. The impulse to act on the instinct of *fighting*, for example, would be paired with a stronger impulse of *flight* for self-preservation. But moral law might guide us to fight to save someone from an attacking creature. These contradicting impulses are like keys of a piano, and moral law is the guiding sheet of music that tells one to play a note and not another for a specific tune. Similarly, the instinct of patriotism gives rise to the impulse to do whatever it takes for the betterment of one's country. But if that impulse means that the neighboring country with its inhabitants need to be destroyed by nuclear weapons, the moral law would stop a person from acting on that impulse at that moment (Lewis 2001, 11–14). This morality saved the lives of millions in America and Russia from mutually assured destruction (MAD) during the Cuban Missile Crisis in 1962 when one of three Russian officers Vasili Alexandrovich Arkhipov refused to authorize a nuclear strike (Krulwich 2016).

Which *guiding morality* or *Godly wisdom* should humanity follow? For Lewis, "There is but one good; that is God. Everything else is good when it turns to him and bad when it turns from him" (Lewis 1996, 96).

If things were conspired differently in the subcontinent, the power game that has been played over this land, its resources, and its people would have been stopped at some point, and the present would have been quite different. If Pakistan and India followed *godly morality*, they would have dealt with Kashmir differently. India would have ceased to harm natives of Kashmir or putting complete lockdowns in the area for gaining control over this territory. Pakistan would have seized to support proxies like JeM. The resulting harmony would have kept a young man like Dar from blowing himself up and causing forty other deaths. These forty saved lives would have prevented the fog of war from rising between two nuclear powers Pakistan and India, and lack of this blinding fog would have banished (in the long run) the need to hold weapons of mass destruction in the first place, even for deterrence.

Thus the third factor of morality in Lewis's thinking, the question of the general purpose of human life is crucial to humanity's transition from *worldly wisdom* to *godly wisdom*. Wisdom guided by godly morality (wisdom of reason) can lead humanity on the paths of wisdom. Without godly wisdom, worldly wisdom perpetuates a vicious cycle of غم *gham sorrow* or *grief* (Eccl 1:18), rendering technologies like nuclear power and ability to control and manipulate water, *havel* (Eccl 1:2, 12:8)!

## Dilemma of Knowing: Sadness

> If some extraterrestrial species were compiling a history of Homo sapiens, they might well break their calendar into two eras: BNW (before nuclear weapons) and NWE (the nuclear weapons era).... NWE starting from August 6, 1945 towards a countdown to the inglorious end of this strange species, which attained the intelligence to discover the effective means to destroy itself, but not the moral and intellectual capacity to control its own worst instincts. (Chomsky 2016, 179)

A lamb does not know it is about to be sacrificed, so it leaps and hops merrily. Humans do not have this liberty. Humanity is not just facing an existential crisis but also enduring a constant state of agony due to the awareness of this self-inflicted threat. This is anticipated in Eccl 1:18b where Waiz declares that promoting "knowledge" (علم *ilm*) leads to "abundance" (فراوانی *farawani*) of "sadness" (دکھ *dukh*).

The only thing worse than total annihilation through climate catastrophe or nuclear Armageddon is the constant fear of it, and this fear comes from knowledge of how close we are to destruction.[8] One wrong move and it will be the end of the world as we know it.

The Science and Security Board at *Bulletin of the Atomic Scientists* kept the Doomsday Clock at two minutes to midnight on 24 January 2019, the closest it has ever been to apocalypse.[9] The Doomsday Clock is a symbol that represents the likelihood of a man-made global catastrophe. Maintained since 1947 by the

---

[8] It has been argued that the most likely trigger for a nuclear exchange could be conflict between India and Pakistan, not North Korea or some other nuclear power. Spiked tensions between the two states within a span of six months in 2019 is testament to this argument. "This Is Where a Nuclear Exchange Is Most Likely. (It's Not North Korea.)," *New York Times*, 7 March 2019, https://www.nytimes.com/2019/03/07/opinion/kashmir-india-pakistan-nuclear.html.

[9] Founded in 1945 by University of Chicago scientists who had helped develop the first atomic weapons in the Manhattan Project, the *Bulletin of the Atomic Scientists* created the Doomsday Clock two years later, using the imagery of apocalypse (midnight) and the contemporary idiom of nuclear explosion (countdown to zero) to convey threats to humanity and the planet. The decision to move (or to leave in place) the minute hand of the Doomsday Clock is made every year by the *Bulletin*'s Science and Security Board in consultation with its Board of Sponsors, which includes fifteen Nobel laureates. The clock has become a universally recognized indicator of the world's vulnerability to catastrophe from nuclear weapons, climate change, and new technologies emerging in other domains (Mecklin 2019). The 24 January 2019 record has only been rivaled in 1953, at the very depths of the Cold War (Spinazze 2019).

members of the Bulletin of the Atomic Scientists, the clock is a metaphor for threats to humanity from unchecked scientific and technical advances.

In his 1948 essay "On Living in an Atomic Age," written just three years after the atomic bombs dropped on Hiroshima and Nagasaki brought an abrupt end to World War II, Lewis argues that we worry a bit too much about the atomic bomb.[10] To the question, "How are we to live in an atomic age?" he responds, "Why, as you would have lived in the sixteenth century when the plague visited London almost every year, or as you would have lived in a Viking age when raiders from Scandinavia might land and cut your throat any night; or indeed, as you are already living in an age of cancer, an age of syphilis, an age of paralysis, an age of air raids, an age of railway accidents, an age of motor accidents" (Lewis 1986, 73).

Ideally the knowledge rendered to us by science should set us free from fear and unite humankind into working together and wisely towards a safer future. Death, natural or otherwise, is a certainty, and accepting this fact makes life easier. Humans can only make efforts to sustain humanity and the environment to which they are stewards. In Lewis's words, "the first action to be taken is to pull ourselves together. If we are all going to be destroyed by an atomic bomb, let that bomb when it comes find us doing sensible and human things—not huddled together like frightened sheep and thinking about bombs. They may break our bodies (a microbe can do that) but they need not dominate our minds" (Lewis 1986, 73–74).

Human efforts did succeed against the ailments that, thanks to vaccines, no longer pose a threat to mass populations. Scientific facts, rather than being ignored and denied, should be accepted and used for human betterment. But for the last few years humanity has backtracked on its commitment to curb climate change[11] and nuclear arms control. Nuclear deals have been abandoned, and the worldwide arms race continues (Holpuch 2018).

The world is losing ground in its efforts to achieve net zero emissions, set against a backdrop of increasing scientific evidence for severe impacts of the warming of earth. Global warming has contributed to the occurrence of catastrophes, including the massive wildfires and the deadly heat waves suffered around the world. Despite clear signs of a progressively disrupted climate, denialists continue to resist action (Mecklin 2019).

Nanotechnologies, robotics, genetics, and artificial intelligence are transforming the world around us, and unless regulations are set in place, such innovations can prove to be more harmful than helpful. There has also been a rise in the intentional corruption of the information ecosystem (knowledge,

---

[10] After its first publication in 1948 in the annual magazine *Informed Reading* (vol 6), this essay has been republished numerous times along with other essays by Lewis.
[11] Global carbon dioxide emissions—which seemed to plateau earlier this decade—resumed an upward climb in 2017 and 2018 (Mecklin 2019).

information, data) on which modern civilization depends. This is another way where knowledge mingled with deceit becomes misinformation and causes anguish. This stands true for India and Pakistan's recent standoffs, where the volatility of Kashmir dispute and the associated *prejudices, biases,* and *ideological differences* augmented the odds of a military conflict growing into a full-grown nuclear war. During the confrontation, media sources in these countries displayed what an Opinion Columnist at *The New York Times*, Farhad Manjoo, calls "miasma of lies" (Manjoo 2019; see also Sidharth 2019). Before it receded for now at least, this miasma of lies pulled these two nations alarmingly close to the thick fog of war.

## Conclusion

Many powerful nations came and went before Pakistan and India; time erased them from the pages of history (Eccl 1:3–11). Their rulers, and the subjects they had power over, perished ultimately (Eccl 11:7–12:7). In the larger scheme of things, it does not matter how strong and technologically advanced these nations were, the reality of time and death rendered their existence *havel*. By declaring this Waiz has taken aim at all the ways humans try to give meaning to this worldly transient life apart from God, including investing it in gaining worldly wisdom and through it, worldly power. Combined, all of those attempts is a "chasing after the wind and can lead to sorrow and sadness" (Eccl 1:17–18).

The worldly wisdom, technology, that has enabled Pakistan and India to acquire weapons of mass destruction and construct dams over mighty rivers can very well be the undoing of these nations as well. What could give this worldly life meaning where time and death consumes all? What would compel humans to follow godly morality when the evil women and men live long but the innocent ones face tragedy and sorrow (Eccl 8:14)?

Waiz answers these questions in the last few verses. Waiz's words cannot be interpreted without reading through these final verses, upon which the anonymous author concludes and summarizes what Waiz has said (Eccl 12:9–14). These verses declare Waiz to be wise, proclaim his words to be upright and true, as he states everything of this world to be *havel*, temporary and filled with enigmas:

> Now all has been heard;
>   here is the conclusion of the matter:
> Fear God and keep his commandments,
>   for this is the duty of all mankind.
> For God will bring every deed into judgment,
>   including every hidden thing,
>   whether it is good or evil. (Eccl 12:13–14)

Judgment is key here. The belief that all deeds will be judged by the creator, the one who determined the destination for humanity is the compelling force to keep worldly wisdom in check. This belief system is the prerequisite for bringing worldly knowledge and wisdom under Godly morality and bringing salvation to humanity from غم *gham* sorrow and دکھ *dukh* sadness.

## Works Cited

Akram, Munir. 2019. "Pakistan's Kashmir Strategy." *Dawn*. 1 September. https://www.dawn.com/news/1502890.

Alter, Robert. 2010. *The Wisdom Books: Job, Proverbs, and Ecclesiastes*. New York: Norton.

Bartholomew, Craig G. 2009. *Ecclesiastes*. Grand Rapids: Baker Academic.

Beckert, Sven. 2014. *Empire of Cotton: A Global History*. New York: Vintage.

Berger, Benjamin Lyle. 2001. "Qohelet and the Exigencies of the Absurd." *BibInt* 9.2: 141–79.

Braswell, Sean. 2015. "The Newspaper Error that Sparked the Nobel Prize." *OZY*. 9 October. https://www.ozy.com/flashback/the-newspaper-error-that-sparked-the-nobel-prize/40007.

de Castella, Tom. 2012. "How Did We Forget about Mutually Assured Destruction?" *BBC News Magazine*. 15 February. https://www.bbc.com/news/magazine-17026538.

Chomsky, Noam. 2016. *Who Rules the World?* New York: Metropolitan Books.

Farooq, Azhar, and Michael Safi. 2019. "Standoff in Kashmir: 'Our Last Hope Is That a War Will Sort This Once and for All.'" *Guardian*. 2 March. https://www.theguardian.com/world/2019/mar/02/kashmir-india-pakistan-stand-off-war-border.

Fleming, James R., and Bethany R. Knorr. 2002. "History of the Clean Air Act: A Guide to Clean Air Legislation Past and Present." *American Meteorological Society: Boston, MA*. https://www.ametsoc.org/sloan/cleanair/.

Fox, Michael V. 1987. "Qohelet's Epistemology." *HUCA* 58: 137–55.

Gettleman, Jeffrey. 2019. "India Threatens a New Weapon Against Pakistan: Water." *New York Times*. 21 February. https://www.nytimes.com/2019/02/21/world/asia/india-pakistan-water-kashmir.html.

Hills, Richard Leslie. 2015. *Papermaking in Britain 1488–1988: A Short History*. New York: Bloomsbury.

Holpuch, Amanda. 2018. "Donald Trump Says US Will No Longer Abide by Iran Deal—As It Happened." *Guardian*. 8 May. https://www.theguardian.com/world/live/2018/may/08/iran-nuclear-deal-donald-trump-latest-live-updates.

Hoodbhoy, Pervez. 2019. "Another India-Pakistan Crisis." *Bulletin of Atomic Scientists*. 7 March. https://thebulletin.org/2019/03/another-india-pakistan-crisis/.

Krulwich, Robert. 2016. "You (and Almost Everyone You Know) Owe Your Life to This Man." *National Geographic*. 24 March. https://news.nationalgeographic.com/2016/03/you-and-almost-everyone-you-know-owe-your-life-to-this-man/.

Lewis, Clive Staples. 1986. *Present Concerns*. Orlando: Harcourt Inc.

———. 2001. *Mere Christianity*. Grand Rapids: Zondervan.

———. 1996. *The Great Divorce*. New York: Touchstone.

Levine, David. 1985. "Industrialization and the Proletarian Family in England." *Past & Present* 107: 168–203.

Manjoo, Farhad. 2019. "The India-Pakistan Conflict Was a Parade of Lies." *New York Times*. 6 March. https://www.nytimes.com/2019/03/06/opinion/india-pakistan-news.html.

Mecklin, John, 2019. "A New Abnormal: It Is Still Two Minutes to Midnight." *Bulletin of Atomic Scientists*. 24 January. https://thebulletin.org/doomsday-clock/current-time/.

Misa, Thomas J. 1998. *A Nation of Steel: The Making of Modern America, 1865–1925*. Baltimore: John Hopkins University Press.

Nabeel, Fazilda. 2017. "How India and Pakistan Are Competing over the Mighty Indus River." *Independent*. 7 June. https://www.independent.co.uk/environment/how-india-and-pakistan-are-competing-over-the-mighty-indus-river-a7769506.html.

Nordlinger, Jay. 2012. *Peace, They Say: A History of the Nobel Peace Prize; The Most Famous and Controversial Prize in the World*. New York: Encounter Books.

Peer, Basharat. 2019. "The Young Suicide Bomber Who Brought India and Pakistan to the Brink of War." *New York Times*. 2 March. https://www.nytimes.com/2019/03/02/opinion/sunday/kashmir-india-pakistan.html.

Peerzada, Aamir. 2019. "Article 370: India Strips Disputed Kashmir of Special Status." *BBC News*. 5 August. https://www.bbc.com/news/world-asia-india-49231619.

Provan, Iain. 2001. *The NIV Application Commentary: Ecclesiastes*. Grand Rapids: Zondervan.

Sidharth, Arjun. 2019. "February Round-Up: Misinformation Industry Feeds Off Pulwama Attack and Indo-Pak Tension." *Alt News*. 12 March. https://www.altnews.in/february-round-up-misinformation-industry-feeds-off-pulwama-attack-and-indo-pak-tension/.

Singh, Vikram J., Colin Cookman, and Richard Olson. 2019. "Kashmir Crisis Raises Fear of Intensified India-Pakistan Conflict." *United States Institute of Peace (USIP)*. 15 August. https://www.usip.org/publications/2019/08/kashmir-crisis-raises-fear-intensified-india-pakistan-conflict.

Spinazze, Gayle. 2019. "It Is Still Two Minutes to Midnight." *Bulletin of Atomic Scientists*. 24 January. https://thebulletin.org/2019/01/it-is-still-2-minutes-to-midnight/.

Steer, George. 2019. "From Suicide Bombing to Captured Pilot: A Timeline of the Latest Crisis in Kashmir." *Time*. 28 February. http://time.com/5541090/india-pakistan-2019-tensions-timeline/.

"This Is Where a Nuclear Exchange Is Most Likely. (It's Not North Korea.)." *New York Times*. 7 March; https://www.nytimes.com/2019/03/07/opinion/kashmir-india-pakistan-nuclear.html?rref=collection%2Ftimestopic%2FIndia-Pakistan%20Relations.

United Nations Development Programme. 2018. "Human Development Indices and Indicators: 2018 Statistical Update." http://hdr.undp.org/en/2018-update.

Zutshi, Chitralekha. 2019. "Kashmir Conflict Is Not Just a Border Dispute between India and Pakistan." *CAN*. 10 March. https://www.channelnewsasia.com/news/commentary/kashmir-conflict-is-not-just-a-border-dispute-between-11323814.

# TOIL(ING) IN TWO CULTURES: AN AUSTRALIAN-SAMOAN READING OF ECCLESIASTES 2:18–23

Brian Fiu Kolia

Toil (work, labor, service) is highly valued among Samoans, both at the home(is)land and among the ones who live overseas. The cultural significance of toil(ing) (*tautua*) is captured in the Samoan proverb *O le ala i le pule, o le tautua*, which asserts that *tautua* (toil, service) is the "path to authority." In Ecclesiastes, on the other hand, toil(ing) is seen with suspicion for Qoheleth (author of Ecclesiastes) characterizes it as *hebel* (vanity). The association of "toil" (*tautua*) with "vanity" (*hebel*) raises several questions: Why would a sage like Qoheleth discourage toil(ing)? Did Qoheleth present the dominant view in his culture or his personal experiential knowledge? Was he troubled with complacency in his society, at the expense of his communal setting? Could *hebel* have other meanings? These questions give the impression that Qoheleth's experiential knowledge disregarded the communal and relational context of life.

For Pasifika islanders, Qoheleth's philosophy is problematic. The islands are perceived as holiday getaways (for resting) by many nonislanders, but our (is)lands are heavily toiled and require ongoing toil(ing) (service). Our (is)lands are for working, not for relaxing. In fact, the majority of islanders are subsistent farmers, and toil(ing) is therefore essential for survival. To assume that life is easy and free of toil is deemed foolish. To address the questions raised above then, I propose a Samoan reading of toil(ing) in Eccl 2:18–23 through the perspective of *tautua*. As a Samoan, I am intrigued with Qoheleth's perception of toil(ing) as vanity and the implications that this perception may have for *tautua* in the Samoan context.

## Toil(ing) as *Hebel*

It is evident in Eccl 2:18–23 that Qoheleth is dissatisfied with toil(ing). The nature of 2:18–23 is repetitive (Murphy 2002, 25), reflecting Qoheleth's frustration regarding human toil and how he deems it *hebel*. In verses 18, 19, and 21, the reason behind his repeated frustration is "inheritance" ("the person who shall be after me"; 2:18). The language suggests uncertainty, as "the person" (*'adam*) does not point to a specific person. Further, there is uncertainty with whether the heir will be foolish or wise (2:19). This leads to Qoheleth's frustration and hate (*šn'*).

The repetitions in this passage accentuate Qoheleth's frustration even further, as Derek Kidner (1976, 35) observes: "The more he has toiled at his life's work … the more galling will be the thought of its fruit into other hands—and as likely as not, the wrong hands." The end clause of verses 19, 21, and 23 ("also, this [is] vanity") confirms Qoheleth's position regarding toil(ing).

The Hebrew word used in Ecclesiastes is *'āmal*, which generally means "toil(ing)" or "labor," but it also has other meanings. In wisdom literature, *āmal* is expected to be positive given Proverbs' positive attitude (see Prov 14:23; 16:26; 18:9; 22:29; 31:13). But in Ecclesiastes, as Doug Ingram (2006, 159) points out, the sense of *āmal* is "very negative, and it therefore gives a decidedly negative answer to the question in 1:3."

The word *āmal* can also mean "suffering" (Jer. 20:18) and "trouble" (Num 23:21; BDB, "עמל" s.v.). David J. A. Clines (2002, 494) identifies this other sense of *āmal* in the book of Job, which "is not generally, perhaps never, the emotional feeling of misery, but typically the objective situation of being hard at work or being oppressed." Taking this nuance of *āmal*, it seems that Qoheleth's experience was one of suffering, as though he was forced to toil. This explains why Qoheleth characterizes it as *hebel*.

*Hebel* is used three times in Eccl 2:18–23, and thirty-eight times in the book of Ecclesiastes out of a total seventy-three times in the Hebrew Bible. *Hebel* is commonly translated "vanity," but the word has an array of meanings. It can mean "breath," "spirit" (Crenshaw 1981, 129), or "wind" (BDB, "הבל" s.v.). Choon-Leong Seow (1997, 102) mentions other meanings such as "air" and "vapour," noting that "in Mishnaic Hebrew the word may refer to breath, air, steam, vapour, gas, and the like." James L. Crenshaw (1981, 129) argues that its usage in Ecclesiastes is usually perceived as a "fleeting significance" (cf. Seow 1997, 102), hence the negative nuances associated with "vanity."

Michael V. Fox (1989, 45) argues "it is difficult to distinguish the contextual meaning of *re'ut ruah* [spirit] from that of *hebel*, since in all but two of the nine times that the former occurs it is appended to a *hebel*-judgment and has precisely the same contexts and referents." This suggests that Qoheleth could have held a spiritual understanding of the word *hebel* as opposed to something transient.

Craig G. Bartholomew and Ryan P. O'Dowd (1990) imply that *hebel* is better defined as "enigmatic" reflecting something that cannot be grasped. Martin Shuster argues that Qoheleth is philosophical, and *hebel* reflects a philosophical assessment of life (Shuster 2008, 220). Alicia Suskin Ostriker (2007, 79–80) argues that *hebel* and "vanity" are not the same: "Vanity is an abstraction, and the Hebrew *hevel* is not. Not quite, though close. As close as a breath. Something perhaps close to nothing, but not quite nothing. A reality, not an abstraction." These various meanings open up opportunities for alternative interpretations, as Qoheleth could have been pessimistic or optimistic about toil(ing) or perhaps somewhere in between (Whybray 1989, 64).

*Tautua*

The deliberations of Qoheleth create a dilemma for Samoan readers who are entrenched in the *faa-Samoa* (lit. "The Samoan Way"). The *faa-Samoa* refers to the Samoan way of life or the Samoan culture. The word *faa* emphasizes the notion that things are done the Samoan way, which is enforced by the elders. Customs, traditions, and general living are all guided by the principles of *faa-Samoa*, and in a village setting it provides its elders with a way of maintaining order and control. The *faa-Samoa* aggrandizes the principles of hard work and determination. Toil(ing) in the Samoan contexts (at home and abroad) is known as *tautua*. *Tautua* is honorable, admirable, worshipped, and vitalizing. From the realities of *faa-Samoa*, Samoans could not agree that toil (*tautua*) is vain (*hebel*).

Definition

*Tautua* is composed of two words, *tau* and *tua*. *Tau* has several meanings: "to strive," "to fight," and "to pluck," as well as "price" or "weather." With regards to "toil," the meanings of "strive" and "fight" are appropriate. *Tua* can mean "back," "behind," or "to rely upon." In relation to toil(ing), physical labor is seen as demanding on a person's back. So, *tau-tua* is commonly understood as referring to service that is strenuous on the back. Nonetheless, *tautua* is service that is done wholeheartedly and committedly.

Why Samoans *Tautua*

The two most common Samoan words for "toil(ing)" are *galue* and *tautua*. The word *galue* describes the *action* of toil(ing). *Tautua*, on the other hand, also conveys an understanding of toil(ing) as encompassing the spirit of service to one's *aiga* (extended family) and to one's village (see Young 2009, 6; Tutuila 2009, 15). As Vaitusi Nofoaiga (2017, ix) explains, *tautua* may be translated as "serve, service, server and servant," and it is a profound and significant component in Samoan life. Makesi Neemia (2018, 147) points to the significance of *tautua* through the Samoan proverb *O le ala i le pule, o le tautua*, "the path to authority/leadership is *tautua* (service, work, toiling)." The proverb explains the importance of *tautua* in family and village contexts, where becoming a *matai* (chief) cannot be achieved without hard work (*tautua*) and service (*tautua*) or without being a server (*tautua*) and servant (*tautua*).

To earn a *matai* (chief) title requires three forms of *tautua*—I highlight these in order to stress the significance of *tautua*: The first is physical service (in the plantation and village grounds), which tends to favor males. The *tautua* is done not just to the *aiga* (relatives) but to the village (*nuu*), and as such the person who performs *tautua* becomes a member of the *aumaga* (group of untitled men). Aiono explains this type of *tautua* in this way:

> The *aumaga* have earned the honorific *o le malosi o le nuu* [strength of the village] because they are the physical strength *api*[1] support upon which the *matai* group (*nuu*) depend. They are the tillers of the soil; the planters; the *tautai* (fishermen or literally those who are involved in the sea and marine activities); the catchers-snarers of birds; the builders; the makers of weapons and tools; the preparers; the cooks and servers of food and drink; the poets, the singers, the dancers, the entertainers; the sportsmen and the fighters in times of war. They are the heirs of *matai* titles who give the uniquely Samoan service called *tautua*, to honour the chosen *matai*. (Aiono 1992, 118–19)

The person who is chosen to be *matai* performs such difficult *tautua* over and over again, thereby catching the admiration and trust of the elders and the community.

Second, *tautua* can be any service that significantly raises the profile of the *aiga* or the *nuu*. This could be through educational or sporting achievements or any equivalent service that would enhance the recognition of the *aiga* and *nuu*.

Third, and resonating with those living away from the village, including those in diaspora, one can *tautua* through monetary contributions to *nuu* and *aiga* commitments. This type of *tautua* does not involve physical service or talent-based accomplishments but financial contributions and gifts of kind (e.g., a box full of clothes or foodstuff sent back to Samoa from families in diaspora).

These three forms of *tautua* are conveyed in the Samoan proverb *O le ala i le pule o le tautua*: the path to authority or leadership is *tautua*. All three forms of *tautua* are done voluntarily and, at some stage, provided that the *aiga* and senior *matai* agree, the individual, as a result of his or her *tautua*, is rewarded with a *matai* title. It is a prodigious reward for all the hard work and toil performed as a service to the *aiga* and *nuu*. Ultimately, the *aiga* benefits as well, as its own status in the *nuu* and the wider context of Samoa is lifted.

*Aiga* "Who Come after Me"

When a person strives for success through *tautua*, the *aiga* is at the forefront of their psyche. The sentiments that Samoans have for their *aiga* form the impetus for them to provide *tautua*. The *aiga* defines who the *tautua* are and how they act

---

[1] The Samoan word *api* often means "rest" but can also mean "rely upon" as Aiono here uses it.

in any society in which they may live. In this regard, the *aiga* motivates Samoans to work harder.

Being an Australian-born Samoan, I am a hybrid. My parents migrated from Samoa in the late 1970s, and I was born in Sydney, Australia in 1981. I am consequently a second generation Australian-Samoan. Life in Sydney during the early 1980s was a struggle for my parents and for many migrant families, as they lacked the necessary skills and training for higher-paid jobs. They were forced to work double-shifts and multiple jobs to make ends meet. Due to the high cost of living in Sydney, we relocated to Melbourne, hoping for more job opportunities.

For most Samoan families, the experience was new and harsh. From toiling the land and the sea, they had to toil in cold and cemented factories and working places. The experience of paying rent replaced living on inherited land. Paying bills became priorities in Australian life, as opposed to family commitments. Nevertheless, *tautua* was still paramount, as Samoans in diaspora fulfilled *tautua* differently in comparison to those who physically remained on the land (*fanua*). *Tautua* connected Samoans in the diaspora back to the *fanua* and *aiga*. The higher incomes of Samoan families in the diaspora became value to the *aiga* back home. So, despite being away from *aiga* and *nuu* back in Samoa, migration to the new lands was never about severing ties with the home(is)land but maintaining them. Migrant Samoan families in the diaspora were away from the *fanua*, but their higher monetary incomes became value to the *aiga* and *nuu* back home. They were able to make higher monetary contributions. This was their *tautua*. In these migratory movements, my parents' *tautua* was for the benefit of our *aiga* and *nuu* back in Samoa.

The *aiga* is important for Samoans. It is not merely a demographical category but a nexus for inheritance, land, identity, religion, village, status, power, and responsibility. The *aiga* is sacred (*paia*). Its significance also extends to chiefly titles and dignitaries, which are also considered as *paia*.

As alluded to above, there is a connection between *aiga* and *fanua* (land). Samoan artist Vanya Taule'alo (1999, 2) reflects that "in Samoa the *aiga* (extended family) is the core of the society, it binds the individual to the group and the soil." This is an important connection because it links *tautua* to both *fanua* and *aiga*. The *fanua* is most valued to *aiga* due to its ancestral links and chiefly titles. *Fanua* is where our ancestors were born. It was the land they tilled, and in the end it will be the land where they are buried.

Our connection to the *fanua*, regardless of where we go, means that we carry with us the significance of the *fanua*. This "carrying" is known as *maota-tau'ave*, which literally means, "house which is carried." We do not physically or literally carry the *fanua*, but in our *tautua* we carry the *maota*. The *maota* means "house," and it houses our *paia*, our spiritual attachment to the *fanua* and the *aiga*. In our carrying, we toil for our *aiga*. Even as we migrate overseas and are physically distanced from the *fanua*, we maintain a spiritual and familial connection through our *tautua*.

## A *Tautua* Review of Qoheleth

Qoheleth's argument against "those who come after me" (2:18) cannot be fully appreciated in the Samoan context because "those who come after me" equates to *aiga*. *Aiga* embodies more than just kinship and inheritance, as the *aiga* encapsulates the Samoan's pride and reputation. *Aiga* is marked by an honorific *matai* (chiefly) title representing its stature and authority, and members of the *aiga* perform *tautua* to ensure that the *matai* title is honored.

Qoheleth's hate (2:18) of his toil due to his *aiga* is therefore problematic in the Samoan context because *tautua* is *for* the *aiga*. The problem then is that Qoheleth is too individualistic (cf. 2:13–16). R. Norman Whybray (1989, 69) too made a similar observation: "we can also see the intense individualism of Qoheleth: the idea that the achievements of individuals might benefit future generations after their death never occurs to him."[2]

Qoheleth's individualism shows that he does not promote the *spiritual* significance of toil(ing) and inheritance. It is as if "Qoheleth's assessment of human wisdom as ultimately valueless, despite its limited successes in particular cases, is closely connected with his preoccupation with human mortality" (Whybray 1989, 69). On this I ask, if human mortality ever ends? The Samoan *aiga* continues on through the generations because the *matai* title and *fanua* are *paia* (sacred, and therefore eternal). From my Samoan world, the spiritual senses appear to evade Qoheleth.

## Rereading Qoheleth

I am a person of two cultures, a cultural hybrid. I am a diasporized Samoan trying to fit into the Australian context (cf. Smith 2008, 9) as well as remain fitting for my Samoan context. I am both Samoan and Australian: an Australian-Samoan. My two cultures present a number of interwoven perspectives that influence my interpretation, and so I read from my hybridity. Hybrid identities are accustomed to various meanings being woven together, and the intention is not to replace an existing meaning but to allow for the different meanings to engage one another, to provide new and alternative meanings. The array of meanings of *hebel* is familiar territory for the hybrid identity and must be seen more as an opportunity for dialogue than as a search for one meaning.

## Alternative *Hebel*

The realities and challenges of my two cultures invite an alternative interpretation. The definition of *hebel* as "vanity" banks on the assumption that Qoheleth was a

---

[2] Bartholomew and O'Dowd (1990, 199) also comment on Qoheleth's individualistic character by stressing Qoheleth's continual use of the pronoun "I."

pessimist. Qoheleth was very much a recognized sage and may not have been a pessimist because he never recommended folly. The twists and turns of Ecclesiastes suggest that Qoheleth was simply philosophical (Murphy 2002, 51). If Roland E. Murphy is correct about Qoheleth being "philosophical," then an alternative view may be entertained.

As mentioned above, the word *hebel* also means "breath" and "vapor." In Isa 57:13 and Prov 21:6, the NRSV translates *hebel* with "breath." Crenshaw argues that *hebel* is linked with the word *reuth ruah* (Crenshaw 1981, 129; cf. Fox 1989, 45; Seow 1997, 102), which means "spirit." Ostriker (2007, 79–80) points out the significance of *hebel* connoting "that which is essential to life," implying a connection to the life-giving aspect of "breath" in Gen 2:7. These meanings are in stark contrast to the negative connotations of "vanity." I therefore wonder if these other meanings of *hebel* would affirm *tautua* (toiling) as opposed to it being rejected as vain.

*Hebel* as *Agaga*

I propose to reread Qoheleth's view of toil(ing) as *hebel* from an Australian-Samoan perspective. The meaning of *hebel* as "spirit" is intriguing. The Samoan word for "spirit" is *agaga*, and like *hebel*, *agaga* can also mean "breath" and even "wisdom" (Tofaeono 2000, 167). So, when Qoheleth considers toil(ing) to be *hebel*, perhaps it was because he could not comprehend the spiritual side of things. Murphy (1987, 259) states that Qoheleth "took God on God's terms. And God's terms were most mysterious for him. So difficult were they that he termed life futile." It was not that toil(ing) was vain but that he could not understand its significance. For Qoheleth, the significance of toil(ing) could only be comprehended by God.

Arthur J. Bellinzoni (2009, 278) states that "Qoheleth was ... a man who admitted that he was without knowledge of the things that matter most in life." The ideals, the dreams and the visions, which were envisioned through toil(ing), failed to reach its fruition as Qoheleth expected. For Qoheleth, things of the spirit were enigmatic (*hebel*) and best understood as God's wisdom (*agaga*). *Agaga* therefore connotes the enigmatic and unexplainable phenomenon that is found in *hebel*, and this is the sense of the word that I find appropriate in this study. Toil(ing) was therefore *agaga* and not *vanity*.

This understanding of *hebel* as *agaga* resonates with the so-called Aussie *spirit* of the battler. The term "battler" originated from colonial times, when the low-class citizens fought against a system that was corrupt and unjust. This spirit of never giving up permeated through to the Australian psyche and was adopted in the life and struggles of the everyday Australian. Living in the Australian context, such was my own prerogative as I struggled to achieve above what society expected of me. Such social expectations were low and often magnified through media, and subtly realized in the work place. Noriko Sekiya (2008, 26) comments on how the *battler* epitomizes this spirit:

> From the "toughness" cultural perspective, Australians admire *battlers* because Australians encourage people not to be overwhelmed by the harsh life which may face them but rather to "bear up" and try to do something for themselves. Therefore, the "fighting spirit" is highly respected in Australian culture.

This is how the Aussie battler struggles, and this is how the spirit is manifested, by fighting above his or her weight to achieve what nobody else would expect. For me as an Australian-Samoan, the Aussie *battler* spirit became the Aussie *agaga*.

Fusing the Two Horizons

The mystifying aspect of the Australian and Samoan spirits contextualizes the *hebel* that baffles Qoheleth. The fact that the spirit carries a certain mysticism thus creating a remarkably relevant rationale behind toil(ing) is enigmatic; and having said that, it is clear that Douglas B. Miller's (2000) realist position documents my own context. The realist position reveals that the voice of Qoheleth is the voice of one who has come to accept that some things do not warrant an explanation. From my hybrid perspective, I understand Qoheleth to be spiritually dumbfounded after coming to the realization that there is a greater being who controls the fate of humankind. It is not that Qoheleth considers toil(ing) to be vain but that he cannot express with words an explanation behind the validity of toil(ing) because it is spiritual. I contend that Qoheleth was a realist as he succumbs to the knowledge that only YHWH has the answer. Qoheleth has come to the conclusion that *tautua* is better left unexplained, for the definition lies with the divine. He is spiritually lacking in this sense and hence this is *hebel / agaga*.

The concept of toil(ing) that perplexes Qoheleth is better explained through the Samoan concept of *tautua* and the Australian notion of *battling*. *Tautua* and *battling* substantiate the phenomenon of pain as entailed in the Hebrew *āmal*, cogitating it as a relevant undergoing for it leads to *pule* (authority) and success. This removes the negative connotation of vanity from the translation of *hebel*, thus giving a positive feel to *toil(ing)*. From an Australian-Samoan perspective, this reading is far more applicable.

*Tautua* and *Battling*

The intersection of my two cultures allows for Qoheleth's voice to be heard in my context as an Australian-Samoan (cf. Gadamer 1989, 305). So we ask the question, what would Qoheleth say about *tautua* and *battling*? Perhaps Qoheleth could be heard through the voice of struggling immigrant families in Australia. Lenore

Manderson (2010, 248) points out that for all one's toil(ing), one is disadvantaged upon migration:

> Immigrant communities are disadvantaged by the loss of certain networks through migration and by the loss of salience of the networks they retain. While cultural capital may be something that one can carry around all the time—language, customs and cultural practices, beliefs and values—social capital only has value in given places and at certain times, and must be re-acquired with relocation. If so, then those who are secure and best educated will inevitably be ahead.

Coexisting with the rest of society when one is an immigrant is successful when cultural networks are established and sustained in the new setting. I nonetheless disagree with Manderson's statement that "those who are … best educated will inevitably be ahead." As I had experienced, educational background was never a guarantee for promotion. Education itself seems to be insufficient to make one be ahead, and Qoheleth probably implies this when he states in 2:22, "What do mortals get from all the toil and strain with which they toil under the sun?" (NRSV). Qoheleth's frustration echoes my own with regards to my hard work and my educational background being disregarded by my former Australian employers (cf. 2:23).

Furthermore, Qoheleth's thoughts may also enforce the question of whether or not I am toil(ing) by force, in order to maintain the status quo while at the same time, upholding the cultural ideology of working towards *pule* (Soo 2008, 164). The cultures of *tautua* and *battling* expect one to work and serve voluntarily, but ideologically they perhaps serve as a way of getting Australian-Samoans to maintain a hard work ethic which translates to a highly efficient society. Also, the Samoan *pule* may seem inviting and perhaps inevitable. But there are some situations where a *matai* title is conferred upon certain members of the *aiga* who have not served or performed *tautua* to the *aiga* and *nuu*. When this happens, Qoheleth is correct: "What do mortals get from all the toil and strain with which they toil under the sun?" (2:22 NRSV).

## Reading in Two Cultures

Australian-Samoans have trouble with understanding *toil(ing)* along with *vanity*, and I strongly expect that this is also the case in many other migrant cultures. The challenge lies therefore in interpreting Ecclesiastes in a manner that is meaningful and relevant for the reader. An alternative reading is needed.

Could the Real(ist) Qoheleth Please Stand Up?

Perhaps the ambivalence of *hebel* is deliberate. The word *hebel* means "breath," "wind," or "spirit," as well as "vanity," which is figurative. The problem with figurative speech is the existential factor behind understanding it. One must be able to relate to the context in order to understand the figurative meaning of a word. As an Australian-Samoan, I fail to comprehend toil(ing) as "vanity" because my context suggests otherwise. I read from my hybrid cultural perspective, and so I give room for other meanings of *hebel*.

It makes more sense to me if Qoheleth was a realist for that is a position that resonates with my two-cultures identity. I follow Miller's (2000, 234) definition of the realist position:

> The exhortations to enjoy life, to be wise, and to find good in one's work are not secondary to Qoheleth's main concern (the position of those who consider Qoheleth a repentant king or an ascetic). They are not half-hearted, wishful thinking, later additions to the book, or inconsistencies in Qoheleth's thought (the position of those who consider him a cynic). Nor are they something to do even though life is actually totally absurd (the position of those who consider him a preacher of joy). Rather, they are exhortations to the elements which, along with the fear of God, constitute the lifestyle which Qoheleth has been advocating all along through a process of destabilization and restabilization. He dispels the false hope that any of them can in themselves be a source of security or satisfaction, and he allows his readers to receive them as a gift from a benevolent, if mysterious deity. As gifts, they may be enjoyed for what they can legitimately provide.

As Miller implies, understanding *hebel* as "meaninglessness" or "nothingness" is a result of perceiving Qoheleth in a negative sense (cf. Bartholomew and O'Dowd 1990, 194). So who is the real pessimist? Perhaps it is not Qoheleth, but the readers!

Is This Reading Vain?

The ambiguity of meaning is a feature of wisdom literature that should not be ignored (Ingram 2006). The limitation of the English translation has been exposed, and this presents a precarious conundrum. We as readers need to realize that there are other nuances of the Hebrew *hebel* whose usage may depend on the context. In this regard, perhaps the ambiguity behind *hebel* was intentional. So that readers bring their context into the act of interpretation!

In wisdom literature, ambiguity is important, as Kathleen O'Connor (1990, 19) rightly argues: "According to wisdom life is not a simple set of truths to be followed scrupulously, but a continual encounter with conflicting truths, each competing claims upon the seeker." Seow (1997, 102) is well aware of this problem and reiterates that *hebel* is difficult to fix and pin down due to the fact that it can mean a number of things according to context. The term *agaga* is one alternative to account for this shortcoming. *Hebel* as *agaga* means that Qoheleth was silent over divine matters (Kruger 2004, 211) and that *'āmal* could only be explained by the divine (see also 3:10–12; 1:4–11; 6:10–12; 7:13–14; cf. Burnett 2010, 112).

## Conclusion

The challenge for readers of wisdom literature, and Ecclesiastes in particular, is not to uncritically accept the text but to allow for an exchange to take place. Allow the text to speak, and for the reader to speak back her or his understanding. The problem occurs when we speak back in terms unfamiliar to us. We need to converse in our own terms and our own concepts, and this is what biblical scholarship needs. This by no means translates into a neglect of modern and Western biblical scholarship. Rather, it allows readers to contribute to the meaning from within her or his two or more cultures or when the two horizons of the text (to borrow Gadamer's language) and the reader meet. In certain instances, such as the theme of toil(ing) in Ecclesiastes has shown, our cultural perceptions may create a newer understanding which had largely been oblivious to those who have already spoken.

This inquiry probes into the questions that Qoheleth asks in relation to toil(ing), and as a result, such questions provide an intriguing insight into *tautua* and *battling*. Am I simply toil(ing), serving *tautua*, and *battling* for the benefit of my *aiga*, family, and inheritance, or am I being forced to maintain the status quo of a working society whilst upholding a cultural ideology? I have never questioned *tautua* or *battling* in this sense, yet Qoheleth's understanding of toil(ing) has such implications for my own understanding.

While the question of inheritance was significant in my understanding of *tautua* and *battling*, had I accepted *tautua* uncritically? Was *tautua* for my pursuit for *pule*, or was it for the *pule* of another? Ecclesiastes 2:18–23 asks questions of our own understanding of whether we are sincere with our toil(ing) or not. Should we have concern for our heir and *aiga*, or should we enjoy it to ourselves as 2:24 suggests? This reading paves the way for an alternative understanding where the response to these questions allows for dialogue to be open.

We now are toil(ing) in a different age and different setting from Qoheleth's. As such, when we question the *hebel* of toil(ing), we should also allow the text to question the *hebel* of our own *tautua*.

## Works Cited

Aiono, Fanaafi Le Tagaloa, and R. G. Crocombe. 1992. *Culture and Democracy in the South Pacific*. Suva: Institute of Pacific Studies, University of the South Pacific.

Bartholomew, Craig G., and Ryan P. O'Dowd. 1990. *A Meditation on Ecclesiastes*. Grand Rapids: Eerdmans.

Bellinzoni, Arthur J. 2009. *The Old Testament: An Introduction to Biblical Scholarship.* New York: Prometheus.

Burnett, Joel S. 2010. *Where Is God? Divine Absence in the Hebrew Bible.* Minneapolis: Fortress.

Clines, David J.A. 2002. *Job 1–20.* WBC. Dallas: Word.

Crenshaw, James L. 1990. "Chapter 10: The Human Dilemma and Literature of Dissent." Pages 235–58 in *Tradition and Theology in the Old Testament.* Edited by Douglas A. Knight. Sheffield: JSOT Press.

Fox, Michael V. 1989. *A Time to Tear Down and Time to Build Up.* Grand Rapids: Eerdmans.

Gadamer, Hans-Georg. 1989. *Truth and Method.* Translated by Joel Weinsheimer and Donald G. Marshall. 2nd rev. ed. London: Continuum.

Ingram, Doug. 2006. *Ambiguity in Ecclesiastes.* New York: T&T Clark International.

Kidner, Derek. 1976. *A Time to Mourn and a Time to Dance: Ecclesiastes and the Way of the World.* Leicester: Inter-Varsity.

Krüger, Thomas. 2004. *Qoheleth: A Commentary.* Edited by Klaus Baltzer. Translated by Orville Cole Dean. Vol. 21. Augsburg: Fortress.

Manderson, Lenore. 2010. "Social Capital and Inclusion: Locating Wellbeing in Community." *Australian Cultural History* 2.3:233–52.

Miller, Douglas B. 2000. "What the Preacher Forgot: The Rhetoric of Ecclesiastes." *CBQ* 62.2:215–35.

Murphy, Roland E. 1987. "The Faith of Qoheleth." *Word & World* 3:253–60.

———. 2002. *Ecclesiastes.* WBC. Dallas: Word.

Neemia, Makesi. 2018. "The Priestly *Ger* (Alien) Meets the Samoan *Tagata Ese* (Outsider)." Pages 147–62 in *Sea of Readings.* Edited by Jione Havea. Atlanta: SBL Press.

Nofoaiga, Vaitusi. 2017. *A Samoan Reading of Discipleship in Matthew.* Atlanta: SBL Press.

Ostriker, Alicia Suskin. 2007. *For the Love of God: The Bible as an Open Book.* Piscataway: Rutgers University Press.

Sekiya, Noriko. 2008. "Aussie 'Battler' as a Cultural Keyword in Australian English." *Griffith Working Papers in Pragmatics and Intercultural Communication* 1:21–32.

Seow, Choon-Leong. 1997. *Ecclesiastes.* AB. New York: Doubleday.

Shuster, Martin. 2008. "Being as Breath, Vapor as Joy: Using Martin Heidegger to Re-read the Book of Ecclesiastes." *JSOT* 33.2:219–44.

So'o, Asofou. 2008. *Democracy and Custom in Samoa: the Uneasy Alliance.* Suva: IPS Publications, University of the South Pacific.

Taule'alo, Vanya. 1999. "Ua Sii le Matalalaga: Creating New Patterns in Pacific Art." *Australia Art Monthly* 121:1–6.

Tofaeono, Ama'amalele. 2000. *Eco-Theology: Aiga—The Household of Life; A Perspective from Living Myths*. Erlangen: Erlanger Verlag für Mission und Ökumene.

Towner, W. Sibley. 1997. *The Book of Ecclesiastes: Introduction, Commentary, and Reflections*. NIBC. Nashville: Abingdon.

Tutuila, Fereti. 2009. "A Critical Analysis of the Meaning of Tautua (Service) in the Lives of Faife'au Samoa (Samoan Ministers): Congregational Christian Church of Samoa (CCCS)." Unpublished Thesis. The University of Auckland.

Whybray, R. Norman. 1989. *Ecclesiastes*. Sheffield: JSOT Press.

Yeo, Khiok–Khng. 1995. *Rhetorical Interaction in 1 Corinthians 8 and 10: A Formal Analysis with Preliminary Suggestions for a Chinese, Cross-Cultural Hermeneutic*. Leiden: Brill.

Young, Loretta. 2007. "Gapatia i Faanoanoaga." Exegesis for the Degree of Master in Art & Design. Auckland: Auckland University of Technology.

# QOHELETH SILENCES WOMEN: REREADING ECCLESIASTES 2:25–26, 4:1, 7:26, AND 28 FROM INDIA

Laila Vijayan

Scripture, history, tradition, dogmas, and doctrines provide the backbones and skeleton of the events through the centuries. All these have taken different forms and varied frameworks but still continue to be the carriers of oppression and violence. Oppression and violence are visible through actions, speech, language, symbols, and so on; thus the people accept or internalize oppression and violence as part of realities, institutional structures, and cultural settings (in domestic and public spheres) that should not be challenged. What makes a person silent? Is it oppression, exploitation, and social rejection, or is it the political power or the experience of the other?

This chapter studies a selection of verses from the book of Ecclesiastes (7:26–28; 2:25–26; 4:1) that can be an oppressive device and a hindrance for the liberation of the people. In this paper, scripture is exposed from the perspective of a marginalized woman, a Dalit woman, a subaltern woman, who has experienced the oppression, exploitation, social rejection, and violence. Case studies are added to highlight the life experience of marginalized women whom people, systems, structures, and literature shame. These marginalized women are vulnerable in the society, victimized, and tortured to an extent that they have lost the power of discernment and the will to speak up as human beings.

The method used in this study is a social-scientific approach with feminist and Dalit perspectives. The honor and shame model is applied in this study to see how honor and shame are within the biblical text as well as affect the life of the Indian woman.

## India: Context of Study

In the Indian context, the life experience of the oppressed, marginalized communities is pathetic, and the social rejection that women experience is difficult to explain with words. The polyphonic expression of the victims of marginalization and oppression is challenging in the present context, but still a number of people are voiceless and continue to be the passive receptors of oppression, marginalization, exploitation, and rejection. I have had personal encounter with two organizations: one organization works for the welfare of the women who are destitute, abandoned, and mentally challenged because of the oppression, exploitation, and rejection, and the other organization stands for the rights of sexual minorities.[1]

Tears were in the voice of a woman who was battered as a wife of a truck driver at a very young age (twelve years) and became the mother of two children by seventeen. She left home and came with her husband and the two children to one of the metro cities in India. She started to work in a medicine factory where the supervisor beat her, found fault with her work, and abused her. After five years of silently bearing the pains for the sake of family survival, she moved to another garment factory. The pain and oppression did not come to an end by changing her workplace. At the new place, the supervisor and other officers in the factory found fault in her work until she compromised with her body. Neither the family nor the work place gave her a happy life; the woman continued to be the victim of sexual exploitation, violence, and oppression. She silently bore these pains because she wanted to provide food for the family and education for the children.

Her husband died from HIV, and she was informed by the doctors that she is also HIV positive. Unwisely, the doctors counseled her to be happy because the children's test results were negative. She was given a separate plate and drinking glass in the house after her husband's death. It was difficult to survive in the midst of torture and oppression, and so she decided to leave the house; she left the children under the care of her husband's sister, and she ran to the street for food, shelter, and clothing (the basic rights of a human being). The man who gave her food that first night became her partner, and eventually she became a commercial sex worker. She was arrested by the police, beaten so badly, abducted by four men, and abused continuously for a day and a night.

Over the last ten years she has lived as a commercial sex worker; now she serves as a leader to raise the voice for the voiceless who experience oppression, exploitation, and violence. She also lives with the realization that neither her family nor the society accepts the women who are in this profession. Still she asserts that her present life is peaceful and a source of income for survival. Her past experience and suffering made her courageous, and therefore she now stands as a voice of the voiceless women in the society and in the streets. She was a fortunate one who withstood the struggles and became a powerful leader, but hundreds of

---

[1] I visited and interacted with the inmates and also with the directors of the organizations. I have not revealed the names of the persons or the organizations for confidentiality. This I have done to make a comparison with the realities of the world today and to compare Qoheleth's statements of contradictions and tensions with the realities of the world.

young women who become victims of violence end their lives (suicide), become mentally sick, or live with the oppression and suffering with the belief that it is fate and God-given.

The twenty-first century witnessed courageous and brilliant women ascending the heights in the sociopolitical and religious arena of Indian society. A number of women have become CEOs of multinational companies and government offices, and the latest news of glory is Neelamani N. Raju, who became the first woman Director General and Inspector General of Police in the state of Karnataka, India. She is a 1983 batch IPS officer. The Chief Minister of Karnataka, Siddaramaiah, stuck to the policy of giving the senior-most officer the top police post, and thus Neelamani was given the position without gender discrimination. In the ecclesial context, the first Indian woman Bishop Right Reverend Eggoni Pushpa Lalitha became the bishop in the Nandyal Diocese of the Church of South India on September 2013.

On the one hand, some women reach the higher levels of service to experience freedom and render service to the society with dignity. But, on the other hand, many women are still victims of exploitation, oppression, rejection, and violence in society. This is the context in which this study explores whether some of the sayings of Qoheleth are oppressive against or liberating toward women who experience oppression, rejection, exploitation, and violence.

Qoheleth and Women

Wise/Wisdom

Traditional understandings of wisdom assign more significance to theological understandings, and therefore the one who "fears the Lord" is considered to be wise and will receive prosperity and blessing. Scriptural references support the view that the fear of the Lord is the beginning of wisdom (Prov 1:7; 9:10). But the biblical notion of wisdom carries a broader worldview. Wisdom is understood as "practical knowledge of life and of the world, based on experience" (Crenshaw 1969, 131). Wisdom is "the ability to cope," "the art of steering," and also "an approach to reality" (131). "The true wisdom is a divine prerogative and is available to humankind only as God chooses to reveal it" (Blenkinsopp 1995, 152). The religious basis of wisdom rests on the assumption that the creator established the world. Wisdom consists of proverbial sentence or instruction, debate, and intellectual reflection on themes such as self-evident intuition, mastering life for human betterment, grouping life's secrets with regard to innocent suffering, grappling with finitude, and the quest for truth, which is concealed in the created order and manifested through Dame Wisdom (Crenshaw 1981, 19).

Wisdom is more than a way of life, and much more than a literary form. It was the common way of thought and speech in which those who are called wise excelled (McKenzie 1967, 2). Wisdom is the total value of the human spirit—

emotional, ethical, and intellectual. These are ultimately the divine qualities, existent in the being of God long before creation (Irwin 1961, 142). The ancient Israelite wisdom has an optimistic view (Gemser 1979, 209). Some scholars consider biblical wisdom to operate in three dimensions—personal, universal, and literary (Bullock 1988, 22). In the personal dimension, wisdom is a skill and a philosophy. Wisdom enables a person "to assimilate, sort, and categorize the elements and issues of life so as to provide synthesis" (Bullock 1988, 22). A person accepts the sovereignty of God; at the same time he or she gives importance to paternal guidance to the people (cf. Prov 12:4; 19:14; 31:10–33; 13:22, 24; 22:6; 5: 1–14; 10:17; 13:13; 10:19; 11:12).

Wisdom as a universal dynamic means that wisdom is a separate entity (Prov 8:22). The word *qānāh* ("to possess or to acquire") is related to wisdom. The personification of wisdom as "an emanation of the divine life" means that God and wisdom are considered as sources of life (Bullock 1988, 25).

In the Hebrew scriptures, wisdom is also a literary dynamic (Bullock 1988, 26). Wisdom is "to know and to keep asking, to remember all our experiencing and to keep having new experiences" (Brueggemann 1972, 91). Wisdom is also understood as the ability to act or perform according to the circumstantial demand, and often it is considered as divine endowment. Walter Brueggemann argues that "wisdom is patient sorting out of what brings life and what does not" (18).

The terms and concepts of wisdom are explained mainly in relation to men. But within the Hebrew scriptures, the title *îšāh ḥŏkmāh* (wise woman) is used six times (Exod 35:25; 2 Sam 20:16, 14:2; Prov 14:1; Jer 9:16; Judg 5:25) but understood as mourning women, skilled women, women who possess special skills (weaving, spinning, trading, wailing), political shrewdness, are wisest among the princes, and so on (Vijayan 2007, 44).

Who really is wise? In the story of the woman discussed above, who is wise? Is the supervisor of the medicine shop or garment shop or the woman who was exploited by others wise? In light of the definition of wisdom as "the ability to cope" and "being crooked/shrewd," could this woman be called wise? Ten years of work in two factories only earned the daily sustenance for the members of the family. She now says that she was a fool because her body was exploited for food. Now being a commercial sex worker (knowing her rights as a worker), she feels that she is standing for the rights of women. She says that she is wiser now; she has attained a sense of self-determination to fight against the social rejection and exploitation.

Some women assert that rejection and exploitation has become a powerful tool for building a victim's self-determination (see Singh 2016).[2] There is a

---

[2] This book is a collection of twenty-one articles, where educators make a critical appraisal of Dalit memoirs. The strategic expressions of Dalit women, who used to consider exploitation and violence as part of Dalit experience, raised their voices by writing Dalit literature and autobiographies.

connection between rejection and creativity. Social rejection is the core experience of Dalit women. Social rejection can provide creative solutions (see Urmila 2008).[3]

In the Indian context, a wife is expected to be passive and do service to all the family members. In this service, she sometimes faces violence, oppression, or exploitation. Through it all, the woman is expected to be silent and also to live for the welfare of the other members of the family. A woman whom I met in one of the NGOs that takes care of destitute women shared stories of being tortured by her husband, father-in-law, and other men within the family. Home is considered to be a safe place and a shelter, but that place has become the source of exploitation and oppression; for her, home was the center of abuse and dehumanization. The continuous torture and sexual violence made her mentally sick; such people are either abandoned by the family on the street, or they ran out of the house to save their life. This is the story of other inmates too, and all these are the consequences of silenced voices within the family and in the society. When tradition and society view silent women as wise, those women are silenced even more.

What Is the Advantage of Being Human?

This rhetorical question is a typical feature of wisdom literature, and the expected response is to find enjoyment in one's toil. The same question has been reiterated in Eccl 2:22, 3:9, 5:6a, 8b, 11, 17 and found in ancient Near Eastern proverbs: "What is the advantage or profit of being a human?"

The use of rhetorical questions is characteristic of Qoheleth's writing. The rhetorical questions are used as a pedagogical device, and it makes the persons attain some kind of answers or conclusions on the basis of empirical observations (Ogden 1979, 342). These rhetorical questions had functional roles as well. The specific type of interrogative sentence offers instructions so it is an indirect form of education. It can be a catechetical-didactic opportunity (von Rad 1972, 18). Qoheleth raises questions from an anthropological position in which human beings are part of the creation (Zimmerli 1976, 176). These human beings have self-understanding that makes them declare that they are the covenant community. Often the rhetorical questions are related with humanity's advantage. The human's temporal situation is compared with the on-going nature of the cosmos and through which the contrast is presented; in other words, humanity is not able to comprehend the mysteries of the created order and its functions (Ogden 1979, 344). In light of the negative context of life, Qoheleth calls the people to enjoy the fruits of their toil. There is no profit or advantage to human beings' toil

---

[3] This is the memoirs of a woman who experienced social rejection, exploitation, and oppression, but she was able to overcome the challenges within the domestic and public spheres and says that her life experience made her have a powerful voice.

(Williams 1976, 375). So Qoheleth argues that the only advantage to the human being is that he or she could enjoy life.

This question could be heard as the cry of the oppressed or a sarcastic saying of the oppressor. If this verse is recognized within the royal testament, then it can be the colonizer's mocking statement to the less powerful nations. In the Indian context, sexual minorities continue to struggle to affirm their status socially, politically, and economically. They struggle to earn their livelihood by begging during the day and by working at night as sex workers. They toil, but they can never enjoy life because society sees them as a sexual minority. What is the advantage or profit they get in their toil, when all they get is only food to eat and nothing more? The silenced pains of alienation, exploitation, and marginalization from the individuals' families and the shelter in the streets are the realities of the society.

Enjoyment and God's Doing (2:24–26)

Contradictions and the polarities within Qoheleth's writings show that enjoyment belongs to a certain group of people but not to all. The purpose or the outcome of the toil must be materialized in the form of enjoyment, and it is mandatory, but then this enjoyment is predetermined by God to a select group of people. The purpose of life in this world is to eat, drink, and find enjoyment in the toil, if God has destined enjoyment for that subject. It is affirmed as the hand of God. To the one who pleases God, God gives wisdom and knowledge and joy, but to the sinner God gives the work of gathering and heaping. For apart from God, who can eat or who can have enjoyment? The one with whom God is pleased will receive wisdom, knowledge, skill, and enjoyment, but to the other it is the toil of gathering and heaping in order to give to the pleasing ones. Enjoyment is only for the one with whom God is pleased. Can this be a part of the scripture that authorizes the suffering of a group of people as God ordained?

Qoheleth divides people into two groups: ones who toil and others who enjoy the profit of others' toil. And it is only the ones to whom God gives the spirit of enjoyment that can enjoy life. Qoheleth repeatedly affirms that life needs to be enjoyed; better to eat, drink, and enjoy the life. This assertion is made because of the uncertainties in life; inheritance can be used wisely or foolishly, and human beings are unaware (ignorant) of the future events; death can encounter anyone at any time without the differentiation of rich or poor, wicked or righteous, wise or foolish, and therefore the advice is to enjoy life. But then this enjoyment is reserved for a group of people as predetermined by God. Nothing can be changed by human choice. Everything is determined by God's doing.

This teaching is a strong oppressive tool for exploitation, oppression, rejection, and violence. It can also be understood as the words of an oppressor who claims that if God was not pleased with you, you cannot enjoy the fruits of your labor. In the Indian society, manual labor is often done by the Dalit communities.

Dalits, who are outside of the *Varnasrama Dharma*, are the deprived communities. They are the lowest ranked people in the society.

This teaching is further intensified in 2:26, which says that "the gathering and heaping is done for others' benefit." Someone else with whom God is pleased will enjoy the fruit of one's labor. God gives to the one with whom God is pleased but not to the one with whom God is not pleased (Murphy 1992, 27). How reasonable is the theocentric approach of the idea, and how might people during Qoheleth's time have understood it? How do we understand this verse in terms of justice and righteousness? A group of people toil, and then someone else enjoys the fruits of their labor, and this was supposed to be God's action. In spite of one's toil, that person can never enjoy it. God's measures and human measures are totally different, and human beings can never fathom it. God is incomprehensible.

Qoheleth is trapped in the views of the oppressors, and it is the oppressors' device to exploit and oppress the working group and the marginalized in the community. The political agenda is theologized, and in a religious background no one can question or challenge God. In this way, the ideology of oppressors and rulers can never be questioned. I. Seligman claims that this is a transposition of motif (in Murphy 1992, 27). Does this transition happen because of the struggle in the mind of Qoheleth? Or is Qoheleth offering theological justification of the oppressor's deeds?

Scripture reaffirms the oppressors' policies, and this results in bondage of the marginalized communities in India. Social and political oppressions are supplemented and authenticated by religious ideology. The wicked's wealth is accumulated from the just and righteous. Who are the wicked in the Indian society? Is it those who challenge the traditional roles of women or those who raise their voices against exploitation wicked? Often the women who challenge the traditional system are denied their daily bread. It is difficult to understand the experience of violence and torture that these women experience, but the desire to live makes them surrender and not challenge the realities of the world. Qoheleth often seems to be oscillating between the tradition and reality. This is one explanation for why Qoheleth concludes every statement with the theme vanity.

Vanity

The Hebrew word translated as "vanity" (*hebel*) occurs seventy-three times in the Hebrew scriptures, with thirty-eight of those in the book of Ecclesiastes. The word *hebel* means "breath or vapor and hence it can designate what is lacking in substance (ephemeral), without any result" (Murphy 1992, 3). The word can also be translated as mist or smoke, and it is related to the ideas of fleetingness, transitoriness, and worthlessness. The figurative and conventional usage of this word is also found in the book of Ecclesiastes (Seybold 1972), referring to ephemerality (cf. Job 7:16; Ps 39:6, 12; see Murphy 1983, 85), triviality, nothingness, incomprehensibility, or mystery (Murphy 1972, 59), and senselessness. Qoheleth treats vanity as absurd. The quality of absurdity is not inherent in the phenomenon, but it is a relational concept. This means that there is always a tension between a certain reality and a framework of expectations (Fox 1999, 30; 1986, 413). Qoheleth commends that human labor produces goods and achievement, but all avails for nothing in the face of chance and death.

Oppression and Oppressor

> And again I saw all the oppressions that are practiced under the sun. Look, the tears of the oppressed—with no one to comfort them! On the side of their oppressors there was power—with no one to comfort them. (Ecclesiastes 4:1; NRSV)

Four phrases in this verse provide a picture of society: oppressions under the sun; tears of the oppressed; none to comfort the oppressed; oppressors have the power. Qoheleth uses these phrases to communicate the tension between reality and tradition. Oppressions are seen under the sun, but there is no specificity regarding whether these oppressions happened in which area of life. It is not clear if real oppression is visible in the social, religious, political, domestic, or public sphere of life. The situation is placed along with the consequences, but it is pathetic that one is not able to overcome the violent act of oppression. Power and authority makes the victim silent and passive bearers of oppression. Neither theocentric approach nor Qoheleth's voice is liberating for the oppressed; instead they elevate the power of the oppressor.

Tears are the visible expressions of unbearable pain and suffering. The pain and pathos of the oppressed ones or the victims are often ignored or silenced by the oppressor. God is identified as the cosufferer with the victims of silenced ones. The silence of Qoheleth is a tool to reaffirm oppression. God never betrays the victims, as God is the God of justice and righteousness. Qoheleth's passive acceptance of the oppressive structures is visible, and that leaves no salvific voice for the oppressed one.

Woman as Trap (7:26) vs. Not Found a Woman (7:28)

> I found more bitter than death the woman who is a trap, whose heart is snares and nets, whose hands are fetters; one who pleases God escapes her. (7:26; NRSV)

> Which my mind has sought repeatedly, but I have not found. One man among a thousand I have found, but a woman among all these I have not found. (7:28; NRSV)

The first woman is compared with death, and the second woman is compared with a man. Qoheleth says in other contexts that death is a better choice for human beings because they do not need to see what is happening in this world.

The woman as a dangerous trap with a heart filled snares and nets, hands with fetters, is taken to be more dangerous than death. To what kind of woman do these images apply? Do they apply to prostitutes, concubines, or the adulterous women in the Israelite society? How about the commercial sex worker and leader of the union whose story I shared above? She told me that when she was abducted by four men, she pleaded with them, saying that she is HIV positive; still the men made mockery and exploited her and later abandoned her in the field. What does 7:26 say to her when she stands as a voice for thousands of women who are the victims of the society? Qoheleth's views are oppressive and offer no empowerment for those women. Both men and women are in prostitution, but often only the women are victimized.

In 7:28 Qoheleth's comparison is with a thousand men and a thousand women, and again the woman is the victim of social rejection. Society continues to use the women in all areas of life for pleasure, enjoyment, and exploitation, but in the social status those women are unidentified, unnamed, and unremembered. The cruel actions, exploitative languages within scripture can never be a positive text for victims of exploitation. Qoheleth betrays thousands of women who can be the power of strength or the means of salvation to make a better world for the whole creation.

## Conclusion

I find it difficult to reread the book of Ecclesiastes from the present day context of India. Ecclesiastes is a book of tensions and polarities. The themes of vanity, fear of the Lord, and enjoyment of life may be interpreted in many ways. Qoheleth pays attention to the number of issues but dilutes the issues either by ascribing them to vanity or to God.

Even in the midst of social rejection and oppression, sexual exploitation, and violence, women who are deprived of their basic rights often rise up and stand for the rights of women in solidarity and with dignity. Authorities and power structures continue to oppress the women in the name of tradition, culture, faith, and modernity, but self-realization strengthens women to be a powerful voice for the liberation, to identify with victims, to struggle and journey with them so that they can experience the fullness of life.

Qoheleth's view on women is limited, and these could be interpreted as justification for the oppression of women, framed as honor to the androcentric community that affirm the power, strength, and actions of men as positive and women as sexual objects presented with the motif of shame. But victimized or oppressed women must challenge the traditional understandings, scriptural engagements, and doctrinal conceptions that continue to oppress them.

Honor is a positive term, and its opposite is shame. Honor is ascribed to the rich, wise, and righteous ones who please God, and these do not come from the margins of the society. But shame is ascribed as the trademark of marginalized people. On the other hand, the women who experience exploitation affirm that the body is not shameful but a powerful tool to give life to other silenced men and women in the society.

## Works Cited

Blenkinsopp, Joseph. 1995. *Wisdom and Law in the Old Testament*. Oxford: Oxford University.

Brueggemann, Walter. 1972. *In Man We Trust*. Atlanta: John Knox.

Bullock, Hasel C. 1988. *An Introduction to the Old Testament Poetic Books*. Chicago: Moody.

Crenshaw, James L. 1969. "Method in Determining Wisdom Influence upon Historical Literature." *JBL* 88:129–42.

———. 1981. *An Old Testament Wisdom an Introduction*. Atlanta: John Knox.

Fox, Michael V. 1986. "The Meaning of Hebel in Qoheleth" *JBL* 105: 409–27.

———. 1999. *A Time to Tear Down and A Time to Build Up*. Grand Rapids: Eerdmans.

Gemser, Berend. 1979. "The Spiritual Structure of Biblical Aphoristic Wisdom." Pages 208–19 in *Studies in Ancient Israelite Wisdom*. Edited by James L Crenshaw. New York: Ktav.

Irwin, William A. 1961. "Where Shall Wisdom Be Found." *JBL* 80:133–42.

McKenzie, John L. 1967. "Reflections on Wisdom." *JBL* 86:1–9.

Murphy, Roland. E. 1992. *Ecclesiastes*. Texas: Word.

———. 1983. *Wisdom Literature and Psalms*. Nashville: Abingdon.

Seybold, Keil. 1972. "Hebel." *TDOT* 3:313–20.

Singh, Bijender. 2016. *Dalit Women's Autobiographies*. Delhi: Kalpaz.

Urmila, Pawar. 2008. *The Weave of my Life: A Dalit Woman's Memoirs*. New Delhi: Columbia University.

Vijayan, Laila L. 2007. "Wisewoman." *In God's Image* 26:43–50.

Williams, James G. 1976. "What Does It Profit a Man? The Wisdom of Koheleth." Pages 375–89 in *Studies in Ancient Israelite Wisdom*. Edited by James L Crenshaw. New York: Ktav.

Zimmerli, Walther. 1976. "Structure of Old Testament Wisdom." Pages 175–207 in *Studies in Ancient Israelite Wisdom*. Edited by James L Crenshaw. New York: Ktav.

# TOILING WITH QOHELETH FOR PASIFIKA, PAPUA, AND PALESTINE: READING ECCL 3:9–13 WITH 7:13–18

Jione Havea

*Ko e hā 'a e 'aonga kiate ia 'oku fai e me'a kuo ne ngangau ai?*
— Eccl 3:9 (*Ko e Tohitapu Kātoa*; Bible in Tongan)

"What benefit is [there, in toil] for the one who does what caused [one's] madness?"

Qoheleth's question—"What gain have the workers from their toil?" (Eccl 3:9; NRSV)—should not be limited to the workers of the land or to the (material) fruits of their labor. This two-part suggestion goes against the grain of the Hebrew text and against the assumption of generations of biblical critics who conclude that Qoheleth's question was raised in the interest of people who work (till, labor, toil) the ground. Without refuting their exegetical findings and scholarly arguments, i offer this reading as, in the first place, a supplement to the Hebrew text and traditional interpretations because those have not come far enough toward Asia and Pasifika.[1] Put differently, and more directly, this chapter seeks to both liquify (dissolve) the text, one of the characteristics of islander criticism (see Havea, Davidson, and Aymer 2015; Havea 2018b), and to flow Qoheleth's question into Asia and Pasifika.

---

Parts of this essay were published in Havea 2018a and are appropriated for this chapter with permission from the publisher.

[1] Since i use the lowercase with "you," "she," "they," "it," and "others," i lowercase the first person also. i do not see the point in capitalizing the first person when s/he *is* in relation to, and because of, everyone/everything else. I use *Pasifika* for the "sea of islands" in the region otherwise known as Oceania, the South Seas, or Pacific Islands; i prefer Pasifika (an indigenizing of *Pacific*) because it flows calmly on native tongues.

## Tools

The second reason (excuse) for my reading against the grain is a decolonizing move: as long as we from Asia and Pasifika privilege the biblical text and the so-called correct translations and readings (as determined by European scholarship), we carry and protect the so-called master's tools. The problem with this is clear, as Audre Lorde (1984, 110–14) explains, because "the master's tools will never dismantle the master's house. They may allow us to temporarily beat him at his own game, but they will never enable us to bring about genuine change."

This essay thus opens by putting the master's tools aside and takes up a native tool (text, translation) that renders Eccl 3:9 as *Ko e hā 'a e 'aonga kiate ia 'oku fai e me'a kuo ne ngangau ai?* ("What use or benefit is [toil] for the one *who does what has caused her or his madness or headache?*").[2] There is no use, benefit or value in doing what makes one mad (*ngangau*) so the answer to the Tongan translation is obvious: stop doing it (the work that makes one *ngangau*). The Tongan text points Qoheleth's question at the *work* that is undertaken, whereas the NJPS directs the question at the *gain* from the work: "What value, then, can the man of affairs get from what he earns?" (see also NRSV and NIV).[3]

The Tongan text breaks from the traditional understanding and creates a space for hearing Qoheleth's question addressed both to the work and to the result (gain). I do not rule out the agricultural setting, which links Qoheleth's question to the garden story in Gen 3 (see below), but the Tongan text extends the scope of Qoheleth's question to toiling in other spheres. The biblical narrators are aware of people who *work* with altars and scrolls, with tabernacle and temples, with traditional knowledge and religious convictions, with other deities and ethnicities, with animals and birds, with bricks and mortar, and even with boats and nets across and over the sea. These workers too expect *gain* from their toil, with some form of wages or in kind(ness). I extend Qoheleth's question to these workers as well, as does the NJPS's "man of affairs," and i wonder why traditional translators

---

[2] I privilege the Tongan translation in this essay and will provide my translation of relevant texts into English in the body of the essay (and indicate where i refer to one of the authorized English translations). The translation of the whole Bible into Tongan was completed in 1903 and *Ko e Tohitapu Kātoa* (The Complete Sacred Book) was presented to the people and church in 1904. This was the result of a twenty-five-year project led by James Egan Moulton (of England) and assisted by four natives: Tēvita Tonga Mohenoa, Tēvita Fīnau, Sione Fekau and Kalisitiane Kolo Fīnau. Moulton gets most of the credit, but i suspect that the four natives (who were helped by other natives) did a lot of the work. It is possible to tell where the translation was by Moulton (e.g., transliterate "eternity" into "'itaniti" in Eccl 3:11) and where it may have been provoked by native speakers (e.g., the use of "ngangau" in Eccl 3:9 and "fakaongosia" in Eccl 3:10); a study of the politics of the Tongan translation is reserved for another opportunity.

[3] In this essay i use *Tongan translation* and *Tongan text* interchangeably.

and interpreters assume that Qoheleth's question applies to blue-collar farmers and agriculturists but not to white-collar professionals. Did traditional translators and interpreters not want to see (or admit) that their line of work was also open to the test of use, benefit and value? The answer to my (a Tongan) ideological and political rhetorical question is obvious, right?

Gain

The second part of my suggestion invites consideration of other forms of gain. Gain comes in many forms, and it could be nonphysical and nonmaterial. Emotional, political, psychological, and spiritual gains are as substantial as stock, produce, and financial gains. There is gain also in the satisfaction with one's toil, in realizing that one has performed a job well done, as well as in the distribution and sharing of the fruits of one's labor, as well as in reflecting on and interrogating texts and traditions. There is gain even in opening and broadening one's thinking about ideas and practices.

Gain is measured contextually, and the standard of measure fluctuates from time to time. What is considered as gain in one context (or generation) may not be welcomed in other contexts (or generations). For instance, a sow that suckles several piglets into good health is welcomed as a mother of gain in many native Pasifika societies but as a nuisance or even as a (means of) curse in other contexts.[4] What gain is depends on context and time, and so it is with loss. What i might consider as your loss might not be such a big deal for other friends and colleagues. The issue for me here is context rather than relevance: i am arguing for contextuality (context influences what gain or loss is) rather than for relativity (gain or loss has no real meaning).

Appreciation of gain also varies, and societies may change their appreciation of gain over time. So something kosher at one time could be banned as an abomination several generations later. The art of tattooing (*tatau*), for instance, was once valued by native Tongans as marks of belonging, of status, and of accomplishment (i.e., success and gain); then it was shunned by the generation of my great-grandfather at the behest of European Christian missionaries; but in the recent past, we have seen a revival of tattooing in Tongan communities at home and in diaspora, with the resurgence of the so-called tribal tattoo patterns (see Havea 2017).[5] Around the time when tattooing was banned in Tonga, some of the tattoo

---

[4] Similarly, what is appreciated as wisdom in some contexts may be laughed at as foolishness in other circles. And over time, the markers of wisdom and foolishness are reassessed and sometimes relocated.

[5] Disney contributes toward the revival of tribal Polynesian tattoo patterns through the tattooed body of the character Maui in the animated feature film *Moana* (2016). Whether Disney does justice to Pasifika legends and cultures will be discussed and evaluated in time, but Disney will surely *gain* at the box office.

patterns jumped from the bodies of natives onto other native art forms like weaving and *ngatu* (or tapa; see Vaka'uta 2017). Something that was celebrated became condemned, but now reaffirmed and regained.

For workers, gain makes a lot of difference. Gain has to do with ability and performance, and it could be condemned, rejected, and regained.

Frustration

Workers are frustrated when, by hook or by crook, they do not receive the gain that they expect. The word *frustration* is appealing with regards to Qoheleth as it translates one of the key themes of Qoheleth—*hebel* (see 8:10 and 8:14 in NJPS)—and it has a less depressing feel than "vanity." When i am frustrated, it is not automatically because of my capacity or my effort but about my expectations. My frustration does not mean that i am hopeless or that i have no hope. On the other hand, my frustration could help me appraise my expectations (and deserts) as well as inspires me to protest against authorities and systems that short shrift me and my work-mates. So there is *gain* in and through *frustration*; in other words, not all are in vain. Frustration is, unfortunately, a regular experience of workers (some of whom expect more than they deserve). Out of frustration, then, this essay explores how Qoheleth is both "frustrating [for] workers" as well as a means of relief for "frustrated workers."

Frustration brings me back to the Tongan translation: frustration is a key component in what gives or makes someone *ngangau* (madness, headache). This term is meaningful for a Tongan reflection on a wisdom text like Ecclesiastes because, in both informal and formal settings, *ngangau* is used in reference to the most useless of fools. The *ngangau* are people for whom not many (except for a few family members) bother or care. They are despised. Rejected. Overlooked. They are expendable. Troublesome. And a nuisance. But they are subjects that deserve recognition and engagement, especially in a reading that flows against the grain of both text and traditional interpretations.

In response to the foregoing reflection, this chapter involves an islander reading against the grain of Eccl 3:9–13 and 7:13–18 in solidarity with people who live and work on (is)lands under occupation in Asia and Pasifika. Those (is)lands include the western part of Papua, under occupation by Indonesia; Kanaky (New Caledonia), Futuna, Mā'ohi Nui (French Polynesia), under occupation by France; Tutuila (American Samoa), Guam, Northern Mariana, and Hawai'i, under occupation by the United States; Rapa Nui (Easter Island), under occupation by Chile; Kashmir, over which India and Pakistan have been fighting since 1947; and Palestine, under occupation by the State of Israel. While occupation is not (experienced as) the same for all, the frustration of workers in occupied (is)lands would be more manifold than the frustration of the workers in independent states (who are not totally free of frustrations). For this essay, because of the limit of space, i will focus on Papua and Palestine, which make Indonesia and Israel *ngangau*.

## Workers / Masters

Characteristics of wisdom teaching[6] are evident in Eccl 3:9–13:

> [9] What benefit is for the one who does what caused one madness? [10] I saw the bravery that Elohim gave to humankind as their burden. [11] For [God] has made everything beautiful in their setting and put eternity into their souls, therefore no one can explain the work that Elohim has done from the beginning to the end. [12] I know nothing is good in the commune, but for one to be happy and do good while one lives. [13] But this also, that every person eats and drinks, and know that all sorts of work have indeed been given by Elohim. (Translation from the Tongan *Tohitapu Kātoa*)

The focus of the pericope is on the worker ("the one who does" or NJPS's "man of affairs") and what she or he has gained (which could cause madness and headache). In the interest of the workers, Qoheleth's opening question is the kind of question that got Karl Marx ticking (see discussion of wages in Marx 1887, 378–99). Qoheleth sets up his answer to the opening question with two assertions:

(1) First, Qoheleth asserts that God "made everything beautiful in their setting" (Eccl 3:11a). It is not that there is *a time for everything* but rather, God has made everything "beautiful" for their setting ("setting" is translation of the Tongan *kuonga*, which applies to both time and space). When there is joy, Qoheleth supposes that God has made joy beautiful for the setting where it occurred; when there is pain, God has made pain beautiful for that setting; when there is sickness, health, laughter, mourning, and so forth, God has made those experiences beautiful for the time and place of their occurrence.

The Tongan "beautiful" (*faka'ofo'ofa*) allows for "bad things" to happen (even though those may not be "suitable," as in the NRSV) or to happen but the precise timing (NJPS) was not appropriate.[7] The Tongan text makes sense of Job's struggles: the bad things that happened to Job, and to his unnamed wife and their household, were not suitable nor at the right time, but they could be beautiful.

---

[6] Like other wisdom writings, Ecclesiastes focuses on living life meaningfully in the present (here and now, under the sun); Ecclesiastes is critical and controversial toward traditional teachings, especially around the doctrine of retribution; and Qoheleth is not bothered by the tensions and contradictions that may arise by the assertions that the book carries. Like other wisdom writings, Ecclesiastes is not the work of a systematic theologian!

[7] Compare to the dominant translations, which do not give room for accident or grace in Qoheleth's assertion: everything is "suitable for its time" (NRSV) and God "brings everything to pass precisely at its time" (NJPS). In the NRSV and NJPS, Qoheleth's assertion is problematized by the debate that Job offered, for the bad things that happened to Job were not suitable at that time. Rabbi Kushner (1981) goes further, asking a broader question concerning whether bad things are suitable *at any time* for good people.

While no suffering is suitable or at the right time to anyone, whether they are good or bad people (Kushner 1981), Job's suffering was beautiful in the sense that it shaped his character and became an opportunity for him to reflect on traditional and religious teachings about life, values, and relations. Suffering is still painful and ugly; the slaughter of people and animals, as well as the destruction of plantations and properties, are painful and ugly—but those are beautiful because they were opportunities for supplementation and alternative thinking. "Beautiful" (*faka'ofo'ofa*) here is a healthier option in contrast to "madness" (*ngangau*).

It helps that the suffering of Job, his wife, and their household, most painful and bloody ugly, is a literary construction. I read it with the Pasifika *talanoa* (story, telling, conversation) lens, in which Job as biblical text does not have to be historical. Nonetheless, there are actual people who suffer in similar ways to Job, like the people who are trapped in (is)lands under occupation—they are beautiful people, but what happen to and around them are painful and ugly. Their experiences are real, and i will return to this concern later.

(2) Qoheleth's second assertion is about the ability to discern and articulate: God "put eternity into their souls, therefore no one can explain the work that Elohim has done from the beginning to the end" (Eccl 3:11b). All that God has done is not known within the limits of time, nor in the presence of eternity. Though God put eternity into the human soul, the ability to know all that God has done is beyond the capacity of the human soul. The Tongan text presumes a distinction between *knowing* what God has done and *understanding* and *explaining* why God has done so, and all three capacities are beyond the human soul in spite of (this is stressed in the Tongan text) being endowed with (time-less) eternity. Human understanding is time-based, but this does not apply to God's business.

There is another way to understand the Tongan text: "God has put eternity into their souls *in order that* no one can explain the work that Elohim has done from the beginning to the end." God inserted eternity into the human "soul" (translation of the Tongan *loto*, which affirms that eternity is inside them) in order to block humans from being able to see and explain the work of God. Eternity is a blockade; filled with eternity, humans become eternal or other worldly so that they end up failing to see what was obvious in front of them—the work of God. That humans cannot discern or explain how God works is purposeful. After all, appropriating Qoheleth's own question, "what use is for the one who can explain what Elohim has done from the beginning to the end?"

God gave humankind (*hako'i tangata*) something as their burden (3:10), but no one really knows what task God has assigned for oneself (individually). It was not Qoheleth's agenda that humans know and/or understand what God has done. To borrow from Indigenous Australians, God's work is "secret business," which means that it is revealed through participation and ceremony. It is ironic that this wisdom text is about the limits on the ability of humans to discern, comprehend and articulate. In this light, the wise person does not know and does not understand. Even the wise person is ignorant of what God is doing (an example of biblical humor).

With those assertions, Qoheleth then provides his answer to the question in 3:9, and this is in two parts: what would be of use (or useful) "is to be happy and do good" (3:12b) and "that every person eats and drinks" (Eccl 3:13b). As suggested above, the Tongan text invites readers to distinguish between toil (labor, work) and fruit of or gain from toil. The question is about toil, gain, and fruits, but the answer focuses on labor. One should "be happy and do good" in what one does, so that "every person eats and drinks" (one gets a glimpse of the relational culture of Tongans in this rendering). The question was in the interest of the worker, but Qoheleth's answer is in the interest of the masters, who stand to gain when their workers and slaves enjoy what they do and the wealth (NJPS) that their toiling gives them. And the clearest sign that workers enjoy their toil is when they are obedient and silent (one gets a glimpse of the feudal Tongan society here). Be happy and be productive for the sake of every person. And be quiet. In this connection, Qoheleth's answer would make Marx turn in his grave (though i do not know if Marx read Ecclesiastes).

Genesis 2–3

Qoheleth's answer points me to Gen 2–3. The garden story opens with the affirmation that *ha'adam* was created for the purpose of tilling the ground (Gen 2:5) and ends with a string of curses (Gen 3:14–19). The serpent and the woman are cursed, and instead of cursing *ha'adam* YHWH cursed *ha'adamah* (the ground). In reading the curse of the ground through the eyes of the land[8] and in the shadows of Eccl 3:9–13 as read above, two elements jump out before me:

(1) First, the ground is cursed to sprout "thorns and thistles" (Gen 3:18) in response to the toil of *ha'adam*. This is a painful curse seeing that, in Gen 2:8–9 and Gen 1:11–12, the ground (land, earth) is appreciated for having the capacity to bring forth life. The Yahwist story affirms the capacity of the ground to bring up water (Gen 2:6, 2:10–14) and vegetation and the Priestly story affirms the life-giving power of the land: in Gen 1:11, God asked the land to bring forth life, and the land in Gen 1:12 responded by bringing forth many kinds of vegetation. In both stories, *ha'adamah* is cocreator with God.

The default stance of the land is to produce and bring forth life, so the curse in Gen 3:18 makes the land go against its natural disposition. The ground is cursed to only bring forth thorns and thistles, and Cain breaks this curse in Gen 4 when he brought "fruits of the land" as an offering to God. I have offered my reading

---

[8] Affirming that *the land has eyes* is common in, but not limited to, Pasifika (see Hereniko 2004). Nonetheless, readers use human lenses when they look for and through the eyes of the land.

of Cain breaking God's curse in another essay (Havea 2003) and will focus here on the curse of the ground.

On the basis of the curse of the ground in Gen 3:17–19, i ask back of Qoheleth: how is one supposed to enjoy working if it involves working with and in contexts that have been cursed? This question is critical for the natives in Pasifika who are struggling with the impacts of climate change, which is a recent form of cursing the land and the sea.

Furthermore, how might people in occupied lands enjoy their toil? This is also a critical question in Pasifika, where many lands are still under foreign occupation. I will come back to these struggles in Pasifika, with special attention to the impact of climate change in Tuvalu and Kiribati, and Indonesia's occupation of West Papua, which results in the brown and black natives not being allowed to enjoy working, to enjoy the fruits of their labor, nor to enjoy the rich resources of their native land and seas.

(2) The second element that makes the curse of the ground painful is God's decision that *ha'adam* will return in the end to dust (Gen 3:19b). With human eyes, we celebrate this decision and declaration as our human destiny—to dust we shall return because from dust we were taken. We imagine that our bodily remains will be a blessing to the ground. But if we look at the curse with the eyes of the land and of the sea, is this really a good thing? Good for whom? According to whose values? What benefit is it to the ground that we humans return to dust? I ask these questions as someone who comes from oral cultures where the return of gifts is insulting, especially if the gifts were received, used, and destroyed and then returned.

YHWH's design of the destiny for *ha'adam* involves returning a gift that the ground had given (Gen 2:7): the ground gave the gift of human body, which God and *ha'adam* used, and God declared that the gift will be returned to the ground so that it may reclaim its gift/dust. Humans, of course, do not wait until the end to return to dust, for we daily excrete components of dust to the ground. To borrow from Eccl 3, what gain does the ground get from human dust and human feces? I point this question back to Eccl 3:13, in order to ask, whose enjoyment matters? The enjoyment of the workers? The enjoyment of the owners? Is there a place for the enjoyment of the ground, the land, and the sea to matter? This last question points me back to Pasifika and the struggles of natives with climate change and against occupation by foreign empires.

Pasifika

The island groups of Tuvalu and Kiribati have caught the attention of environmentalists and politicians in the recent past because of the havoc that climate change brings upon low-lying lands especially, and the threats to the world as a whole. Tuvalu and Kiribati are not the only island nations threatened by climate change (resettlement has already taken place in PNG and Solomon Island), and there are more populous nations (e.g., Bangladesh) under threat from climate change. In the case of Tuvalu and Kiribati, i call attention to two less-known struggles of the two groups:

First, ecological disaster is not new to Tuvalu and Kiribati. These two culturally distinct groups used to be combined as one British colony named Gilbert and Ellice Islands until 1976 when the group was separated into two countries and gained independence. While still a British colony, two of the islands were resettled to islands in Fiji: natives from Banaba (an island in today's Kiribati) were moved to the island of Rabi beginning in 1945, because their home island had been devastated by phosphate mining (so the island of Nauru); and natives from Vaitupu (an island in today's Tuvalu) were moved to the island of Kioa in Fiji beginning from 1947 to 1983.[9] Both Banaba and Vaitupu suffered because of human civilization: the destruction of Banaba was hurried by economic and developmental endeavors, while overcrowding and soil erosion made Vaitupu inhospitable.

With regard to Qoheleth's question, the natives of Banaba and Vaitupu, and by extension the groups of islands in Kiribati and Tuvalu, could no longer gain from their toil. In fact, other peoples, corporations, and nations were toiling and enjoying the gain from their (is)lands. The natives had to be moved because their home islands, once rich with resources, became cursed grounds.

Second, Kiribati and Tuvalu were in the front line of the so-called Pacific War. This war was not between Pasifika islands, but between the United States and Japan. The capital islands of Funāfuti (Tuvalu) and Tarawa (Kiribati) still bear the scars of this war, with corroding war machineries on shore and the open pits (in Funāfuti) dug up for the construction of the airstrip used in the war. There are a lot of references to the highest point on Tuvalu being 4.6 meters above sea level (at Niulakita), but not enough conversations around how the Americans dug several points on Funāfuti below sea level. Those pits are filled with sea-water twice a day, when the tides come in.

Climate change is not new to Kiribati and Tuvalu, and war contributed to the ruining of both island groups. The natives of Kiribati and Tuvalu, and of Pasifika in general, have had to live with and through ecological disasters, but the world community only pays attention when they realize that their existence is also threatened. Adding to the pains of the natives, the world community conveniently forget that war between superpowers—both the actual fighting and the testing of weapons of war in Pasifika waters during the Cold War—is a contributing factor to the ecological disasters in Pasifika. It is difficult for native workers to enjoy their toil, and the world community is not keen on seeking climate justice.

---

[9] It was only in 2005 that the Fiji government decided to grant full citizenship to the Kioa and Rabi islanders.

## Papua

The case of West Papua is painful because the natives do not have the freedom to toil. The largest island (in terms of land, population, and languages) in Pasifika is split between two nations—Papua New Guinea (PNG) to the east with West Papua to the west. West Papua was colonized by the Netherlands in 1898 and called it Irian Jaya. The Dutch government also colonized Indonesia but granted independence for Indonesia in 1945 (however it was not until 1959 that Indonesia was recognized as an independent nation). West Papua meanwhile remained a Dutch colony.

The Dutch government promised independence for West Papua in 1961, and by 1 December 1961 West Papua had a national flag, a national song, a national parliament, and a national police. Indonesia shortly afterwards invaded West Papua and made it a province of Indonesia (Papua Barat), and the Dutch government did not fight the Indonesians for the sake of West Papua. As expected, the native Papuans had no chance against the stronger Indonesian forces.

In 1962 the United States stepped in and brought West Papua under the protection of the United Nations, but in 1963 the United Nations gave control over West Papua to Indonesia. This move was not questioned because it was supposed that the black natives were too primitive to "cope with democracy" and that they could not lead national affairs. Since Indonesia occupied West Papua, Indonesian forces have slaughtered more than 500,000 native West Papuans and tortured, raped, and imprisoned thousands more.[10]

West Papua is fenced off from PNG and excluded from the rest of Pasifika. In September 2016, finally, seven Pasifika nations spoke up at the United Nations General Assembly in solidarity with West Papua and in protest against Indonesia's occupation of West Papua. Time will tell what becomes of West Papua, but Qoheleth's question is painful for the natives of West Papua. How could people whose home(is)land is under occupation gain from, much less enjoy any fruit of, their toil?

## Palestine

I am interested in Palestine as part of Asia, as well as one of the lands that have paradisiac appeal in the Bible. Viewing Palestine as paradise, insofar as the biblical version of the Abrahamic story is concerned, stems from YHWH's call of Moses, which many read partially, focusing on the spacious land overflowing with milk and honey but overlooking the fact that it is remembered as occupied land:

---

[10] Further information available at the international Free West Papua Campaign website (https://www.freewestpapua.org).

> So I have come down to save them from the hand of the Egyptians, and to bring them up from that land to a good and spacious land, a land overflowing with milk and honey, *the place of the Canaanite and the Hittite and the Amorite and the Perizzite and the Hivite and the Jebusite*. (Exod 3:8, a translation from the Tongan *Tohitapu Kātoa*; my italics)

The NIV is poignant, identifying this land as "*the home* of the Canaanites, Hittites, Amorites, Perizzites, Hivites and Jebusites." The destination for the rescued Israelites was a home, and it was not empty.[11] The natives were not faceless, so they could not be forgotten in the hinterland.[12] This biblical awareness is not new. Canaan-Palestine has always been remembered as occupied land, from the very beginning of the biblical Abrahamic story. Shortly (in narrative space) after receiving the mission and promises from YHWH (Gen 12: 1–3), Abram moved:

> Abram went on through the land as far as the place of Shechem, up to the tree of Moreh. *The Canaanites were in the land at that time*. The LORD appeared to Abram and said, "[to] Your offspring, I shall give this land." So he built an altar there to the LORD, who appeared to him. (Gen 12:6–7, a translation from the Tongan *Tohitapu Kātoa*; my italics)

The home(land) of native people are desired by another people whose forbearers were not indigenous to that land/home. Promising the land to an incoming foreign people requires the removal of the native people. Fast forward to the present time, and Palestinian Christian theologian Mitri Raheb's assertion rings loud and painfully clear:

> Our [Palestinians'] history, roots, and presence in the Holy Land are overseen so that we become invisible; as if this land were "a land without a people" for "a people without a land." What happens here is a real "displacement theology": the Palestinians were theologically replaced by the modern State of Israel and politically displaced from the land of their ancestors. (Raheb 2011, 11)

The Jewish settlers who are now occupying Palestine, encouraged and pardoned by the world's guilt because of the Holocaust and set apart by walls of separation, do so by displacing native Palestinians. These Jewish settlers are not all sons and daughters of native people of Palestine:

> Many of the Jewish emigrants to Palestine were actually not the descendants of those native people who were exiled but mainly the descendants of North African

---

[11] Those who assume that the land was vacant upon the call of and promise to Abram, or later in the 1880s or in 1948, were wrong (so Ateek 1989, 26).

[12] A parallel could be drawn with the situation in Australia: when white settlers arrived, they pretended that the land was empty (*terra nullius*) and claimed it without respect to the Indigenous Australians (the majority of whom were in the hinterland).

Berber tribes or Eastern Europeans "Khasar" tribes who converted to Judaism. For them Jerusalem was like Rome for Catholics. One should be careful when talking about the "return" of the Jews, as if they are experiencing something of a homecoming to their original land. (Raheb 2012, 16)[13]

The sum of the foregoing reflection is obvious: the Jewish Zionist settler project seeks the "ethnic cleansing of Palestine,"[14] and this is "a crime against humanity, punishable by international law" (Pappe 2006, 1). Yet, the world turns a blind eye, preferring to forget (see Masalha 2012, 120–34).[15] And mainline theologians are deconscientized by hermeneutics that justify occupation and displacement (so Ateek 1989, Raheb 2012).

In Pasifika, we call forced entry into native people's homeland invasion. Other people may give it a different name, but invasion by a different name is still invasion; displacement by another name is still displacement; ethnic cleansing by another name is still ethnic cleansing; colonization by another name is still colonization (see Havea and Neville 2014). Natives of Pasifika could therefore easily identify with Palestine and Palestinians—"a people not fighting to destroy its neighbor, but a people fighting for the right to be a neighbor" (Ateek 1989, 47).

Like the people and land of Papua, the people and land of Palestine are under occupation and Qoheleth's question applies to them also: what use is for them to do what cause them madness?

Toiling Qoheleth

I read Eccl 3:9–13 as *a response to the event* that is Gen 2–3, with my preferred living context of Pasifika in the background. My reading is unapologetically contexted. I privileged a native text and translation, and i enable two texts in the closed canon to listen to one another, and for me, readings of those texts that do not address the struggles with climate change and with political occupation have no relevance for Tuvalu, Kiribati, West Papua, Palestine, and many (is)lands and

---

[13] Raheb draws on the work of Shlomo Sand, professor of history at Tel Aviv University, who asserts: the "fact is: most of these European Jews were but descendants of European tribes that converted to rabbinic Judaism in the middle ages; so their ancestors were never ever in Palestine; they were never exiled; and their connection to Canaan was more like the connection of Catholics to Rome. This invented 'mythistory' became the foundation for Zionism that created the political ideology connecting 'the people' with 'the land' with the aim of creating there a 'Jewish State'" (cited in Raheb 2011, 13).

[14] Pappe refers to the 1948 occupation of Palestine and displacement of the Palestinians as "ethnic cleansing" rather than "Nakba" (catastrophe) because "ethnic cleansing" gives a human face to the atrocity (see also Masalha 2012).

[15] Loss of memory is a painful ailment for oral preferring peoples. While talanoa and orality may not always be historically precise, as far as record-keeping historians are concerned, talanoa and orality are in the battle against memory loss.

nations in Asia and Pasifika. Those readings might pass as contextual biblical interpretations but they are useless for us in Asia and Pasifika.

The two-part assertion that Qoheleth offers are not satisfactory when assessed through the realities of Tuvalu, Kiribati, West Papua, and Palestine. What do workers in climate affected and occupied lands gain from their toil? Qoheleth's answer is useless for those workers. But Qoheleth's question rings with hope, so his question—"What use is for the one who does what caused one madness?"—is more useful than his answer.

What gain have i received from this reading? Simply this, that with regards to Eccl 3:9–13, the question is more relevant than the answer. This gain is non-material, but *beautiful*.

*Muna*

To close this essay, i turn to one of the concepts for which Qoheleth is remembered—*hebel*, usually translated as "vanity"—through Eccl 7:13–18:

> [13] Look properly at the work of Elohim. Who can correct what [Elohim] has made to be crooked? [14] On a good day be well, and on a bad day look goodly at this: Elohim has made *this* and *that* to be stable, so that no one will guess things after death. [15] The various things that I have seen in my illusive days: a righteous person was lost in spite of being righteous; and a wrongdoer prevailed in spite of doing wrong. [16] Don't be too righteous; and don't be too wise: what use is in your becoming wasted? [17] Don't do too many wrongs; and don't be a fool: what use is in your dying before your time? [18] It is better that you hold on to *this* but don't pull your [other] hand from *that*; for the one who fears Elohim will be spared from it all. (Translation from the Tongan *Tohitapu Kātoa*, my italics)

Qoheleth's tune changes. This time, a human can see the work of God (7:13a; compare 3:11) on both good and bad days (7:14a). However, no one can make straight what God has made to be crooked (7:13b). One could see but could not adjust God's crooked work. Whether this makes Elohim a crooked God is not Qoheleth's concern. What seems more important for Qoheleth is to declare that God has made the crooked things to be "stable" (for *fakatoukatea*, double-outrigger; 7:14b). The Tongan *fakatoukatea* refers to a canoe with two outriggers (*katea*), both of the same size and both could carry travelers and cargo.[16] Though crooked, God's work is *fakatoukatea* and could carry burden (cf. 3:10). And as long as God's work is *fakatoukatea*, there is no need to correct it. God's work is useful even in its crookedness.

In 7:15, Qoheleth turns to the crooked things that he observes among humans during his "illusive [*hbl*] days": a righteous person was lost, while a wrongdoer

---

[16] Compare to canoes made of one outrigger with a float-attachment (not for carrying people or baggage) to help keep the canoe from tipping over.

prevailed. Things do not turn out as expected. Life is crooked. Such was what Qoheleth observed during his "illusive [*muna*] days" (compare NJPS: "In my own brief span of life"). Like his days passing like an illusion (*muna*), the things that passed before his eyes, the things that he saw, were also like an illusion.

Because *muna* also refers to the "pretend play" (*faka-muna*) of children, Qoheleth teases the imagination of readers: through his "brief span of life," he simply played pretend (*muna*, *hebel*, illusion). He was not stuck in some deep theological position or some high moral ground; rather, he found the work of God and the unfolding of life to be, simply, *fakamuna*. In other words, he did not take things too seriously. This makes sense of his advice:

> Don't be too righteous; and don't be too wise.
>
> Don't do too many wrongs; and don't be a fool.
>
> It is better that you hold on to *this* but don't pull your [other] hand from *that*. (7:16–18)

Qoheleth observed that God made things to be crooked and that life was crooked, and advised readers to be crooked also. If workers toil according to Qoheleth's directions, they will not reach *ngangau* (madness, headache) and frustration. Rather, they will come to appreciate and celebrate *muna* (*hebel*, illusion, pretend play) as an effective way of coping with the crookedness of the work of God and the crookedness of life. In this regard, the Tongan text makes *hebel* (*muna*) beautiful as well.

Qoheleth's advice can help workers on climate changed and occupied (is)lands in Asia and Pasifika cope with the crookedness of God and of their life situations. And it would be useful for them to see their burden as *muna*. But Qoheleth did not come far enough, for he did not condemn, for instance, the carbon civilization that is the biggest contributor to climate change nor the occupying governments of Indonesia and the modern State of Israel. Of course, these modern struggles were not part of his worldview. Qoheleth is excused, but not readers who toil with his (and other biblical) texts, whether in Hebrew or in any of the vernacular languages of the world.

## Works Cited

Ateek, Naim Stifan. 1989. *Justice, and Only Justice: A Palestinian Theology of Liberation.* Maryknoll: Orbis.

Havea, Jione. 2003. "To Love Cain More than God, in Other Words, 'Nody' Gen 4:1–16." Pages 91–112 in *Levinas and Biblical Studies.* Edited by Tamara C. Eskenazi, Gary A. Phillips, and David Jobling. Atlanta: Society of Biblical Literature.

———. 2013. "Diaspora Contexted: Talanoa, Reading, and Theologizing, as Migrants." *Black Theology* 11.2:185–200.

———. 2015. "Sea-ing Ruth with Joseph's Mistress. Pages 147–61 in *Islands, Islanders, and the Bible: RumInations*. SemeiaSt 77. Edited by Jione Havea, Margaret Aymer, and Steed Vernyl Davidson. Atlanta: SBL Press.

———. 2017. "*Tatau*ing Cain: Reading the Sign on Cain from the Ground." Pages 187–202 in *The Bible and Art, Perspectives from Oceania*. Edited by Caroline Blyth and Nāsili Vaka'uta. New York: Bloomsbury.

———. 2018a. "What Gain Have the Workers from Their Toil? (Con)Texting Ecclesiastes 3:9–13 in Pasifika." in *The Five Scrolls*. Edited by Athalya Brenner-Idan, Gale A. Yee, and Archie C. C. Lee. Texts @ contexts. New York: Bloomsbury.

———, ed. 2018b. *Sea of Readings: The Bible in the South Pacific*. Atlanta, SBL Press.

Havea, Jione, and Neville Naden. 2014. "Colonization Has Many Names." Pages 1–8 in *Indigenous Australia and the Unfinished Business of Theology: Cross-cultural Engagement*. Edited by Jione Havea. New York: Palgrave.

Havea, Jione, Steed Vernyl Davidson, and Margaret Aymer, eds. 2015. *Islands, Islanders, and the Bible: RumInations*. SemeiaSt 77. Atlanta: SBL Press.

Hereniko, Vilisoni. 2004. *The Land Has Eyes* [Film: *Pear ta ma 'on maf* in Rotuman]. Suva: PBS.

*Ko e Tohitapu Kātoa.* 1966. Suva: Bible Society of the South Pacific.

Kushner, Harold. 1981. *When Bad Things Happen to Good People*. New York: Random House.

Lorde, Audre. 1984. *Sister Outsider*. New York: Crossing.

Marx, Karl. 1887. *Capital: A Critique of Political Economy*. Moscow: Progress.

Masalha, Nur. 2012. *The Palestine Nakba: Decolonising History, Narrating the Subaltern, Reclaiming Memory.* London: Zed.

Pappe, Ilan. 2006. *The Ethnic Cleansing of Palestine.* Oxford: Oneworld.

Raheb, Mitri. 2011. "Displacement Theopolitics: A Century of Interplay between Theology and Politics in Palestine." Pages 9–32 in *The Invention of History: A Century of Interplay between Theology and Politics in Palestine.* Edited by Mitri Raheb. Bethlehem: Diyar.

———. 2012. "Toward a New Hermeneutics of Liberation: A Palestinian Christian Perspective." Pages 11–27 in *The Biblical Text in the Context of Occupation: Towards a New Hermeneutics of Liberation.* Edited by Mitri Raheb. Bethlehem: Diyar.

Vaka'uta, Nāsili. 2017. "Art as Method: Visualising Interpretation through Tongan Ngatu." Pages 97–116 in *The Bible and Art, Perspectives from Oceania*. Edited by Caroline Blyth and Nāsili Vaka'uta. New York: Bloomsbury.

# JUSTICE IN ECCLESIASTES (3:16–4:3 AND 8:10–17)
# A MISSIONAL READING FROM AND FOR PALESTINE

Anton Deik

My interest in Ecclesiastes goes back to East Asia. I started reading the book in the Philippines—a context of severe economic oppression. I witnessed in Manila how thousands of families live in extreme poverty at dump sites. These families made their livelihood from garbage, toiling from the early hours of the morning in search of plastic containers and food leftovers. They sold the plastic for a few pesos, and the leftovers of the rich people became food for their children. In a striking contrast, moving to Hong Kong after a year-long ministry in the Philippines, I had my first encounter with extreme luxury in Tsim Sha Tsui near the Victoria Harbor. There, I saw people lining up under the sun for hours in front of Gucci and Louis Vuitton to buy luxury bags priced at 10,000 HKD upwards. I also saw jewelry stores displaying watches with 12M HKD price tags. So, I cried with Qoheleth: *vanity of vanities!*[1]

My reading of Ecclesiastes continues in Palestine, my homeland, with another kind of oppression. My people, the indigenous people of Palestine, have been living under an iron-fist military occupation since the establishment of the State of Israel in 1948. To establish the Jewish state, the Zionists had to ethnically cleanse Palestine from its indigenous population, expelling more than 750,000 Palestinians (among them my grandfather and his family), depopulating more than five hundred Palestinian towns and villages and committing no less than twenty-four massacres against the Palestinian people. The result was the occupation of

---

[1] In this chapter, *Ecclesiastes* refers to the whole book and *Qoheleth* refers to the author of Eccl 1:3–12:7. The introduction of the book and its epilogue (1:1–2 and 12:8–14) I take as written by another person, referred to here as the (frame) narrator.

78 percent of historical Palestine in 1947–1949. This is known in Palestine as the *Nakba* (the catastrophe).[2]

In 1967, Israel occupied the remaining 22 percent of historical Palestine: the West Bank, Gaza Strip, and East Jerusalem, referred to today as the Occupied Palestinian Territories (OPT). East Jerusalem has been fully annexed by Israel since 1980, and although Palestinian governments are present in Gaza and 40 percent of the West Bank (Areas A and B according to the Oslo Accords), the entire area of the West Bank and the Gaza Strip remains under full Israeli military control. Furthermore, 60 percent of the West Bank has already been confiscated by Israel for their ever-expanding settler-colonial project. Life in Bethlehem, where my family has been living for at least a millennium, is marked by Israeli military checkpoints, eight-meter-high apartheid wall, confiscation of land, continuous expansion of settlements, forced separation of families (what my wife and I are going through at the time of writing this chapter), illegal military arrests in the middle of the night, water shortage in order to fill the swimming pools of the Israeli settlers, and the list goes on and on.[3] Zionist perpetrators and oppressors remain unpunished. On the contrary, they live in prosperity and their actions are seen by many as self-defense. Moreover, many Christians who worship Jesus as their Lord and Savior do not hesitate to defend and justify the ongoing *Nakba* of the Palestinians, interpreting it as an act of divine faithfulness. For me as a Palestinian Christian living under Israeli military occupation, this is absurd, *hebel*!

In this chapter, I stand in twenty-first-century Palestine in solidarity with readers from Asia and Pasifika, trying to understand and relate to the struggles of Qoheleth, who battled with oppression and injustice in ancient Palestine. In what follows, I uncover a missional dimension in Ecclesiastes and relate it to modern-day Palestine-Israel. I have two goals. First, to offer a Palestinian Christian missional reading of the text that I hope could motivate other biblical interpreters to consider a missional hermeneutic in reading Ecclesiastes. Second, to offer the church a missiological paradigm that helps it act differently in contexts of oppression and injustice, especially in Palestine-Israel. I accomplish these goals by focusing on two parallel passages that reflect the gist of Qoheleth's thinking on justice and oppression: Eccl 3:16–4:3 and 8:10–17.

The chapter is organized as follows. I first briefly explain my hermeneutical approach and present my exposition of the passages. I then synthesize and summarize my Palestinian Christian missional reading of the text and relate it to

---

[2] For more about the Palestinian Catastrophe (*Nakba*) of 1948, or what Israeli historian Ilan Pappe rightly calls the *ethnic cleansing* of Palestine, see Pappe 2007 and Masalha 2012.

[3] For an introduction on the situation of the West Bank, East Jerusalem, and Gaza Strip since 1967, see White 2014, 62–109. The Palestinian Lutheran theologian Mitri Raheb also provides an excellent first-hand account of the situation in post-1967 West Bank (Raheb 1995, 29–32).

Palestine-Israel, focusing in particular on the role of the Christian church in the Palestinian-Israeli conflict.

## Reading with Two Lenses

Palestinian Christian interpreters typically use two hermeneutical lenses to read Old Testament texts: a Christian lens and a Palestinian lens.[4] I too use both lenses. First, I read Ecclesiastes as scripture; that is, I read the text theologically (see Vanhoozer 2005). Ecclesiastes is part of my spiritual heritage as a Christian, and I believe its inclusion in the scripture, despite ancient debates, is purposeful. The text contains significant theology; as Bartholomew (2009) maintains chapter after chapter in his commentary, there are important "theological implications" to the text. In particular, I read Ecclesiastes with what has been referred to as a "missional hermeneutic" (see Wright 2006, 33–69; Goheen 2016).[5] The Bible tells the story of the mission of God "under the sun," and Ecclesiastes is part of this grand narrative. Rather than reading Ecclesiastes as the musings of a distant intellectual, I read the sayings of Qoheleth as "goads" (Eccl 12:11) that are meant to move the reader into mission. In doing this, I hope to motivate Bible interpreters to look at Ecclesiastes as a missional text. The outpourings of Qoheleth, as will be shown below, are cries that are meant to provoke action.

Second, I read Ecclesiastes as part of my Palestinian heritage. Following the Palestinian Christian theologian Mitri Raheb (2014), I consider the text part of the *longue durée* history of Palestine.[6] Qoheleth most likely lived in Palestine when it was under the Greek Empire,[7] and thus the text he wrote represents the cry of a sage from ancient Palestine, who lived in the context of empire, oppression, and injustice. Using a Palestinian hermeneutical lens allows me to use my modern-day Palestinian experience of occupation, injustice, and oppression, to better

---

[4] This hermeneutical framework is used by the majority of Palestinian Christian interpreters of the Old Testament. But it is defined differently by different interpreters (see e.g., Ateek 2008, 53–56; Ateek 1989, 74–86; and Raheb 1994, 55–64). For a more conservative use of this hermeneutic, see Katanacho 2013. It is worth mentioning that Raheb modifies his hermeneutic in his *Faith in the Face of Empire* (2014), where he uses a *longue durée* reading of the history of Palestine to construct a Palestinian Old Testament hermeneutic.

[5] For a convincing basis to consider missional hermeneutics as theological interpretation, see McKinzie 2017.

[6] The *longue durée* approach to historiography was first proposed by the French *Annales* School. The approach came as a reaction to traditional historiography, which focuses on events of brief time spans (*histoire événementielle*). *Longue Durée*, on the other hand, studies long-term historical structures. For a definitive introduction to *longue durée* by one of its founders, see Braudel 2009.

[7] There are competing views on dating Ecclesiastes either in the Hellenistic or the Persian eras, with the inclination of scholarship to a Hellenistic dating (Murphy 1992, xxii). In both cases, Ecclesiastes was written under empire.

understand the struggles of Qoheleth in ancient Palestine. This does not mean I can violate the text or ignore its grammar or context. Rather, I use a Palestinian lens (together with my Christian lens) as exegetical aid that helps me better understand and appreciate the text as it stands. This lens also allows me to relate the struggles of ancient Palestine to modern-day Palestine. One of the upshots of this exercise is the recovery of the Old Testament as part of the history of the indigenous people of Palestine.[8]

So, in a nutshell, what motivates my hermeneutic is a double-stranded thread that connects me to Qoheleth. First, Ecclesiastes, for me, is part of the scripture of the universal catholic people of God, ancient and modern, including the Palestinian church today. Second, as a voice from ancient Palestine, Qoheleth is part of the *longue durée* struggle of the people of Palestine, ancient and modern—the struggle against injustice and oppression.

Justice and Oppression in Ecclesiastes
(3:16–4:3 and 8:10–17)

The subjects of justice and oppression are central themes in Ecclesiastes. This is understandable when one notices that Qoheleth lived and wrote in the context of empire. In fact, the themes are so central that Qoheleth's *hebel* carries the connotation of injustice and oppression within its semantic range, as rightly noted by Jewish scholar Michael Fox (1986, 410). For example, what leads Qoheleth to "hate life" in Eccl 2:17 is the fact that both the wise and the fool are treated the same in the end; they both have the same fate—death (see Eccl 2:14b–17). For Qoheleth, this is *rā'* (2:17) and *hebel* (2:15); grievous/oppressive and absurd/unjust. Similarly, it is *hebel* and *răbbā rā'ā* (great evil) that a wise should toil with "wisdom and knowledge and skill ... [and] ... leave all to be enjoyed by another who did not toil for it" (2:21).[9] In both cases, *hebel* is associated with *rā'ā* (cf. 6:1–2, 9:1–3). That is, "for Qoheleth *hebel* is an injustice, nearly synonymous with *rā'ā*, 'inequity, injustice'" (Fox 1986, 410). It is no surprise therefore to find one passage after the other in the text dealing with issues of injustice and oppression. Two passages are central: Eccl 3:16–4:3 and 8:10–17—both of which are the focus of this chapter (see also 5:8–9, 7:15–18, 8:2–9, 9:1–10, 9:11–12).

Before delving into the details of our exegesis, two points are worth clarifying regarding the selection of Eccl 3:16–4:3 and 8:10–17 for this study. First, a

---

[8] In recognizing the distinction in the identity of modern-day Palestinians vis-à-vis the ancient people of Palestine, I use the label *Palestinians* only in reference to modern-day Palestinians, whereas the term *people of Palestine* is used interchangeably to describe both the ancient people of Palestine (including ancient Israelites) and modern-day Palestinians. In this way, I emphasize the *longue durée* connection between modern-day Palestinians and the ancient people of Palestine, while recognizing the distinction in their identities.
[9] All English translations are based on the NRSV.

number of commentators deal with Eccl 3:16–22 and 4:1–3 separately, especially since 4:1 starts with "again I saw" which signals a change of subject (see Longman 1998, 125, 132; Bartholomew 2009, 175–76, 183–85; Eaton 1983, 83–84, 90; *contra* Murphy 1992, 28; Kidner 1976, 41). However, the unity of theme, namely, injustice and oppression, is hard to neglect, and thus treating the two passages as one unit is more convincing. Therefore, our first passage covers all of Eccl 3:16–4:3. Second, Eccl 8:10–17 is best seen as a continuation of the thoughts that start in 8:2–9 (the king as an oppressive authority) and continue in 9:1–10 (lack of justice—same end for all). However, due to space limitation, I choose to focus only on 8:10–17 without neglecting the immediate context. The following is an outline of both passages.

| Ecclesiastes 3:16–4:3 | Ecclesiastes 8:10–17 |
| --- | --- |
| Observation: Wickedness prevails (3:16) | Observation: Wickedness unpunished (8:10–11) |
| Confession: God will judge in due time (3:17) | Confession: God will judge eventually (8:12–13) |
| Struggling with justice in the here and now (3:18–21) | Struggling with justice in the here and now (8:14) |
| Conclusion: Ironic expression of deep struggle (3:22) | Conclusion: Ironic expression of deep struggle (8:15) |
| Observation: Powerful oppress powerless (4:1) | Conclusion: Unable to comprehend (8:16–17) |
| Conclusion: Hyperbole expressing deep sorrow (4:2–3) | |

By placing the two passages in juxtaposition, one notices the striking parallel of thoughts in both. Each passage contains four main elements that Qoheleth goes through in facing injustice and oppression.[10] The first element is the observation of injustice and oppression. Qoheleth then moves into faith response or confession (the second element). Qoheleth does not stop there. Central to both passages is Qoheleth's deep struggle with the absence and perversion of justice in the here and now (the third element). The intensity of Qoheleth's struggle is expressed in his conclusions (the fourth element) using a mixture of hyperbole and irony. I discuss each element in turn, demonstrating that Qoheleth's canonized struggle with injustice and oppression under the sun can inform hermeneutical and missiological praxes in contemporary contexts of injustice and oppression, especially in Palestine-Israel.

---

[10] While in 3:16–22 and 8:10–17 Qoheleth moves from *observation* to *confession* to *struggle* to *conclusion*, he jumps directly from a troubling *observation* in 4:1 to a *conclusion* in 4:2–3. This should be understood in light of the unity between 3:16–22 and 4:1–3. Since Qoheleth has just finished his struggle in 3:16–22, in 4:1–3 he brings a similar observation about injustice and oppression that leads him again to a troubling conclusion.

First Element: Observation (3:16, 4:1, 8:10–11)

Our passages are marked with three main observations, what Bartholomew (2009, 176) calls "statement of the problem." The three observations are related to the perversion of justice (3:16 and 8:10–11) and the oppression of the weak by the powerful (4:1). In 3:16 (cf. 7:15), Qoheleth notices that wickedness is prevailing in the place of justice and righteousness, which implies that wickedness remains unpunished. Instead, the wicked/guilty are treated as innocent, while the righteous/innocent are condemned (Longman 1998, 126). Qoheleth picks this up again in 8:10–11 observing how the wicked are unpunished in due time, and their actions never condemned in the here and now—which is the reason why wickedness increases on earth.[11]

Some commentators are quick to declare that in these passages "Qoheleth does not attack the system; he simply notes miscarriages of justice" (Murphy 1992, 36). Those interpretations miss the point that seeing and noticing the perversion of justice (and writing about it) implicitly challenges the political and legal systems. It should be remembered that in ancient Israel the king was ultimately responsible for political and legal justice (Longman 1998, 127). Therefore, by mentioning the perversion of justice, Qoheleth is challenging the rule of the king himself. Furthermore, as rightly noted by Tremper Longman, the abrupt Hebrew of 3:16 "communicates the outrage Qoheleth feels at the situation. It is as if the outrage outpaces his ability to articulate words" (127). Therefore, we are not talking about a disinterested observation, but rather a passionate cry that challenges political and legal systems to vindicate the innocent and punish the wicked.

It should be noted, however, that while Qoheleth does not hesitate to point out the perversion of justice and the oppression exercised by a political establishment, he is also fully aware that one needs to exercise caution when dealing with the ruler. For instance, while Qoheleth observes and writes about the way a person with authority rules over another "to the other's hurt" (8:9), he realizes that "the word of the king is powerful, and who can say to him, 'What are you doing?'" (8:4). What is in front of us here is how Qoheleth uses wisdom to challenge unjust political systems, by "know[ing] the time and way" (8:5). This also can explain the connection between 8:1 (wisdom) and 8:2–9 (dealing with an authoritarian and oppressive ruler).

---

[11] The textual issue in 8:10 revolves around the rendering of the MT Hebrew *yiš$^e$ttăkk$^e$hû'*. Commentators choose one of two options; they either maintain the reading as it stands in the MT, i.e., *forgotten* (Murphy 1992, 79; Bartholomew 2009, 289) or amend it following other ancient witnesses as *praised* (Longman 1998, 218–19; Eaton 1983, 121–22; see also NRSV; ESV; NIV). Regardless of this choice, Qoheleth's point remains the same. For if the wicked are *praised* in the city (amended reading), this for sure is vanity. And if they are forgotten after their burial (MT reading as it stands), this is still vanity, for even after they die, their actions are not condemned as evil (see Bartholomew 2009, 289–90).

In 4:1, Qoheleth focuses on oppression. Again, Western commentators remind us that Qoheleth is only descriptive—he notices the issue but does not do anything about it. Longman (1998, 133) comments that Qoheleth "does not personally engage the subject or enjoin others to resist the oppressor. He simply resigns himself to the situation." Roland Murphy (1992, 37) states that "He simply registers the fact without condemnation." Similarly, for Fox, in all passages related to oppression, "[Qoheleth] is just sorry that we must see these things" (1989, 201 as cited in Longman 1998, 134). In my opinion, these interpretations miss an important point that is clear in my Palestinian lens, that is, the importance of *seeing and noticing situations of oppression and injustice.*

In a careful reading of 4:1, the following details are critical. First, as mentioned above, the immediate context of the passage (3:16) reveals how Qoheleth was outraged at the sight of perverted justice. This outrage intensifies to a point where being dead—or better, never being born—is much better than seeing the oppressions done under the sun (4:2–3). Second, there is an implicit cry for compassion and solidarity with the oppressed in 4:1 as evident by Qoheleth's repetition of "with no one to comfort them." Third, the "evil deeds" mentioned in 4:3b refers back to the acts of oppression described in 4:1, indicating that Qoheleth is doing much more than "simply registering the facts." Describing oppression as an "evil deed" is rather a condemnation of the act. Finally—and importantly—one should not neglect the depth of insight that Qoheleth has. Not only does he see "the tears of the oppressed" (4:1a), but he also recognizes the power imbalance between the oppressed and the oppressor ("on the side of their oppressors there was power"; 4:1b). Furthermore, Qoheleth notices that all this is part of a bigger governmental system of oppression, what Roland Murphy (1992, 51) calls "hierarchy of powers," which goes all the way up to the king himself (5:8–9).[12]

Therefore, in *observing* injustice and oppression and *writing* about them the way he did, Qoheleth does the following. First, he wisely and passionately challenges the unjust political and legal establishment to administer justice by vindicating the innocent and punishing the wicked (3:16; 8:10–11). Second, Qoheleth's observation is a cry for compassion and solidarity with the powerless and the oppressed (4:1). Third, in his observation, Qoheleth does not hesitate to

---

[12] Again, as is the case in many places in Ecclesiastes, the interpretation of 5:8–9 is uncertain especially verse 9 (see the footnotes of the ESV and the NRSV). Verse 8, nevertheless, seems to explain the reason that causes oppression, rather than describing a system of checks and balances (Fox 2004, 35; Murphy 1992, 51; Bartholomew 2009, 217; Longman 1998, 157–58). However, it is not certain whether the king in verse 9 is administering justice or whether he is part of the system of oppression. It seems to me that the latter is a stronger reading, especially if we maintain that verse 8 speaks about the reason behind oppression, and given the bleak image Qoheleth depicts of the king in other places such as 8:2–9 (see Longman 1998, 158–59; *contra* Eaton 1983, 101–2 and Bartholomew 2009, 217–18).

condemn the acts of the oppressor as evil (4:3b). Finally, Qoheleth's observation is that of an intellectual who does not only notice the miscarriages of justice, but also understands the power imbalance and hierarchy of powers behind them. Those, in a nutshell, make up what it means to observe injustice and oppression for Qoheleth.

Second Element: Confession (3:17, 8:12–13)

In both of our passages, Qoheleth moves from observing injustice and oppression to faith confession. After observing the prevalence of wickedness in the place of justice and righteousness in 3:16, Qoheleth moves to declare that "God will judge the righteous and the wicked, for he has appointed a time for every matter, and for every work" (3:17). Similarly, in 8:10–11 Qoheleth states his troubling observation of how wickedness remains unpunished in the here and now and then moves into confessing that God will eventually bring about justice (8:12–13). Some interpreters, however, note that Qoheleth quickly nullifies his faith confession in the subsequent verses (e.g., Longman 1998, 220). In 3:18–21, he meditates on how humans (both righteous and wicked) die in the end as animals, before justice takes place at the appointed time (contrary to what he just confessed in 3:17). Similarly, at a first glance it seems that Qoheleth in 8:14 is nullifying his faith confession in 8:12–13. However, the question that should be asked here is whether Qoheleth holds onto his faith confession despite being problematized and challenged by his observations.

There is a tension between 3:17 and 3:18–21, and similarly between 8:12–13 and 8:14. However, it seems to me that Qoheleth does not nullify his faith in a just God. Rather, he holds his faith in tension with his struggle to see justice in the here and now. Qoheleth's struggle does not nullify his faith that God will judge the righteous and the wicked in the appointed time (3:17, cf. 8:12–13). What deeply troubles Qoheleth, however, is that he is not seeing this happening under the sun, in the here and now. Furthermore, he does not know when justice will take place, for he cannot "find out what God has done from the beginning to the end" (3:11b, cf. 8:17). What he sees in the here and now is perverted justice. This, nevertheless, does not hinder him from proclaiming his faith again and again. For after his first confession in 3:17, he proclaims his faith again in 8:12–13.

The confession of Qoheleth in 8:12–13 is not to be passed quickly. First, this comes *after* problematizing his first confession in 3:18–21, and despite of it. Second, the wording of 8:12–13 indicates that Qoheleth is aware of the tension between his faith and what he observes in the here and now, yet he still holds on to his faith and proclaims it. This is evident in his own words: "sinners do evil a hundred times and prolong their lives, *yet I know that* ... it will not be well with the wicked, neither will they prolong their days" (8:12–13; emphasis mine). Not only does this indicate that Qoheleth is aware of the tension (Bartholomew 2009, 293), but also that he maintains his faith in the justice of God despite his deeply troubling observations. Eaton (1983, 123) rightly notes that, whereas Qoheleth's observations are usually marked with "I saw" (e.g., 8:10), his confession here is introduced by "yet I know," indicating that Qoheleth's troubling observations do not demolish his internal knowledge and faith. Furthermore, although Qoheleth's confession in 8:12–13 is challenged by his observation in 8:14, his confession is not nullified. This is clear in the epilogue (11:7–12:7), where the idea of judgment is brought back in the instructions to the "young man"—eventually "God will bring ... judgement" (11:9b).

Qoheleth continues to point out injustice and oppression in a way that challenges the system and calls for solidarity with the oppressed; he continues to be deeply troubled by oppression and injustice; yet at the same time, he holds fast to faith in a just God.

Third Element: Struggling with Justice in the Here and Now (3:18–21; 8:14)

While one may label the whole of 3:16–4:3 and 8:10–17 as "Qoheleth's struggle with justice in the here and now," it is also fitting to use this title specifically in reference to 3:18–21 and 8:14 for they represent the climax of Qoheleth's struggle. These verses come *after* Qoheleth's faith response to his initial observations. Qoheleth's faith in the justice of God does not mean he can stop pointing out the perversion of justice or being deeply troubled by it. It is important to note here that while Qoheleth in 3:18–21 and 8:14 problematizes traditional faith confession, his main focus is on justice in the here and now. It does not seem to me that Qoheleth is set on a journey to problematize faith, but rather to make sense of what is happening on earth (1:13a)—and he struggles with God along the way.

In 3:18–21, Qoheleth brings the reality of death, one of his predominant themes, into his quest for justice on earth. This is brought as a response to his faith confession that God has "appointed a time" for judgment (3:17). Qoheleth's passion to see justice prevail under the sun leads him to struggle even with God. He observes how the end of all humans, righteous and wicked, is the same as the end of animals. They all die and "return to dust" (3:20). Qoheleth makes two points here. The first point is related to time: "God has made everything suitable for its time" (3:11a). However, this traditional confession is challenged by the inability of Qoheleth to understand God's timing (3:11b). The link between the theme of time in 3:1–15 and the topic of justice in 3:16–22 is evident by the reference to time in 3:17, where Qoheleth declares his faith again in God's timing but now in relation to the execution of justice. The point of 3:17 is not only that "God will judge the righteous and the wicked" (v. 17a) but also that God "has appointed a time" for that (v. 17b). Since 3:18–21 comes as a response to the faith confession in 3:17, Qoheleth might have brought the motif of death into the picture to show that justice is not executed *in due time before death comes*, that is, in the here and now, "under the sun" (cf. 8:11).

The second point Qoheleth makes in 3:18–21 is more obvious. For him, it is *hebel* (absurd, unjust) to see the same "fate" (death) befalling all humans, wicked and righteous, as well as animals (3:19–20). What makes the situation more difficult for Qoheleth is the uncertainty he finds when he tries to glance at whether justice lies after death (3:21). Even though the question posed in verse 21 "does not necessarily deny the possibility of the afterlife, ... it does deny a certainty about it" (Longman 1998, 130). This renders death for Qoheleth as the same unjust *end* that meets everyone, whether they are wicked or righteous. Qoheleth here is clearly struggling with God and with understanding what God is doing (cf. 3:11b). However, this struggle should be understood in the context of Qoheleth's faith confession and of a Hebrew experience of God as intimate and near, rather than a Hellenistic understanding of the gods as far and unreachable. Therefore, in a nutshell, Qoheleth in 3:18–21 is still struggling to find justice in the here and now, even after his faith confession in 3:17. He realizes that death comes before justice is executed on earth and that death in itself is not a just end, since it befalls everyone equally, wicked or righteous, and no one knows what awaits after death.

Qoheleth's quest to find justice executed in the here and now does not stop here. As noted by Longman (1998, 20–21), Qoheleth's struggle in 8:10–14 should also be read in the context of death. Underlying Qoheleth's observation in 8:10 is his belief that justice could still be achieved under the sun, *despite death*, for either the wicked who die should not be praised in the city where they have committed evil or their evil should not be forgotten (but rather remembered) after they die.[13] In here is an implicit challenge to the ruling establishment to expose and perhaps condemn the acts of the wicked after their death. But even that is not happening, and this is from where Qoheleth's *hebel* comes at the end of 8:10.

Qoheleth's subsequent confession in 8:12–13 highlights his belief that the timing of death could be a reward to the righteous and an acceptable judgment of the wicked: "it will be well with those who fear God ... but it will not be well with the wicked, *neither will they prolong their days like a shadow*" (8:12–13; emphasis mine). Qoheleth's response to this in 8:14 is that the opposite is the reality. Righteous people are treated as the wicked deserve; that is, they die young. The wicked people are treated as the righteous deserve; that is, they die old (Longman 1998, 221). Qoheleth revisits the matter of death in 8:10–14 as it relates to justice, in a continuous struggle to find justice somehow executed on earth despite the reality of death. He declares his faith in the justice of God (8:12–13), yet his struggle continues, reaching a climax in 8:14 where he observes how justice is "turned upside down" (Bartholomew 2009, 291), and this is where Qoheleth cries out his *hebel* twice; at the beginning and the end of 8:14—indicating his outrage at the complete perversion of justice in the here and now.

---

[13] These two possible readings of 8:10 depend on whether we are to follow the rendering of the MT or other ancient witnesses (see n. 11).

We have seen how Qoheleth challenges the ruling establishment and exposes the imbalance and hierarchy of powers that lie behind injustice and oppression—all the while maintaining his faith in a just God. The perversion of justice under the sun is deeply troubling to Qoheleth, as manifested in his struggle with God and with finding justice on earth. One may thus conclude that Qoheleth's deeply troubled heart is behind his penetrating observations.

Fourth Element: Qoheleth's Conclusions (3:22, 4:2–3, 8:15, 8:16–17)

There are two ways that modern scholarship has chosen to look at the so-called *Carpe Diem* conclusions in 3:22 and 8:15. One way considers Qoheleth a "preacher of joy" (Whybray 1982; cf. Bartholomew 2009, 150–153; Eaton 1983, 89, 124), and scholars who follow this approach interpret 3:22 and 8:15 as positive faith-based conclusions. R. Norman Whybray, for example, argues that in these conclusions, Qoheleth gives answers and solutions to the enigmas and vanities of life. This leads him, for instance, to read 8:15 ("I commend/praise enjoyment") as the "sentiment ... which ... Qoheleth above all wished to commend to his readers" (Whybray 1982, 94). A second way of looking at these *Carpe Diem* conclusions is with a more pessimistic lens. For many interpreters, these conclusions express Qoheleth's "strident desperation, or perhaps resignation" (Longman 1998, 221; cf. Murphy 1992, 39, 87).

Read with Palestinian eyes, however, these *Carpe Diem* conclusions are hyperbolic and ironic utterings flowing out of a heart deeply troubled and perplexed by the injustices of life. They are neither to be taken seriously as the "practical solutions" (Eaton 1983, 124) of a "preacher of joy" nor as hopeless resignations. In the context of Qoheleth's outrage against injustice and oppression, it is difficult to see how Qoheleth's solution to injustice and oppression is to drink, eat, and enjoy life. In juxtaposition with Qoheleth's conclusions in 4:2–3 and 8:16–17, such interpretations are problematic. Soon after his *Carpe Diem* conclusion in 3:22, Qoheleth expresses another almost antithetical conclusion, in which he utters his outrage at the sight of oppression to the point of envying the dead and the unborn, who have not seen injustice and oppression (4:2–3). Similarly, the *Carpe Diem* conclusion in 8:15 is followed by another conclusion (8:16–17) that reveals how deeply troubled Qoheleth is because of the complete perversion of justice and his inability to comprehend what is happening around him. In fact, Qoheleth's statement in 8:16–17 is his rather serious conclusion that challenges the simplistic knowledge claims of the wise of his time (Murphy 1992, 86).

This does not mean, however, that we should read Qoheleth's conclusions as hopeless resignations. Qoheleth did not write his poetic essay to advocate hopelessness, as I demonstrated in my exposition above. The sharp contrast between Qoheleth's outrage at injustice and oppression and his *Carpe Diem* conclusions in 3:22 and 8:15 should lead interpreters to consider irony as a possible explanation. The plausibility of this interpretation increases when one notices the poetic influence in Qoheleth's writing, which includes the use of repetition, imagery and hyperbole (see Murphy 1992, xxviii–xxix; Longman 1998, esp. 24). Qoheleth's conclusions in my opinion employ a mixture of irony (in 3:22 and 8:15), hyperbole (in 4:2–3 as well as in 3:22 and 8:15), and straight-forward challenging statements (8:16–17) to express his troubled and pain-stricken heart (cf. 2:17)—thus revealing the intensity of his struggle with injustice and oppression.

## A Missional Reading of Ecclesiastes

Bartholomew helpfully summarizes Western theological readings of Ecclesiastes as attempts to level the book into one of two poles (Bartholomew 2005, 184). The first is the pole of the *hebel* conclusions, which reduces the message of Qoheleth into hopelessness and pessimism. In this mode, Qoheleth is a representative of a type of ancient skeptics that deny the goodness—if not the very existence—of God (Longman 1998, 36). For Longman, the normative theological contribution of Ecclesiastes lies in the frame narrator, whose epilogue basically demolishes Qoheleth's dark and pessimistic theology (37–39).

The second pole is that of the *Carpe Diem* conclusions—interpreted in a positive light—which renders the message of Qoheleth as providing practical, faith-based, joy-affirming answers to the grim realities of life. For instance, Michael Eaton (1983, 44), who sees the frame narrator in harmony with Qoheleth, considers Qoheleth's speech "an essay in apologetics … that defends the life of faith in a generous God."

Bartholomew (2005, 184–85; 2009, 93–96) tries to resolve this polarization by proposing a reading that looks at the epistemology of Qoheleth. The theological contribution of Ecclesiastes for Bartholomew lies in Qoheleth's ironic exposure of an empiricist autonomous epistemology that leads Qoheleth to *hebel*, as opposed to a faith-based epistemology that enables him to enjoy life (the *Carpe Diem* conclusions). This, however, is still a polarized reading that favors the *Carpe Diem* conclusions and interprets them as hopeful answers to the enigmas of life, while at the same time reducing the value of Qoheleth's *hebel*.

Although these readings have enriched my understanding of the text, they miss an important point towards which Ecclesiastes points. Read in its canonical form with the narrator's epilogue, the nature of Qoheleth's speech and his message become clearer. First of all, I take the words of the narrator seriously when he says that Qoheleth "wrote words of truth plainly" (12:10). Second, along with the frame narrator, I believe that the sayings of Qoheleth are given by "one shepherd" which I take as referring to God (cf. Ps 23:1, 80:1; Eaton 1983, 154). Therefore, what is in front of us is a canonized, God-breathed, truthful speech of an Israelite sage in ancient Palestine. It is not the speech of some dark sage who doubted the goodness or the existence of God.

The purpose of Qoheleth's speech is plainly and excellently given by the narrator in the epilogue. "The sayings of the wise," the narrator tells us, "are like goads" (Eccl 12:11). This, for me, summarizes Qoheleth's speech. Like a goad moves an animal, so should Qoheleth's words move the reader into action. This is a convincing basis for a missional reading of Ecclesiastes. But what kind of action does the text, particularly Eccl 3:16–4:3 and 8:10–17, provoke in the reader?

Based on our exposition above, Qoheleth moves the reader into being deeply troubled and agonized about what is going on under the sun, especially with regard to injustice and oppression. Qoheleth warns against simplistic answers and knowledge-claims and instead motivates the nurturing of a heart deeply troubled at the sight of injustice and oppression. Furthermore, Qoheleth warns against dismissive attitudes towards injustice and oppression. Instead, the preacher encourages wise and passionate resistance that deeply observes issues of injustice and oppression in a way that challenges unjust systems, and exposes power imbalance and the hierarchy of powers behind them. Such resistance calls for the just vindication of the oppressed and the condemnation of the acts of the wicked. Moreover, Qoheleth encourages the reader to proclaim faith in God and God's justice, all while struggling for justice in the here and now. In fact, it is out of this faith-abiding struggle that Qoheleth provides penetrating observations that challenge the oppressor and provide hope for the oppressed.

For the Church in the Context of Palestine-Israel

Although the missional reading presented above can be applied to the Palestinian-Israeli context in a variety of ways, I focus on its application on the church. This is vital both to the Palestinian Christian community and the wider church, especially at a time when people (like US Vice President Mike Pence) speak loudly in the name of Christianity. Mike Pence was the first US Vice President to speak at the Israeli Knesset. His historical speech on 22 January 2018 was closer to a sermon, where he did not hesitate to quote the Bible directly and connect biblical Israel with the modern-day settler-colonial State of Israel. His aim was clearly to proclaim his conviction of how modern-day Israel is a sign of God's faithfulness to his ancient promises. Such Christian Zionist[14] interpretations of the Bible lead Pence to turn a complete blind eye to the suffering of the Palestinian people. This is what he proclaimed with confidence:

> And so today, as I stand in Abraham's Promised Land, I believe that all who cherish freedom, and seek a brighter future, should cast their eyes here to this place and marvel at what they behold.... You have turned the desert into a garden, scarcity into plenty, sickness into health, and you turned hope into a future. Israel is like a tree that has grown deep roots in the soil of your forefathers, yet

---

[14] For an introduction to Christian Zionism and its historical and theological roots, see Sizer 2004 and Smith 2013.

as it grows, it reaches ever closer to the heavens. And today and every day, the Jewish State of Israel, and all the Jewish people, bear witness to God's faithfulness, as well as your own. (*Haaretz* 2018)

As rightly noted by Palestinian-Israeli member of Knesset Ahmad Tibi (2018), although Pence encouraged his listeners to "cast their eyes here," he never looked at the reality in front of him. For if he had done so, he would have seen and recognized the historical oppression of the Palestinian people since the inception of the State of Israel on their homeland.

What hurts Palestinian Christians the most is that many followers of Christ around the world would nod with an "Amen!" at the sermon of Pence. Many Christians today are blinded by false theologies and misappropriations of scriptures. This hinders them from seeing the injustice and oppression that have befallen the people of Palestine. For example, at the time of the 2014 Israeli war on Gaza, when Israel killed 2,251 Palestinians (most of whom are civilians), the only thing that a premier Bible website (biblegateway.com) could do is post a Christian Zionist ad that read "Israel under attack." This ad failed to see the power imbalance between Israel and the Palestinians or notice the innocent Palestinian civilians who were murdered in cold blood by one of the most powerful armies in the world (which is supported by a hierarchy of world powers).

Even more moderate Christians fail to see the root of the problem and instead relativize the Israeli occupation. In 2016, the Lausanne Movement, which I dearly respect, brought together a group of Messianic Jews and Palestinian Christians (some of whom are dear friends) in an effort to reconcile the body of Christ in the land. The meeting resulted in a statement referred to as *the Larnaca Statement* (Harvey et al. 2016), which represents an important effort towards reconciliation. Although the Palestinian Christian group tried to push for the recognition of the Israeli occupation as a fact, this unfortunately did not pass into the final edition of the document. What appeared eventually is a relativized depiction of oppression and injustice. Such examples show the blindness that the church suffers when it comes to Palestine. This blindness permeates the church in all its spectrums. For liberal Christians, especially in the West, who in many cases advocate for the rights of the oppressed and the marginalized, are often blinded by postholocaust theology and guilt when it comes to Palestine-Israel.

Furthermore, many of our brothers and sisters in Christ who hear our stories try to comfort us by saying that Jesus will come in the end to fix all this. While, for me, this is a truthful faith confession, it is rarely accompanied by a passion for justice in the here and now. In fact, this confession can do more damage than good, when held in simplistic ways without understanding the full scope of the situation or being really troubled by it.

In light of all this, I believe the message of Qoheleth could not be more relevant for the church and its mission, especially in the context of Palestine-Israel. At a time when the Israeli occupation has been relativized, dismissed and even justified by many Christians, Qoheleth challenges the church to observe intensely the colonial history behind the establishment of the State of Israel and the continuous violations of the basic human rights of the Palestinian people. The issue is primarily that of *seeing* and *acknowledging* reality—both historical reality, and reality on the ground. Qoheleth reminds us that there is a reality out there, especially when it comes to injustice and oppression, and that it is not relative.

Qoheleth challenges the church to keep confessing the goodness and justice of God, and to do it ever more clearly and publicly. Like Qoheleth, our confession should flow out of hearts troubled and agonized at the sight of people suffering under oppression and injustice; hearts that would open our eyes to see acts of injustice and oppression as they really are—as "evil deeds" (Eccl 4:3b). This kind of seeing, Qoheleth tells us, should expose powers, challenge political establishments, and call for the vindication of the oppressed and the condemnation of the acts of the oppressor. This is a message of hope for Palestine.

## Works Cited

Ateek, Naim. 2008. *A Palestinian Christian Cry for Reconciliation*. Maryknoll: Orbis.

———. 1989. *Justice, and Only Justice: A Palestinian Theology of Liberation*. Maryknoll: Orbis.

Bartholomew, Craig G. 2009. *Ecclesiastes*. Baker Commentary on the Old Testament Wisdom and Psalms. Grand Rapids: Baker.

———. 2005. "Ecclesiastes, Book of." Pages 182–85 in *Dictionary for Theological Interpretation of the Bible*. Edited by Kevin J. Vanhoozer. Grand Rapids: Baker Academic; London: SPCK.

Braudel, Fernand. 2009. "History and the Social Sciences: The Longue Durée." Translated by Immanuel Wallerstein. *Review (Fernand Braudel Center)* 32.2:171–203.

Eaton, Michael A. 1983. *Ecclesiastes: An Introduction and Commentary*. Tyndale Old Testament Commentaries 16. Leicester: InterVarsity.

Fox, Michael V. 1986. "The Meaning of Hebel for Qohelet." *JBL* 105:409–27.

———. 1989. *Qoheleth and His Contradictions*. JSOTSup 71. Sheffield: Almond Press.

———. 2004. *Ecclesiastes*. The JPS Bible Commentary. Philadelphia: The Jewish Publication Society.

Goheen, Michael W., ed. 2016. *Reading the Bible Missionally*. Grand Rapids: Eerdmans.

Haaretz. 2018. "Full Text: U.S. Vice President Mike Pence's Speech at Israel's Knesset." *Haaretz English Edition* (22 January): https://www.haaretz.com/israel-news/full-text-u-s-vice-president-mike-pence-s-speech-at-the-knesset-1.5751264.

Harvey, Richard, et al. 2016, "The Larnaca Statement." *The Lausanne Initiative for Reconciliation in Israel/Palestine (LIRIP)*. https://www.lausanne.org/content/larnaca-statement.

Katanacho, Yohanna. 2013. *The Land of Christ: A Palestinian Cry*. Eugene: Pickwick.

Kidner, Derek. 1976. *The Message of Ecclesiastes*. The Bible Speaks Today. Downers Grove: InterVarsity.

Longman, Tremper. 1998. *The Book of Ecclesiastes*. The New International Commentary on the Old Testament 23. Grand Rapids: Eerdmans.

Masalha, Nur. 2012. *The Palestine Nakba: Decolonising History, Narrating the Subaltern, Reclaiming memory*. London: Zed Books.

McKinzie, Greg. 2017. "Missional Hermeneutics as Theological Interpretation." *JTI* 11.2:157–79.

Murphy, Roland. 1992. *Ecclesiastes*. WBC 23A. Dallas: Word Books.

Pappe, Ilan. 2007. *The Ethnic Cleansing of Palestine*. London: Oneworld.

Raheb, Mitri. 2014. *Faith in the Face of Empire: The Bible through Palestinian Eyes*. Bethlehem: Diyar.

———. 1995. *I Am a Palestinian Christian*. Minneapolis: Fortress.

Sizer, Stephen. 2004. *Christian Zionism: Road-Map to Armageddon?* Leicester: InterVarsity.

Smith, Robert O. 2013. *More Desired than Our Own Salvation: The Roots of Christian Zionism*. Oxford: Oxford University Press.

Tibi, Ahmad. 2018. "We Protested Mike Pence's Speech, and Israel Could Not Tolerate It." *Newsweek U.S. Edition* (27 January). http://www.newsweek.com/we-protested-mike-pences-speech-and-israel-could-not-tolerate-it-792898.

Vanhoozer, Kevin J., ed. 2005. *Dictionary for Theological Interpretation of the Bible*. London: SPCK.

White, Ben. 2014. *Israeli Apartheid: A Beginner's Guide*. 2nd ed. London: Pluto.

Whybray, R. Norman. 1982. "Qoheleth, Preacher of joy." *JSOT* 7.23:87–98.

Wright, Christopher J. H. 2006. *The Mission of God: Unlocking the Bible's Grand Narrative*. Nottingham: InterVarsity.

# Sophia, Untameable like Moana: An Oceanic Reading of Sirach 24 with Ecclesiastes 7:10–12

Mariana Waqa

The Wisdom of Sirach[1] emulates the tradition of Proverbs with its synthesis of observations, commands, and prohibitions (Barton and Muddiman 2001, 667). Sirach 24 is a poetic interjection by Sofia (Wisdom) that mirrors the personification of Hokma (Wisdom) in Prov 8.[2] In Sir 24, Wisdom (for Hokma and Sophia, both of which are feminine) tells her story. She speaks of her glory and begins with a liquid reminisce of her earthly and aquatic bearings.[3] However, the flow of her story comes to a sudden halt in 24:5–6 when she is commanded by the Creator to make her dwelling in Jacob.

My oceanic[4] reading challenges Ben Sira's (assumed author of Sirach) account of Sophia seeking and being given rest within the confinements of Israel's narrative and geographical borders. What might have been the reasons for Ben Sira wanting to give a "resting place" for Wisdom (24:7)?[5] Who would have benefitted from locating Wisdom or Sophia within Israel's boundaries? Could Israel's

---

[1] This book is also known as the Proverbs of Sirach, and in Latin it is *Liber Ecclesiasticus*—"the Church book" (MacKenzie 1983, 13).
[2] The Hebrew word for Wisdom—Ḥokma—has a feminine ending that personifies her as a divine figure in Prov1, 8, and 9:1–12 (Penchansky 2012, 27–28).
[3] Note the following liquid images (in italics) in Sir 24:3–6: "covered the earth like a *mist* ... my throne was in a pillar of *cloud* ... traversed the depths of the *abyss*. Over *waves of the sea, over all the earth*" (NRSV).
[4] By *oceanic* I am referring to the ocean. I am also alluding to *Oceania*, referring to the islands of the Pacific or Southern Seas.
[5] Prior to this, Wisdom's dwelling is in the "highest heavens" (24:4). If she already has a dwelling place, why is she in search of a "territory" (24:7) to rest in? Wisdom's "sways" (24:6) over the seas and earth also show no indication of a need for the "rest" which the author remedies with her dwelling in Jacob (24:8).

Torah contain the depths of Sophia's profundity? Or like the ocean, is Sophia both uncontainable and untameable?

## Oceanic Reading

Unlike the desert borders of Israel and her neighbors, the South Pacific islands (Pasifika, Oceania) are surrounded by the expanse of the world's largest ocean.[6] *Island space* consists of more water than land; it is *fluid* and *volatile*, a *liquid continent* (Havea 2004, 43). In our Pasifika island space one of the many names given to the ocean is *Moana* (Havea 2010, 135). For Micronesian, Polynesian, and coastal Melanesian Islanders, Moana is like a mother who provides food for her children—she embraces and sustains their livelihood, but she also has the power to teach and discipline from her recondite (a subject that is little known) depths. Moana is alive, her tides ebb and flow, and her waves surge and break. She is fluid and rhythmic, with the ability to swell beautifully or crash with torrential rapidity. Moana envelops; she overlaps and crosses boundaries. In one moment Moana may be shallow and playful, and at another she becomes as deep and dark as the Mariana Trench.[7] Moana's motions and flow are not fully definable; they are wild, often turbulent and profoundly enigmatic.[8] My oceanic reading endeavors to claim that the biblical text, much like the Moana, is both fluid and wild; it is also life-sustaining; its words have the power to teach and discipline from the depths of its flow.

To read oceanically therefore means that one cannot be fixated on surface matters. Sure, it is important to establish and examine thoroughly what is apparent to the eyes, but like the concocted superficiality of an island "paradise,"[9] those native to the South Pacific Ocean know that this façade often masks deeper realities. It is important here to distinguish that where some other methodologies work their way up from the surface towards astral and incorporeal dimensions, the Oceanic dives deep into the textual abyss, seeking to swim through the torrents of language, seeking to uncover concealed agendas and biases in order to yield forth hidden and sometimes forbidden truths.

---

[6] The Pacific Ocean is the largest of the five oceans and covers one third of the earth's surface at 63,800,000 square miles.

[7] The Mariana Trench is the ocean's deepest point, with declinations as low as 10,911m (35,800 ft).

[8] Winston Halapua explains that "the word *Moana* is closely associated with words that suggest depth of feeling, thought or experience. Moana suggests mystery" (Havea 2010, 138).

[9] The South Pacific Islands are synonymous with the word *paradise* because of their picturesque settings and laidback ambiance. But behind these idealistic notions, a reality of struggle and poverty is common in local communities.

In this essay I plunge beneath the surface of Sir 24 with an oceanic reading of Sophia's story. To set my reading up, within the context of wisdom literature, I first offer a frame for reading Sophia through the lens of *hebel* (vanity) in Ecclesiastes.

## Sophia's Vanity in Ecclesiastes

In the book of Ecclesiastes, Qoheleth the teacher reproaches with "Vanity of Vanities! All is vanity!" (1:2). This statement is repeated several times throughout the book, and it helps conclude the book in chapter 12— "Vanity of vanities, says the Teacher: all is vanity." David Penchansky (2012, 51) comments that the repeated phrase "functions as a kind of motto or thesis statement" to summarize the theme of the book. The Hebrew word *hebel* is often translated as *vanity*, but *hebel* cannot be fully defined in the English language because it has a variety of meanings. Used thirty-eight times in Ecclesiastes, *hebel* has also been understood to also mean absurd, enigmatic, futile, and breath (Bartholomew 2009, 105). Many scholars translate *hebel* as *breath* or *vapour*, with some explaining that there's a sense of insubstantiality to the word which occasionally connotes an entity or force outside of human understanding.[10] In Isa 57:13 for example, *hebel* is analogous with *rûaḥ* (wind): "The wind will carry them off, a breath [*hebel*] will take them away" (Bartholomew 2009, 105).

Most scholars refrain from rendering *hebel* indefinitely. Craig G. Bartholomew explains that scholars retain the English translation of *vanity* for want of an "adequate alternative" (Bartholomew 2009, 105),[11] but Tremper Longman (1998, 61) adds that the use of *vanity*, made famous by the KJV, is problematic because of its reference to self-pride. Longman preferred the use of *meaningless* instead.[12] Antoon Schoors (1998, 887) argues that *vanity* as triviality or futility is "insufficient" and that the best translation of *hebel* is *absurdity* in both the logical and existential sense. Schoors adds, "the essence of the absurd is a disparity between two phenomena that are supposed to be joined by a link of harmony or causality but are actually disjunct or even conflicting.... It is not only incongruous or ironic: it is oppressive, an injustice." Whichever way the word *hebel* is translated, whether *vanity* (Bartholomew), *meaningless* (Longman), or *absurdity* (Schoors),

---

[10] "The word comes from the sound a breath makes, *hebel*. Then, by extension, it means 'breath' or 'vapor' having the sense of something insubstantial, and occasionally something 'not real'" (Penchansky 2012, 52).
[11] "Seow, with others, maintains that Ecclesiastes uses *hebel* in a variety of ways, so that no one translation covers all uses. He retains 'vanity' as the translation for want of an adequate alternative" (Penchansky 2012, 105).
[12] "The phrase *completely meaningless* literally reads 'meaninglessness of meaninglessnesses'" (Longman 1998, 61).

it remains that *hebel* highlights negative connotations about human life and experience in Ecclesiastes (Bartholomew 2009, 105).

If *hebel* is translated as *breath*, then the motto of Eccl 1:2 reads as "breath of breath! All is breath!" This rendering anticipates the *chasing after the wind* that Qoheleth references as a meaningless and ineffectual activity in Eccl 1:14, "I saw all the deeds that are done under the sun; and see, all is vanity and a chasing after wind" (Penchansky 2012, 52). But two verses later Qoheleth continues, "I said to myself, 'I have acquired great wisdom, surpassing all who were over Jerusalem before me; and my mind has had great experience of wisdom and knowledge.' And I applied my mind to know wisdom and to know madness and folly. I perceived that this also is but a chasing after wind" (Eccl 1:16–17).

Qoheleth does not appear to have a comfortable handle of Sophia's enigmatic bearings. He acquires her in 1:16[13] only to bemoan her in 1:18—"for in much wisdom is much vexation." Qoheleth was disillusioned with the wisdom theology of Israel that derived its knowledge from "careful observation and passed-down traditions" which perpetuated God's righteous governance over life and the universe.[14] Instead of finding certainty through knowledge, Qoheleth is faced with Sophia's enigmatic tendencies. As *breath*, she cannot be fully grasped and therefore controlled by sage, priest, or prophet;[15] so Qoheleth cautions that to pursue her is a "chasing of the wind," a quest that "increases sorrow" (Eccl 1:18) for men like him who desire and attempt to possess her.

It seems that despite Sophia's breath-like origins, which she will elaborate later on in Sir 24:2–3, her essence is something that is not to be taken lightly. Qoheleth's acclamation of "vanity of vanities!" is more than just exasperation on his part. It is a warning of Sophia's volatile nature—she stations herself for no one and moves according to her own ways.[16] Qoheleth uses a double analogy of wind and sea from verses 6–7: First she is *wind* blowing to the south before turning north, then round and round she goes. Next, Qoheleth likens her to the element of water—streams flowing to the sea and yet, the sea is never full. To the place from where the streams begin, there they will return again. Qoheleth is left bewildered by Sophia's volatility. It seems that every time Qoheleth thinks he's grasped wisdom she escapes him and overthrows his human need to secure wisdom,

---

[13] "I have acquired great wisdom, surpassing all who were over Jerusalem before me; and my mind has had great experience of wisdom and knowledge."

[14] "For Qoheleth, his own observations of nature and human lives have caused him to question the tradition which taught that God governed the universe in an orderly manner" (Penchansky 2012, 52).

[15] "What is *hebel* cannot be grasped—neither physically nor intellectually. It cannot be controlled" (Bartholomew 2009, 106).

[16] "The wind blows to the south, and goes around to the north; round and round goes the wind, and on its circuits the wind returns" (Eccl 1:7).

knowledge, success, and prosperity.[17] Sophia moves with the changing times but will repeat the seasons and lessons with each generation ("A generation goes, and a generation comes, but the earth remains forever"; 1:4 NRSV). Even YHWH comes under scrutiny in her path as she has Qoheleth making observations that the prophets and priests would deem sacrilege—in the places of justice, wickedness reigned (3:16); humans have no advantage over beasts, for as one dies so dies the other (3:18–20); God gives wealth and honor but does not allow the bearer to enjoy them (6:2); the righteous suffer and die while the wicked prosper in their evildoing (7:15; 8:14).[18] Qoheleth finds all of those as total absurdity—*hebel*!

Sophia teaches Qoheleth to *breathe*—to exhale assumed and perceived realities in order to inhale the vagaries of life that surround him—this being a paradox in and of itself. Indeed, the righteous do suffer while the wicked curate places of honor and power. Qoheleth finds that knowledge is a commodity of sorrow (1:18) and that the heart of the wise is in the house of mourning (7:4). Success is futile, and people will not be remembered by those who come after them (1:11). A stillborn child is lucky to enter into darkness without taking breath, for it will never have to toil under the sun and rather finds immediate rest (6:3–5). The impermanence of *hebel* teaches Qoheleth that Sophia is someone who cannot be possessed. She is too powerful an enigma to be contained by mere human aspirations. Qoheleth surrenders to Sophia's profundity in Eccl 7—"All this I have tested by wisdom; I said, 'I will be wise,' but it was far from me. That which is, is far off, and deep, very deep; who can find it out?" (7:23–24)—as Ben Sira will discover later in Sir 24.

Sophia as *hebel* in the book of Ecclesiastes serves a warning for sages like Ben Sira. Qoheleth's declaration of "Vanity of vanities! All is vanity!" cautions those who seek to control Sophia (wisdom). Her dosage can be lethal if she is not taken with measured restraint, for with great wisdom comes much affliction (1:18). Ben Sira will learn this for himself in chapter 24—that the possession of wisdom is indeed *hebel* and done in vain for the fool who attempts.

## Sophia's Story in Sirach 24

The poem of Sir 24 is considered to be the centerpiece of the book (Barton and Muddiman 2001, 682). It has thirty-four lines with the first twenty-two lines in an alphabetic acrostic pattern (Skehan and Di Lella 1987, 331). The poem divides into three major sections: Sophia's speech in 24:1–22; revelation of Torah in 24:23, 25–29; and Sirach's autobiography in 24:30–34.

---

[17] "Qoheleth declares all things to be *hebel* and then examines wisdom, pleasure companionship, fame, and wealth to see if they will support this claim. In each case, the desired object (wisdom, pleasure, etc.) turns out indeed to be *hebel*" (Penchansky 2012, 53).

[18] "There is a vanity that takes place on earth, that there are righteous people who are treated according to the conduct of the wicked, and there are wicked people treated according to the conduct of the righteous" (Eccl 8:14, NRSV).

Sophia introduces herself through an aretalogy in which her origin and cosmic influence over the rest of creation is described. The tune of her story changes when she suddenly reveals in 24:7 that she is in search of a "dwelling place" where to "abide." God enters the story in 24:8 with a command that Sophia make her dwelling within Israel, and in 24:10 we are told that her dwelling in Zion included religious ministry. From 24:11–22 Sophia's story and glory are firmly attached to Israel. Her growth and fertility are compared to the trees and flowers, the fruit and the scents of her geographical surroundings (24:13–17). In 24:19–22 Sophia invites those who "desire" wisdom to eat, drink and obey her. Ben Sira reveals his total control of the final eleven verses, and in 24:23 he emphatically reveals that Wisdom is to be found in the Torah—"the book of the covenant of the Most High God" (cf. Exod 24:7). In alliance with the preceding eulogies to nature, 24:25–27 go on to compare the Torah to bodies of water that "overflow," "run over," and "pour forth" understanding and instruction.[19] Ben Sira confesses in 24:28–29 that Sophia will never be fully fathomed. Here, he likens her to "the sea" (NAB, NRSV) or the "ocean" (NEB), possibly in tribute to Eccl 1:7 ("All streams run to the sea, but the sea is not full; to the place where the streams flow, there they continue to flow"; NRSV), where all streams flow into the sea but never fill it.

Ben Sira closes with a short autobiography and emulates his contribution to the fluidic notions asserted of both Sophia and the Torah in the previous 29 verses. He rates himself as a canal that waters his own garden, when "suddenly" (NAB), his canal became a river, and his river a sea. The curtain call of this lustrous poem in praise of Wisdom ends with the praise of its own author, while remaining all but silent on his failed coup on Sophia through the use of Israel's Torah.

Possessing Sophia

The first wave of this oceanic reading shows that Sophia has a voice with which she speaks. The wisdom which sages timelessly sought shows that she is more than just an objectification of morality, knowledge, and discernment. Sophia is first and foremost an experience, a ripple that convolutes into a rolling tale of beginnings. Revealing that beneath the surface of objectivity and astral projections, wisdom is a lived-out experience with a voice that has echoed throughout the space of time.

Misty Waters

Verses 1–6 show Sophia to be bold and free, and much like the waves of Moana her story begins with an all-inclusive surge before breaking into an exclusive story

---

[19] NEB uses the word "flood" in its translation of 24:25—"He sends out wisdom in full flood like the river Pishon or like the Tigris at the time of first fruits."

of her relationship with Israel (Skehan and Di Lella 1987, 331).[20] In 24:1–2 Sophia glories in her divine heritage before her Creator and his "hosts."[21] She describes her origins as a spoken word which poured forth from God's mouth and covered the earth like a mist (24:3).[22] Scholars such as Patrick W. Skehan and Alexander A. Di Lella interpret the mist-like formation of Sophia from God's mouth as *spirit*.[23] However, if one was to dive back beneath the meaning of the word *mist*, it becomes apparent that *mist* is not an incorporeal substance; rather, *mist* consists of tiny airborne drops of water that possibly pertain to the mist in Gen 2:6—where a mist rises up from the earth to water the face of the ground (Snaith 1974, 121).[24] Therefore, Sophia as the spoken word of God was breathed out over creation and traversed the heights and depths of the heavens and the earth (24:5)

Verses 4–6 show Sophia as mist clouding over creation in its primordial form; she drenches creation with wisdom and embeds knowledge into the surrounding cosmos. The heavens, the earth and its inhabitants therefore became a sacred text on which God writes his commands with the ubiquitous ink of Sophia. Penchansky comments that through observation of nature and human behavior, sages learnt diligence from the work ethic of ants or the roots of poverty from a lazy farmer who does not plant in time (Penchansky 2012, 2). Hence the moral regulations that would later become the backbone of wisdom literature were attainable through the careful observance and experience of *life*. Whether this *life* was in the Semitic-Arab desert terrain or the liquid space of the Pacific Ocean, Wisdom or Sophia would have been present in both experiences and contexts.

To Whom Is Sophia Speaking?

Things however change in 24:7 when Sophia begins to look for a resting place.[25] We are not given an explanation for the sudden search of a resting place, but this part of Sophia's aretalogy ends with her asking a question—"In whose territory

---

[20] The mention of "her people" could refer to one of two things: (1) the Israelites, which befits her later linkage to Jacob in 24:8 or (2) the heavenly companions or host.

[21] Angelic attendants that reside with God (cf. 17:32; Ps 82:1; Skehan and Di Lella 1987, 331).

[22] The ancient Hebrews believed that a word, once spoken, was irreversible (Snaith 1974, 121).

[23] "Because she is a spirit, Wisdom is compared to a mist covering the earth" (Skehan and Di Lella 1987, 332).

[24] NRSV states that the watering of the earth in Gen 2:6 was through a stream, but other translations name the stream as a *mist* that arose from the earth (ESV, The Complete Jewish Bible, NAB).

[25] "Sophia, who traveled over all lands and the seas, was now compelled to accept limits and boundaries, to reduce herself to one nationality alone (Jacob, another name for Israel) and only one locality" (Penchansky 2012, 88).

should I abide?" Was this a rhetorical question, or was Sophia addressing the question to someone? We cannot answer these questions with certainty, but her creator responds in 24:8 as if Sophia's question was for him. Her creator commands that she makes her dwelling in Jacob. I suggest that this is a shallow interpretation of a deeper and more perplexing encounter between Sophia and the author of this poetic centerpiece. Since 24:1, this is the first time Sophia conspicuously flows from an aretalogy to conversation. With whom was Sophia suddenly conversing? Why does she have to settle in Israel when the whole of creation was her dwelling place? Verse 4 tells us that Sophia's dwelling was in the highest heavens and her throne was a pillar of clouds; so what need was there for her to settle in Israel? Was it God who commanded that she makes her tent and dwelling in Jacob, or was it somebody else?

Compared to Sirach, the first three wisdom books have a universal flavor that was not restrained to Israel's geographical borders (Penchansky 2012, 12). In this epic poem, Sophia is commanded to "rest," "minister," and be "established" in Jacob. I therefore ask, who gains or benefits from issuing Sophia an abode in Israel?

Marrying Sophia to Jacob

An oceanic reading that dives deep into the currents that ripple in the text suggests a façade on Ben Sira's part to domesticate Sophia, for the sake of preserving his Jewish identity and tradition in a world of Hellenistic occupation. It is not God who commands Sophia to settle, but Ben Sira who reigns Sophia in from her universal dance and sprays her erudite waters into the dry and arid region of Israel. Ben Sira fills Sophia's mouth with praise and admiration for Israel's honored people ("I took root in an honored people, in the portion of the Lord, his heritage"; 24:12). He changes her language so that Sophia no longer speaks of traversing and compassing the heavens and the abyss, but instead she is now "rooted" in Jacob (24:12). In 24:13–14 Sophia begins to grow like the trees inside Israel's borders—she is like a cedar of Lebanon, or a cypress tree on the heights of Mount Hermon. In 24:15 she begins to smell like Israel—picking up the fragrance of choice myrrh and onycha[26] (24:15). In 24:17 Ben Sira has Sophia protruding forth through the blossoms and fruits of Israel and in 24:20 compares her in sweetness to the honey that flows from its land (cf. Exod 33:3). All these endearing comments lead to the climactic revelation of the poem—*Sophia is the Torah of Israel* (24:23; Skehan and Di Lella 1987, 336).

No longer is she the misty waters that drenched creation with wisdom and understanding. Sophia is now "instruction," "teaching," and "guidance" (Soulen

---

[26] *Onycha* (Greek: ονυξ), along with equal parts of stacte, galbanum, and frankincense, was one of the components of the consecrated *Ketoret* (incense) that appears in the Torah book of Exodus (Exod 30:34–36) and was used in the Jerusalem temple.

and Soulen 2011, 219). The proclaimed revelation which Ben Sira makes of Sophia being Torah in 24:23 (cf. 20:19)[27] not only changes Sophia's ubiquitous bearing but that of her name and identity too.

Wild Waters Cannot Be Tamed

Although we are told that the mist-like Sophia is now the written Torah, in 24:26–29 Ben Sira recaptures her watery bearings. Sophia, who is now known as Torah is closed in between the riverbanks of the ancient Near East—Torah overflows like the Pishon River with wisdom and runs over like the river Euphrates with understanding. In 24:25–27 Ben Sira describes this abundant overflow of Wisdom as "the first fruits," "the time of harvest," as well as "the time of vintage."

However, an oceanic reading exposes and counters Ben Sira's façade, suggesting instead that the abundance to which the text witnesses is actually a *flood*. Israel cannot fully capture or contain the profundity of Sophia's depths. By trying to annex Sophia to Israel's geographical and narrative borders, Ben Sira realizes that Wisdom's erudite waters cannot be solely possessed or controlled by one place or people—no matter how exclusive or honored that place or people may think they are. His masterful attempt to enclose and domesticate Sophia results in a cataclysmic overflow that neither Jacob nor Torah could retain. Sophia's powerful waters can indeed bring abundant *life* but as Ben Sira learns, her waters can just as easily destroy. He realizes this in 24:28–29 where he confesses that no one is able to "fathom" her; "for her thoughts are more abundant than the sea, and her counsel is deeper than the great abyss."

This Oceanic reading of Sir 24 plunges beneath the temperate and systematic delivery of Ben Sira's poetic *talanoa* and in turn reproaches him by exposing the egocentric bias of his Jewish rendering to the exclusion of others. Wisdom cannot be confined to any one space or controlled by any one group; instead she is ubiquitous by way of saturating all peoples, places, and creation with her mysteries. The rivers show that though Sophia should indeed be embraced as something that can sustain a prosperous livelihood, her flood also shows that she is an entity who cannot be restrained or controlled, especially by human prejudice.

The Vanity of Sophia

Sophia proves too much to handle for both Qoheleth and Ben Sira. In Ecclesiastes she is *hebel*, which Qoheleth finds a total absurdity as she perplexes him with the futility of life; while in Sirach, Sophia is mystified water, reigned into the land of Israel before flooding his honored people under the guise of abundance. The translation of *hebel* has often taken on the meaning of "vanity" or something being

---

[27] "The whole of wisdom is fear of the Lord, and in all wisdom, there is the fulfilment of the law" (Sir 19:20, NRSV).

done "in vain." Qoheleth certainly views it in the latter since all his toil, success, and possessions in Eccl 2 proved futile as he pitifully concluded, "I considered all that my hands had done and the toil I had spent in doing it, and again, all was vanity and a chasing after wind, and there was nothing to be gained under the sun" (Eccl 2:11, NRSV).

Ben Sira later collides with the full meaning of this when his attempt at possessing and renaming Sophia as Torah meets with the full force of her torrents. He deflects his mistake by celebrating the "overflow," "running over," and "pouring forth" as a symbol of Israel's abundance but, like Qoheleth, ends by confessing that *the first man* did not know wisdom fully nor shall the *last one* fathom her. For her thoughts are more abundant than the sea, and her counsel deeper than the great abyss (cf. Eccl 7:23–24). The depths of Sophia confront the two sages in the midst of their pursuit, causing them to acknowledge their failure to possess her.

Sophia's dealings with both sages reveal the power of her essence as *hebel*. Although this is interpreted as the vanity of life in Ecclesiastes, her aretalogy in Sir 24:1–6 indicates that the vanity Qoheleth lamented about in his book might also suitably apply to Sophia. Indeed, she praises herself and speaks of her glory in the presence of YHWH and his hosts. Announcing that she originated from the mouth of the Most High as mist, she then covered the earth. Sophia dwelled in the highest heavens, passed over the depths of the abyss, and held sway over peoples and nations. She tells of her throne in a pillar of cloud (Sir 24:4, NRSV), which can signify sovereignty, royalty, or priestly bearings. The Hebrew word for "throne" (*kisse*) connotes "power, authority, kingship, dynasty, and the seat of any important person" (cf. Ps 47:8; Isa 6:1), while the pillar of cloud symbolizes divine guidance and communication. As *hebel* which emerged from God's mouth, Sophia holds sovereignty over creation and is a channel through which YHWH guides and communicates.

Sophia's vanity in Sir 24 shows that as the *hebel* of God she was aware of both her power and prowess. Perhaps part of the wisdom she shares is that by vainly announcing her majestic origins, the tale shows restraint and almost a sense of tenderness. Compared to the two sages who *chase after the wind (hebel)* and *root her in Jacob*, Sophia describes her ways in Sir 24 as "coming forth," "dwelling," "compassing," "traversing," and "holding sway" (NRSV), all of which connote movement and life. As YHWH's *hebel*, Sophia's dance over creation was both glorious and powerful.

Breath and Death

Qoheleth and Ben Sira make attempts to attain and possess Sophia to their own detriment. Qoheleth concludes that all is vanity or meaningless, while Ben Sira retracts his claim on her as Torah—the written law of Israel. Sophia as the breath of YHWH displays a certain fickleness to her nature: not only does she move and sway, but she is also transient, which contradicts Ben Sira's call for rest in 24:7 as well as Qoheleth's cynical praise of rest in association with *death* in Eccl 6:4. There is both life and death in Sophia. When *hebel* is removed from a child that is yet to be born into this world, it finds rest because it will never have to toil under the sun (cf. Job 3:11).[28] Sophia as breath can elicit death when she is made to rest, because in order for her to function as *hebel* she requires space and the free movement displayed in her aretalogy,[29] making Ben Sira's goal of claiming her for Israel problematic and deadly. Not only does he change the narrative and have Sophia look out for a resting place, he also speaks on behalf of YHWH and commands her to make a dwelling in Jacob. He submits Sophia's aretalogy to Jacob, culminating in Sophia changing from *hebel* to *law*.

Untameable Sophia

Ben Sira fails to take heed from preceding sages such as Qoheleth, who forewarn of Sophia's volatile nature. In Sir 24 Ben Sira elucidates quite clearly of his desire to acquire wisdom as a national possession and by doing so attempts to deny all accessibility to Sophia through the exclusive rights of Israel as YHWH's portion. Sophia would radiate Israel's glory through the world of nature which preceding sages viewed as a sacred text (Sir 24:13–17); however, now with Sirach, this sacred text turns into law. Sophia as written law is accosted by regulatory measures pertaining to the nation and people of Israel, leaving behind the ubiquitous essence of her origin as *hebel*. Ben Sira did not learn from Qoheleth the futility of pursuing or acquiring wisdom; it is Sophia herself who reprimands him by flooding the poem of Sir 24 and freeing herself from his patriotic clutches.

Sophia as wisdom holds no allegiance to a group of people because as the *hebel* of YHWH, her domain is over all peoples and nations (24:6). Before Ben Sira interrupts her aretalogy with a request for rest, Sophia mentions that she holds sway over seas and land, showing that it was his own will that tries to tie her down to Israel. The overflow of wisdom later in verse 25 shows the reprimand of Sophia that no one nation or people can contain her. Like the Moana, Sophia is wild and untameable. The laws and instructions that often go alongside her proverbial words of wisdom can preserve life, but they can also highlight the absurdity and meaninglessness of life. This is why when Ben Sira tries to attach Sophia to Torah; she bursts the banks of his homeland and has him surrender her back to the great abyss of her counsel (24:29). It is also the reason why when Qoheleth pursued her in Ecclesiastes, he proclaims that it was all in vanity. Sophia as the *hebel* of YHWH cannot be possessed exclusively by sages or kings. She avails herself to

---

[28] "Why did I not die at birth, come forth from the womb and expire?"
[29] Even her throne, which would imply some sort of being still or rested, is said to be in a pillar of cloud which indicates transience rather than being stationed.

all who drink of her waters (24:21) but will also test and teach from her enigmatic depths.

## The Fear of YHWH

Wisdom is to be feared because like the Moana of this oceanic reading, her ways are not safe. Her ways are not the ways of the law although they encompass it; her depths and motions are too profound to be understood by anyone else but YHWH. She has the capacity to unearth the contradictions and absurdities of life and shake up the secure foundations upon which Israel stand. Qoheleth with all his riches and possessions on the promised land cried out that "All was vanity!" Sophia reprimands Ben Sira that no man will ever know her fully. Yet there is wisdom in all of this, if Sophia cannot exclusively belong to one people or nation then she could be shared amongst all of creation.

This challenges the assumption that wisdom belongs to certain peoples with exclusion to others. YHWH's ubiquitous *hebel* breathes over all creation and cannot be harnessed by the insatiable desires of humans. Perhaps this is why the ancient sages of the Bible did not reference Israel and its patriarchs (besides the illusory use of David and Solomon in Ecclesiastes; cf. Penchansky 2012, 2). They concealed their identity and "demonstrated the more universal nature of their work" because they knew that the wisdom of YHWH stretched beyond their own understanding and context—wisdom existed beyond the borders of the chosen people and promised land. Ben Sira takes it upon himself to safeguard the Jewish state and people by assimilating Sophia to Torah because as YHWH's *hebel*, which sways over creation, possessing her equated to divine knowledge and power. What Ben Sira failed to remember was that as the breath of YHWH, Sophia brings with her elements of danger which previous sages warned against by cautioning the *fear of YHWH* (cf. Ps 111:10; Job 28:28; Prov 1:7; Eccl 8:12–13).

Wisdom has a voice that speaks through all creation and all peoples. Her vastness as *hebel* of YHWH cannot be contained to one thing, one place, or one people. Ben Sira had to learn this for himself despite those who preceded him, proving that Qoheleth was right when he said that generations come and go but *there is nothing new under the sun*. Despite the foretold wisdom by the authors of Job, Proverbs, and Ecclesiastes, generations later Ben Sira faced the reprimand of YHWH's *hebel*–Sophia—and she is indeed to be feared.

## Conclusion

Sirach 24 reveals Sophia's elusive powers to teach from her recondite depths by teaching and rebuking Ben Sira from within his own poetic centerpiece. Ben Sira may have had his reasons for trying to root Sophia within the borders of Israel, but the safeguarding of Jewish tradition and Mosaic law is no excuse and indeed no match for Sophia's literary rebuke of the acclaimed sage. Sophia teaches Ben

Sira within the confinements of his own writings that she will not bow down to his or Israel's assertion of their exclusive rights to YHWH.

Wisdom as *hebel* is available to all living creatures and is too great and profound to be attained or understood. Qoheleth finds this out in his own pursuits of wisdom and ends up finding that all of it had been in vain because chasing after *hebel* is a tireless activity—a person can find nothing better than to eat and drink and find joy in their daily toil. Ben Sira follows this advice in his final verses when he waters his own gardens and drenches his flowerbeds. In doing so he learns that when one tends to his own people and nation, wisdom will naturally emanate—"I will water my garden and drench my flower-beds. And lo, my canal became a river, and my river a sea."

## Works Cited

Bartholomew, Craig G. 2009. *Ecclesiastes*. Grand Rapids: Baker Academic.
Barton, John, and Muddiman, John. 2001. *The Oxford Bible Commentary*. Oxford: Oxford University Press.
Fowler, H. W., and F. G. Fowler. 1976. *The Concise Oxford Dictionary of Current English*. 6th ed. Oxford: Oxford University Press.
Havea, Jione. 2004. "Numbers." Pages 43–51 in *Global Bible Commentary*. Edited by Daniel Patte. Nashville: Abingdon.
———, ed. 2010. *Talanoa Ripples: Across Borders, Cultures, Disciplines*. Massey: Directorate Pasifika.
Longman, Tremper. 1998. *The Book of Ecclesiastes*. Grand Rapids: Eerdmans.
MacKenzie, R. A. F. 1983. *Sirach*. Delaware: Michael Glazier.
Penchansky, David. 2012. *Understanding Wisdom Literature: Conflict and Dissonance in the Hebrew Text*. Michigan: Eerdmans.
Schoors, Antoon. 1998. *The International Bible Commentary: A Catholic and Ecumenical Commentary for the Twenty-First Century*. Minnesota: Liturgical.
Skehan, Patrick W., and Di Lella, Alexander A. 1987. *The Wisdom of Ben Sira*. New York: Doubleday.
Snaith, John G. 1974. *The Cambridge Bible Commentary on the New English Bible: Ecclesiasticus*. London: Cambridge University Press.
Soulen, Richard N., and Soulen, R. Kendall. 2011. *Handbook of Biblical Criticism*. 4th ed. Kentucky: Westminster John Knox.

# Understanding Ecclesiastes 7:15–18 Through The Lens Of Zhuangzi's Perspectivism

Clement Tsz Ming Tong

Ecclesiastes 7:15–18 is a difficult passage in a number of ways.[1] Most notable is in verses 16 and 17, when Qoheleth advocates against an "excessive" (*harbēh*) kind of righteousness and claims that wicked people can live long despite their wicked ways, even to the point of implying that wickedness is alright as long as one does not go too far.[2] Common explanations given by commentators to explain this passage include:

1. The phrases "righteousness" and "wise" should not be taken at face value, but rather as a self-indulgent form of "righteous" and "wisdom," hence just a pretense to these virtues.[3]
2. This is advice against believing in one's own righteousness and wisdom, since no one can ever attain that level of goodness to avoid any errors, such as suggested in 7:20 (Seow 1997, 267).
3. The verse suggests one should follow the golden mean principle—Qoheleth is asking the readers to avoid extremism and advises them to take the middle ground.[4]

---

[1] Walter C. Kaiser (1979, 85) states that "few verses in Ecclesiastes are more susceptible to incorrect interpretations than 7:16–18."

[2] This is in contrast to the retribution theology that other Old Testament books, such as Proverbs, appear to suggest (see e.g., Prov 10:2, 27; 11:4, 21; 12:21).

[3] For instance, R. Norman Whybray argues that the *hithpael* allows such an understanding, like in Num 16:13 and 2 Sam 13:5 (Whybray 1978, 191–204; so. G. R. Castellino 1968, 24).

[4] "Don't be too holy and don't be too wicked. Sin to a moderate level!" (Kaiser 1979, 85; see also Longman 1998, 195–97; Ginsburg 1861, 379–80; G. A. Barton 1908, 143–44; Tse 2012, 228–30; Hsieh 1981, 185–86).

4. The admonition is against a form of fanaticism (Murphy 1992, 69–70) and Pharisees-style legalism,[5] an explanation that finds strong support among some Chinese commentators (Cheung 2005, 128).[6]
5. The phrases "do not be too righteous" and "do not act too wise" are quotations used by Qoheleth, like when Paul states "all is permissible" (*panta exestin*) in 1 Cor 10:23, so they do not represent the actual advice of Qoheleth but are statements he quotes to make his point.[7]
6. It is a warning against an overreaction to the truth of Eccl 7:15 (DeHaan and Vander Lugt 1974, 107–8).

All of these explanations have their problems. A major concern is the parallel formation of verses 16 and 17. For instance, if being "too righteous" is to be understood as a pretense (1), must not being "too wicked" be understood as a pretense too (Jarick 1990, 339–40)? In the same way, a warning against having too much faith in being righteous and wise may sound reasonable (2), but a warning against being too confident in one's wickedness is quite improbable and incomprehensible (Tse 2012, 227–28). The golden mean (3) and legalistic (4) explanations are not without problems either, since both seem to endorse wickedness, as long as it is at a moderate level.[8] The quotes approach (5) offers an interesting and different suggestion but provides little textual or hermeneutical support. Finally, the suggestion to read 7:15–18 as a warning against adhering too strongly to the anticipated outcome of retribution theology (6) offers yet another approach, as Qoheleth has often challenged his audience about commonly held logic and expectations, especially the traditional wisdom expressed in Proverbs.[9] The suggestion that the teaching has something to do with questioning and challenging our whole concept of reasoning opens up a new way to understanding these verses, rather than just trying to literally take them as Qoheleth's command.

---

[5] "So perhaps the writer here meant religious or ritualistic, like the Pharisees who strained at a gnat and swallowed a camel" (Powers 1952, 95).

[6] Similar to the NIV, the Chinese New Version (新譯本) adds "extremes" after "two" in verse 18b, dictating the way this verse should be understood.

[7] "This worldly maxim is the counsel of the wicked man, not the maxim or teaching of Solomon" (Coleman 2004, 37).

[8] Seow (1997, 253–54) does a parallel reading with the Aramaic Proverbs of Ahiqar to support his avoid-the-extremes reading. Yet he is very vague when he uses it to explain verse 17, only alluding that "perhaps the proverb is capable of double meaning, illustrating the fact that wisdom cannot be easily distinguished from folly." Cheung (2005, 130) interprets "too wicked" as "getting more and more wicked" but explains "too righteous" as being Pharisees-like hypocritical. Again there is inconsistency in the hermeneutic approach for the two parallel verses.

[9] Mark Sneed (2002, 118–19) thinks Qoheleth is trying to deconstruct the traditional Old Testament beliefs, such as retribution theology. But Sneed also realizes that Qoheleth is not a true Deconstructionist, because he still insists on retribution principle (e.g., 11:9; 12:14) and stops from rejecting it totally.

This essay seeks to develop a way to understand Eccl 7:15–18 as a whole through a shift of perspective, making use of Chinese philosopher Zhuangzi's (Chuang Tzu's)[10] idea of *perspectivism*. By borrowing from this ancient Chinese way of thinking, we will hopefully be able to understand this passage in Ecclesiastes in a new light.

## Perspectivism in Zhuangzi

The concept of perspectivism is commonly understood in two ways. First, all knowledge is relative and objective, dependent on one's perspective,[11] hence an absolute or greater truth does not exist. Second, human limitation is brought about by a limited perspective, hence more knowledge can be gained by looking at things from more and different perspectives (Connolly 2011, 487–88). Early study of perspectivism focused on Friedrich Nietzsche, and for a long time scholars generally agreed that Nietzsche's perspectivism was closer to the first view—that he was skeptical of the existence of objective and absolute knowledge.[12] Scholarship has recently shifted under the influence of works by researchers such as Brian Leiter. In support of the second view, Leiter uses Nietzsche's optical analogue in *On the Genealogy of Morals and Ecce Homo* 3:12 to illustrate the point that even if our viewing of an object is perspectival, we still observe it from a particular perspective. Hence by seeing things through many perspectives, even if some of them may distort the true nature of the object, the plurality of perspectives will still ensure some characteristics of the subject to be observed (Leiter 1994, 344). Similarly, by applying this analogy to the understanding of knowledge, the use of multiple perspectives will still be beneficial, because perspectivism "emphasizes that knowledge is always interested (and thus partial) and that differing interests will increase the breadth of knowledge, but it does not imply that knowledge lacks objectivity or that there is no truth about the matters known" (Leiter 2002, 21).

A methodological potential of perspectivism can also be found in the works of Zhuangzi, who lived during the Warring States Period (475 to 221 BCE) in ancient China. For years, scholars have been examining the similarities between Zhuangzi and Nietzsche. Comparing Nietzsche's *Thus Spoke Zarathustra* and *Zhuangzi*,[13] one scholar remarks that "the style of the two texts is so similar and

---

[10] "Chuang Tzu" is the translated name according to the Wade Giles system, which has been in use for quite some time. "Zhuangzi" is the more modern translation according to the pinyin system. Both are still in use today.

[11] Donald Sturgeon (2015, 893) defines "perspective" as "some set of background assumptions, cognitive and affective attitudes, and physical and psychological states that have a bearing upon how one thinks, feels, acts."

[12] Such as interpreted by Cinelli (1993, 43): "For Nietzsche, the world is a product of perspectival interpretations, not perspectives of some true world."

[13] The works of Zhuangzi by the same name.

their philosophical content so uncannily congruent that a careful comparison is called for, on several grounds" (Parkes 1983, 235). Others observe different similarities between the two, such as regarding the transevaluative consciousness of the two (Allinson 1994) or their use of deconstructive approaches to get to the root of reality (Wawrytko 2008). The similarity in their views towards the importance of perspectives has also been discussed (e.g., Chen 1991), and more recently Tim Connolly (2011) explores the methodological aspect of perspectivism found in the two philosophers. Connolly argues that Zhuangzi's perspectivism, similar to Nietzsche's (as understood by Leiter), is "interested more in furthering our individual well-being than in the ideal of disinterested knowledge" and that through an embracement of as many perspectives as possible the ideal state of *da zhi* (大知), the greater knowledge, can be attained (Connolly 2011, 488, 502). Donald Sturgeon (2015, 892) puts forward a similar argument, claiming that Zhuangzi is "far from promoting 'epistemological nihilism'" but is attempting to help us understand the *da zhi*, while at the same time "warning us of the ultimate limits of what we can come to know."

At a quick glance Zhuangzi does appear to question the human ability to understand absolute truth, given all the constrains. For example, in *Qiushui* Zhuangzi stages a conversation between Hebo (the River Elder) and the Beihai Ruo (the North Sea Ruo), in which Beihai Ruo says that "a frog in a well cannot be talked with about the sea—he is confined to the limits of his hole. An insect of the summer cannot be talked with about ice—it knows nothing beyond its own season" (*HY Zhuangzi Yinde*: 42/17/5–6).[14] Another story in *Xiaoyiuyao* tells of the mystical bird called Peng, which was so big and majestic that when its wings hit the water the splashes went up 3,000 *li*,[15] and when it flew it soared above 90,000 *li* in the sky, heading to the Southern Ocean and would not need to rest until after six months of flying. When a cicada and a little dove heard about Peng they laughed and ridiculed it, saying "we make an effort and fly towards an elm or sapanwood tree; and sometimes before we reach it, we can do no more but drop to the ground. Of what use is it for this (creature) to rise 90,000 *li*, and make for the South?" (*HY Zhuangzi Yinde*: 1/1/8–9).[16] Both stories speak to the limitation of human understanding and argue that our knowledge is very much constrained by our own experience and the context of our existence. As hard for a small insect to comprehend the vast outside world and the mystical creatures, it is equally

---

[14] Original:井蛙不可以語于海者，拘于虛也；夏蟲不可以語與冰者，篤于時也. All references to the text of the *Zhuangzi* are given in the appropriate volume of the Harvard-Yenching Institute Sinological Index Series concordance (*HY Zhuangzi Yinde*). Unless otherwise indicated, all translations of *Zhuangzi* come from the English translation by James Legge.

[15] 里, traditional Chinese unit of distance, which roughly equals to 500 meters.

[16] Original:蜩與學鳩笑之曰：「我決起而飛，槍榆枋而止，時則不至而控於地而已矣，奚以之九萬里而南為？」

difficult for humankind to comprehend what lies outside of their experience and beyond their imagination.

Another famous story told by Zhuangzi that seeks to explore the limitation of human knowledge through the angle of differing perspectives is the butterfly dream in *Qiwulun*. Zhuangzi dreamt he was a butterfly flying about and enjoying itself. All of a sudden it woke from the dream and realized that he was Zhuangzi again. Yet he began to wonder: was it Zhuangzi dreaming of himself being a butterfly earlier or a butterfly dreaming of himself being Zhuangzi right now? (*HY Zhuangzi Yinde*: 7/2/94–96). Zhuangzi takes a common human experience and digs deep, asking if the human perspective should always take priority when it comes to cognitive awareness. What if other perspectives are equally valid and important?

Two other stories can help us understand better Zhuangzi's view on perspectives, both of which are found in *Xiuyaoyou*. Huizi one day told Zhuangzi about a large tree, which people called the Chu.[17] Although it has a huge trunk, it is not straight enough for easy carpentry, and its branches are small and crooked. So even though they are planted alongside the roads, the carpenters have no interest in them. Hence they should well be called big but useless. In reply, Zhuangzi asks why Huizi should be troubled by such a tree and suggests that it should be planted at a place where there is little plantation or a wide and barren area. Since no one would ever bother to cut it, it can provide a resting place for people and a canopy for a traveler to sleep underneath (*HY Zhuangzi Yinde*: 3/1/42–47). Here, Zhuangzi points out that viewing the same object with two different perspectives can yield vastly different results: what is considered useless in the eyes of a carpenter can be seen as very useful to those who can "think through it." Zhuangzi is clearly also presenting himself as the wiser one in this conversation; hence, not only is he stressing how different perspectives can shape understanding; he is implying that some perspectives are indeed more superior to others.

The second story again features Huizi and Zhuangzi in a conversation.[18] Huizi is complaining about the large calabashes he grew using the seeds given by the king of Wei. He says they are too heavy to make into a water container and too odd-shaped to make good drinking vessels. In reply Zhuangzi calls Huizi's ability to use large objects "clumsy"[19] and shares the story of a man from the country Song, whose family had a lotion that could keep the skin from getting chapped; hence his family had worked as silk bleachers for generations. When a stranger learned of the formula, he offered to purchase it by a large sum, and the Song man thought it was a great deal, because he could now make much more in

---

[17] James Legge translates it as "Ailantus" (*HY Zhuangzi Yinde*: 3/1/42).
[18] The story actually comes before the one about the Chu tree in *Xiaoyaoyou* (*HY Zhuangzi Yinde*: 2/1/38).
[19] 夫子固拙于用大矣—Legge translates it even more ungraciously: "You were indeed stupid, my master, in the use of what was large."

a single stroke than generations of his silk bleaching ancestors could. Later, the stranger took the formula and went to the king of Wu, who was fighting the king of Yue at the time. The stranger was made a commander of the Wu army, and when he engaged in a naval battle against Yue he made good use of the formula and dealt the Yue army a great defeat. As a result he was given a portion of the conquered land (*HY Zhuangzi Yinde*: 2/1/35–42). At the end of the story Zhuangzi provides a commentary: using the same formula, one managed to gain the reward of lands, while the other does bleaching better. The key is to not let one's heart be closed to different possibilities—it is like Huizi being troubled by calabashes just because he held onto his limited definition of usefulness and would not think outside the box.

Zhuangzi's perspectivism also has both characteristics. On the one hand, he accepts that human limitation can hinder us from envisioning the incomprehensible. On the other hand, being able to see things from different perspectives may help us overcome our limitation. A closer look reveals that the beneficial and methodological side of perspectivism in fact receives more than just a casual mention in Zhuangzi. He seems to advocate the advantage of having better perspectives through the discussion and distinction between *da zhi* (greater knowledge) and *xiao zhi* (lesser knowledge). This is pointed out by both Connolly (2011, 495) and Sturgeon (2015, 897). The place where Zhuangzi makes a clear distinction between the two is in *Qiwulun*, where he says *da zhi* is "wide and comprehensive" but *xiao zhi* in comparison is "partial and restricted"[20]—a trivial kind of knowledge (*HY Zhuangzi Yinde*: 3/2/9). If we go back to the story of the cicada and the little dove poking fun at the majestic Peng in *Xiaoyiuayo*, not only is Zhuangzi expressing how the limitation of the small creatures prevents them from conceiving things much greater; at the end of the section he is also advocating for having the greater knowledge to overcome such limited existence, saying that "the *xiao zhi* is no match to the *da zhi*, and shorter in years [*xiao nian*] is no match to greater in years [*da nian*]" (*HY Zhuangzi Yinde*: 1/1/10).[21] Zhuangzi then goes on to define what he means by *xiao nian*: it is like a morning mushroom that does not know what's going on between the beginning and the end of a month, and the short-lived cicada does not know what's going on in spring and fall (*HY Zhuangzi Yinde*: 1/1/10–11). In this context, Zhuangzi ties longevity to the acquiring of the greater knowledge and appears to suggest that with more time one can gain more perspectives, thus elevating one from the peril of acquiring just the lesser knowledge.

Another interesting commentary comes after the story of the frog in the well and the summer bug in *Qiushui*, as mentioned previously. After Beihai Ruo

---

[20] Original: 大知閑閑，小知閒閒.

[21] Original: 小知不及大知，小年不及大年, which Legge translates as: "the knowledge of that which is small does not reach to that which is great; (the experience of) a few years does not reach to that of many."

speaks of the limitation of the frog in the well and the summer bug, Hebo asks if he can consider heaven and earth as big while the point of a hair as small. To that Hebo replies, "No. The capacities of things are limitless; time never stops, people's lot changes, and things begin and end without reason," so given such unpredictable trends in life, "the person with greater knowledge must look at things both far away and close by, do not take small as insignificant, or big as too much, and be aware of limitless possibilities" (*HY Zhuangzi Yinde*: 42/17/14–15).[22] In this dialogue Zhuangzi makes it even clearer that *da zhi* must be acquired by someone who does not try to understand the world by making simple and easy assumptions but by pushing the boundaries to allow one to gain more perspectives. To Zhuangzi, the greater knowledge can only be achieved by those who do not hold onto simple assumptions but who strive to see and understand things from as many perspectives as possible.[23]

Finally, there is one more intriguing story in Zhuangzi that illustrates his concept of perspectivism. It is found in *Qiwulun*, with Chang Wuzi challenging Qu Quezi on the common view that life is better than death. He asks: "How do I know that the love of life is not a delusion? And that the dislike of death is not like a young person's losing his way, and not knowing that he is going home?" (*HY Zhuangzi Yinde*: 6/2/78–79).[24] Chang Wuzi goes on to tell the story of a lady by the name of Li, who was the daughter of a warden of Ai. At the beginning when the State of Jin got possession of her, she was very unhappy and cried all the time. But after arriving at Jin, she lived in the palace, shared the king's bed, and ate well, so that she regretted that she had ever cried in the first place (*HY Zhuangzi Yinde*: 6/2/79–81). So again, Zhuangzi speaks against overconfidence in a certain perspective, even if it is a view as commonly held and accepted as living is better than death. Because without knowing what is to come in death, no one can judge with certainty.

Perspectivism in Ecclesiastes

Throughout Ecclesiastes Qoheleth challenges his audience with the uncomfortable facts of life. For instance, he discusses how both the wise and the foolish will face the same fate (2:16), and he often sounds very pessimistic about life, even to

---

[22] Original: 是故大知觀於遠近，故小而不寡，大而不多，知量無窮。
[23] Donald Sturgeon also includes the story in *Waiwu* about the divine-tortoise (*HY Zhuangzi Yinde*: 74/26/28–31) as one of those that speak about *da zhi* (897), because of the line 去小知而大知明 ("the greater knowledge will become clear after removing the lesser knowledge"). However, the main point of the story seems to emphasize that even with the greater knowledge one can face perils but not to suggest the way of gaining *da zhi*.
[24] Original: 予惡乎知說生之非惑邪！予惡乎知惡死之非弱喪而不知歸者邪！

the point of wishing never to be born (4:3).[25] Yet, what he is doing may simply be preparing the audience for his ultimate view. This becomes apparent when some of Qoheleth's statements are just blatantly contradictory, making it difficult to take all of them at face value, but rather to regard them as rhetorical in nature.[26] Such can be seen with his discussion of having wisdom and being wise, one of the major themes of the book. In the opening chapter Qoheleth speaks of the fallacy of having much wisdom, as he claims that "for in much wisdom is much vexation, and those who increase knowledge increase sorrow" (1:18). Soon after affirming that "wisdom excels folly as light excels darkness" (2:13), he quickly questions his own conclusion again, as he confides that "the same fate befalls all of them" (2:14)—both the wise and the fool. Yet later on in the book he is more consistent in the benefit of having wisdom, saying that "wisdom gives strength to the wise more than ten rulers that are in a city" (7:19), "it is better to hear the rebuke of the wise than to hear the song of fools" (7:5), and "words spoken by the wise bring them favor, but the lips of fools consume them" (10:12). What appears as an endorsement and affirmation of wisdom comes amidst the questioning of the point of being wise, and Qoheleth is fond of shaking up the confidence of his audience in their assumptions (e.g., in this case of the superiority of wisdom), even when he is in agreement with them. Similarly he challenges his audience's assumption about death, and questions if living is ever better. In 2:16–17, Qoheleth asks:

> For there is no enduring remembrance of the wise or of fools, seeing that in the days to come all will have been long forgotten. How can the wise die just like fools? So I hated life, because what is done under the sun was grievous to me; for all is vanity and a chasing after wind. (NRSV)

Since both the wise and the foolish are destined to die and be forgotten in the same manner, Qoheleth claims that he hated life, because it seems to offer a kind of hope that is not sustainable. In 7:1 he strikes a similar tone, saying that "a good name is better than precious ointment, and the day of death, than the day of birth." Yet later on in the book Qoheleth strongly refutes his earlier statements, saying in 9:4–6:

> But whoever is joined with all the living has hope, for a living dog is better than a dead lion. The living know that they will die, but the dead know nothing; they have no more reward, and even the memory of them is lost. Their love and their

---

[25] Such negativity prompts Frank Zimmermann (1973, 8) to write that Qoheleth is neurotic, that he is "a pathological doubter of everything stemming from a drastic emotional experience, a psychic disturbance. He is doubtful about himself as a person of worth and character. He has no self-esteem or value of himself. His doubt has destroyed all values."

[26] Rhetorical questions and statements are a typical feature in wisdom literature and used often in Ecclesiastes (Murphy 1992, 7).

hate and their envy have already perished; never again will they have any share in all that happens under the sun. (NRSV)

By comparing the contradictory statements, I propose that Qoheleth sees living as better than death for two reasons. First, he makes a more direct comparison between life and death in 9:4–6 and chooses life. Second, life enjoyment is a major theological theme in Ecclesiastes and is considered a gift of God.[27] Qoheleth is not constantly switching positions and changing his mind; rather, he uses 2:16–17 to challenge the commonly accepted view that living is better than death, only to achieve a rhetorical climax and answer it himself in 9:4–6. The reasoning that living is better because the living know but the dead do not resonates with what Zhuangzi says in *Xiaoyiuyou*, where *da zhi* (the greater knowledge) is tied with longevity. The one who exists will continue to gain perspectives of things, but the one that has perished will not know anything anymore—which in the language of Ecclesiastes is that they no longer have a share.

Realizing that Qoheleth often uses contradiction to question and challenge long-held Israelite wisdom,[28] it is possible to understand that he is doing the same thing when he explores the vanity of righteous people perishing in their righteousness but wicked people enjoying long life in their wickedness in 7:15–18. Qoheleth does not often speak directly about righteousness, but when he does in 3:16–17 he sounds far from optimistic, as he accepts the pervasive presence of wickedness, even in the place of righteousness:

> Moreover I saw under the sun that in the place of justice, wickedness was there, and in the place of righteousness, wickedness was there as well. I said in my heart, God will judge the righteous and the wicked, for he has appointed a time for every matter, and for every work. (NRSV)

Some authors have chosen to read 3:17 as a reference to the eschatological judgment to come. Yet, as Choon-Leong Seow (1997, 175) argues, "God will judge" does not necessarily suggest a futuristic judgment. He points out that Qoheleth seems to discourage looking ahead to the future (e.g., 3:22). Instead, we find that 3:17 strongly relates to the view of differing perspectives. Some commentators have identified the phrase "under the sun" as referring to a particular worldview, not just whatever is happening on earth. Tremper Longman (1997, 66) argues that the use of the phrase "highlights the restricted scope of [Qoheleth's]

---

[27] As Bruce Waltke (2007, 962) writes: "But when [life enjoyment is] accepted as a gift from God and used responsibly in the fear of God, there is nothing better under the sun: 'I know that there is nothing better for men than to be happy and to do good while they live. That everyone may eat and drink, and find satisfaction in all his toil—this is the gift of God' (3:12–13)."

[28] "Instead of upholding traditional wisdom's teachings and assumptions, Qohelet appears to be critical of them throughout the book" (Sneed 2012, 6).

inquiry" and that it "does not allow him to take a transcendent yet immanent God into consideration."[29] Timothy San-Jarn Wu (2015, 144) thinks that 3:17 speaks of the limitation of what humankind can observe in this world, and only with the above-the-sun perspective, the perspective of God, can one see beyond the situation.

### Reexamining 7:15–18 using Zhuangzi's Perspectivism

A number of researchers have used Chinese philosophical concepts to try to understand Ecclesiastes, and many have noticed similar concepts shared by Qoheleth and Chinese philosophers.[30] If 3:16–17 appears to speak about perspectives, we may be able to use a similar approach in trying to understand 7:15–18. Using the concept of perspectivism found in *Zhuangzi*, a simple outline can be used to show how Qoheleth makes his point:

> 7:15 A realistic observation about life "under the sun";
> 7:16–17 Advice against two unrealistic human assumptions—relying on retribution too much, or rejecting it outright;
> 7:18 Approach life with a new ("above the sun") perspective.

Verse 7:15 serves as the introductory statement of this paragraph, in which Qoheleth challenges the widely held assumption that the righteous will enjoy bountiful blessings whereas the wicked will suffer retribution consequences. Warning those who refuse to see things otherwise, Qoheleth describes two scenarios. First, those who have too much faith in the former will be disappointed if doing many good deeds does not bring about the expected good outcome (7:16). The Hithpolel imperfect of "ruin" or "desolate" (*šāmēm*) can carry a reflexive meaning, implying that it may be something that the person brings onto themselves. Elsewhere in the Bible the term can mean "be shocked" or "be

---

[29] Tse (2012, 30) says "under the sun" refers to everything that is happening within the realm of mankind, and does not include God." Farmer (1991, 150) also suggests that the "expression seems to imply that the speaker thinks a distinction can be made between what happens in human experience and what happens elsewhere.... Once convinced that the traditional doctrine of retribution fails to reflect human experience, one either has to give up the idea of justice or one has to push its execution into some realm beyond the evidence of human experience."

[30] For example, John Choi (2002, 343) argues that the "golden mean" is not a Greek product but rather a universal concept, such as that found in the Confucian beliefs. Chan Yiunam (2010, 64–66) also relates the golden mean principle to the idea of *zhongyong* (中庸, the art of taking the middle ground) in Confucianism. On the other hand, Thomas Merton (1965, 11) writes that "the book of the Bible which most obviously resembles the Taoist classics is Ecclesiastes."

devastated."³¹ Bob Utley (2008, 79) points out that it denotes a "self-deceiving spirit that trusts too much in its own efforts," and in this case it likely refers to people going an extra mile to be righteous *and* expecting reward accordingly. Qoheleth warns them: do not bother, because when disappointment sets in, one will be devastated, hence bringing destruction to oneself by some unrealistic assumption of life.³² The second scenario is in the parallel verse (v. 17), in which he warns that those who totally forgo the concept of retribution in favor of the other extreme are risking premature death. Qoheleth uses the more regular *qal* imperfect for "kill" (*mût*), which contrasts with "ruin" in verse 16 and does not have the sense of self-inflicted destruction. Hence, he seems to suggest that the premature death in verse 17 is brought upon by others through committing too much wicked behavior. As a whole, both denote an undesirable outcome for those who place too much confidence in and insisting on a particular assumption and belief, and both lead to disaster.

In verse 18, Qoheleth offers a solution to understanding verse 15 but not by following the examples in verses 16 and 17—"It is good that you should take hold of the one, without letting go of the other; for the one who fears God shall succeed with both." While to "take hold of" or "grab" may refer to either "physical or intellectual grasping" (Seow 1997, 255), in this case it means the latter. Though Qoheleth has not made clear what the "this ... that" (*zeh ... zeh*) formula is referring to,³³ it likely means the two perspectives found in the previous two verses.³⁴ Naoto Kamano (2002, 168–69) uses a rhetorical-critical approach to examine 7:15–18 and concludes that Qoheleth's advice "concentrates on the limitation of wisdom and righteousness" and teaches that "those (who) fear God accept this vulnerability of wisdom-righteousness and try to accommodate themselves to this reality." John Jarick (1990, 178) too thinks that the line refers to one "who is mindful of human powerlessness over against God." Further evidence for interpreting 7:15–18 as Qoheleth's call to avoid overconfidence in a certain human view and an advocate for a change of perspective comes in 8:10–17. These verses deal with the issue of apparent injustice in the world and centers on the fear of God. Qoheleth again confirms his observations that "because sentence against an evil deed is not executed speedily, the human heart is fully set to do evil" (8:11),

---

³¹ Such as in 2 Chr 7:21, Ps 143:4, Isa 52:14, 59:16, 63:5, and Dan 8:27.
³² Seow (1997, 254) agrees that the *hithpolel* form of "ruin" may "also connote emotional or psychological devastation."
³³ Coleman (2004, 142) finds verse 18 "ambiguously formulated."
³⁴ The Message's translation may help put this verse in a clearer perspective: "It's best to stay in touch with both sides of an issue. A person who fears God deals responsibly with all of reality, not just a piece of it." What the translation makes clearer is that Qoheleth finds holding firm onto one perspective (a piece of reality) is not wise, and overreliance on one view is not advisable; rather, those living with the fear of God knows humbleness, have learned to embrace different views, and see things from many perspectives.

and "there are righteous people who are treated according to the conduct of the wicked, and there are wicked people who are treated according to the conduct of the righteous" (8:14b). Yet Qoheleth still offers assurance:

> Though sinners do evil a hundred times and prolong their lives, yet I know that it will be well with those who fear God, because they stand in fear before him, but it will not be well with the wicked, neither will they prolong their days like a shadow, because they do not stand in fear before God. (8:12–13, NRSV)

Qoheleth reveals that he is not endorsing wickedness and is on the side of those "who fear God." The opposite to the wicked here are not the wise or the righteous but those who fear God, because this is what Qoheleth believes is the most important quality. It is implied that those who fear God will shun evil and do good, but they also come with a sense of humility that keeps them from overreliance on their own wisdom or righteousness.[35] Qoheleth continues:

> When I applied my mind to know wisdom, and to see the business that is done on earth, how one's eyes see sleep neither day nor night, then I saw all the work of God, that no one can find out what is happening under the sun. However much they may toil in seeking, they will not find it out; even though those who are wise claim to know, they cannot find it out. (8:16–17, NRSV)

For Qoheleth, the fear of God is the great understanding that keeps us humble and in our right place, that guides us from leading a life of wickedness but also from indulging in our own sense of righteousness and wisdom. This perspective teaches us to enjoy what has been given to us in life, accept things that we cannot change or explain, and hold out the hope that God will bring justice in his own time and in his own manner.

For Zhuangzi, the equivalent term for the fear of God would be *da zhi*, the great understanding. Zhuangzi's teaching that we should not dwell on a particular perspective but try our best to expand our horizon is similar to what Qoheleth advises his audience. Qoheleth's advice of taking "hold of the one, without letting go of the other" in 7:18 also speaks to the need of embracing different perspectives and not being overconfident and stubborn in holding onto just one particular view—what Zhuangzi would call the *xiao zhi*.

Although both thinkers seem to agree on expanding one's horizon through embracing perspectivism, there are two crucial differences. The first difference is that Zhuangzi argues that *da zhi* comes from the accumulation of perspectives (hence the longer one lives the more advantage one has), but Qoheleth's focus is

---

[35] "Both recommendations (7:16–17) illustrate the failure of human wisdom to understand what God is about. It is the God-fearer who will come out of it all in the best shape. Fear of God is more basic for living than doctrines about wisdom and moral conduct. The spirit of v 18 is close to 3:14 and 5:6" (Murphy 1992, lxv).

less on the number and more on avoiding overconfidence. Though we can argue that by wanting to embrace more views Zhuangzi is essentially advising against focusing too much on a particular perspective, there is still a subtle difference between the two. The second and more important difference is that the paths of the two thinkers lead to different outcomes. To Zhuangzi the acquiring of *da zhi* is a great achievement, and wisdom is achieved by those who have the ability to see things through many perspectives. To Qoheleth the fear of God shows how little one knows, even those who claim to be wise (8:17). Hence those who fear God avoid overconfidence and do not rely on a particular view or assumption. Their ultimate goal is not to accumulate perspectives and feel enriched but to let go of persistence and to feel humbled, to accept things that cannot be explained, and to believe that God will right the wrong.

Qoheleth and Zhuangzi can thus be seen to represent two forms of ancient Asian perspectivism. Both take a similar approach to life, trying to understand and overcome life's difficulties and adversaries by forgoing assumptions and seeing things from different perspectives. Zhuangzi tries to make sages who hold all perspectives and have the *da zhi* and who can rise above all others with just the *xiao zhi*; Qoheleth tries to put humans in their right place, humbled with the fear of God that shuns human arrogance, which allows them to enjoy their portion in life and gives them hope even when things cannot be explained by earthly perspectives.

## Works Cited

Allinson, Robert E. 1986. "Having Your Cake and Eating It, Too: Evaluation and Trans-evaluation in Chuang Tzu and Nietzsche." *Journal of Chinese Philosophy* 13:429–43.
Barton, George A. 1908. *A Critical and Exegetical Commentary on the Book of Ecclesiastes*. ICC. New York: Scribner.
Castellino, George R. 1968. "Qohelet and His Wisdom." *CBQ* 30:15–28.
Chan, Yiu-nam. 2001. *Chuandaoshu yu Zhongguo Sixiang* [*Ecclesiastes and the Chinese Thoughts*]. Hong Kong: China Alliance Press.
Chen, Guying. 1991. "Zhuang Zi and Nietzsche: Plays of Perspective." Pages 115–39 in *Nietzsche and Asian Thought*. Edited by Graham Parkes. Chicago: University of Chicago Press.
Cheung, James M. 2005. *Chuandaoshu* [*Ecclesiastes*]. Jian Dao Bible Commentary Series. Hong Kong: Alliance Bible Seminary.
Choi, John H. 2002. "The Doctrine of the Golden Mean in Qoh 7.15–18: A Universal Human Pursuit." *Bib* 83:358–74.
Cinelli, Albert. 1993. "Nietzsche, Relativism and Truth." *Auslegung* 19:35–45.
Coleman, John N. 2004. *Qoheleth, A Commentary*. Edinburgh: Augsburg.
Connolly, Tim. 2011. "Perspectivism as a Way of Knowing in the Zhuangzi." *Dao* 10:487–505.

DeHaan, Richard W., and Herbert Vander Lugt. 1974. *The Art of Staying off Deadend Streets*. Wheaton, IL: Victor Books.
Farmer, Kathleen A. 1989. *Who Knows What Is Good? A Commentary on the Book of Ecclesiastes*. ITC. Grand Rapids: Eerdmans.
Ginsburg, Christian D. 1970. *Coheleth, Commonly Called The Book of Ecclesiastes; The Song of Songs and Coheleth*. New York: Ktav.
Gordis, Robert. 1968. *Koheleth: The Man and His World*. 3rd ed. New York: Schocken.
Hsieh, Andrew Yu-Wang. 1981. *Xukong yu Chongman* [*Vanity and Verity*]. Hong Kong: Seedpress.
Jarick, John. 1990. *Gregory Thaumaturgo's Paraphrase of Ecclesiastes*. SCS. Atlanta: Society of Biblical Literature.
Kaiser, Walter C., Jr. 1979. *Ecclesiastes: Total Life*. Everyman's Bible Commentary. Chicago: Moody.
Leiter, Brian. 1994. "Perspectivism in Nietzsche's Genealogy of Morals." Pages 334–57 in *Nietzsche, Genealogy, Morality: Essays on Nietzsche's On the Genealogy of Morals*. Edited by Richard Schacht. Berkeley: University of California Press.
———. 2002. *Nietzsche on Morality*. New York: Routledge.
Longman III, Tremper. 1998. *The Book of Ecclesiastes*. NICOT. Grand Rapids: Eerdmans.
Merton, Thomas. 1965. *The Way of Chuang Tzu*. New York: New Directions.
Murphy, Roland. 1992. *Ecclesiastes*. WBC. Texas: Word.
Naoto Kamano. 2002. *Cosmology and Character: Qoheleth's Pedagogy from a Rhetorical-Critical Perspective*. New York: de Gruyter.
Parkes, Graham. 1983. "The Wandering Dance: Chuang Tzu and Zarathustra." *Philosophy East and West* 33:239–45.
Power, A. D. 1952. *Ecclesiastes or The Preacher: A New Translation*. London: Longmans.
Seow, C.L. 1997. *Ecclesiastes*. AB. Doubleday: Anchor Bible.
Sneed, Mark. 2002. "(Dis)closure in Qohelet: Qohelet Deconstructed." *JSOT* 27:115–26.
———. 2012. *The Politics of Pessimism in Ecclesiastes: A Social-Science Perspective*. Atlanta: Society of Biblical Literature.
Sturgeon, Donald. 2015. "Zhuangzi Perspectives, and Greater Knowledge." *Philosophy East and West* 65:892–917.
Tse, Mary Wai-yi. 2012. *Chuandaoshu* [*Ecclesiastes*]. Ming Dao Commentary Series. Hong Kong: Ming Dao.
Utley, Bob. 2008. *Bible Lessons International Old Testament: Wisdom Literature; The Mysterious Books of Ecclesiastes and Song of Songs*. Marshall, TX: Bible Lessons International.
Waltke, Bruce K. 2007. *An Old Testament Theology: An Exegetical, Canonical, and Thematic Approach*. Grand Rapids: Zondervan.

Wawrytko, Sandra A. 2008. "Deconstructing Deconstruction: Zhuang Zi as Butterfly, Nietzsche as Gadfly." *Philosophy East and West* 58:524–51.

Whybray, R. Norman. 1978. "Qohelet the Immoralist (Qoh 7:16–17)." Pages 191–204 in *Israelite Wisdom: Theological and Literary Essays in Honor of Samuel Terrien*. Edited by J. G. Gammie, W. A. Brueggemann, W. L. Humphreys, and J. M. Ward. Missoula: Scholars Press.

Wu, Timothy San-Jarn. 2015. *Chuandaoshu* [*Ecclesiastes*]. Tien Dao Bible Commentary. Hong Kong: Tien Dao.

Zimmermann, Frank. 1973. *The Inner World of Qoheleth: With Translation and Commentary*. New York: Ktav.

# "SHE IS MORE BITTER THAN DEATH": READING ECCLESIASTES 7:23–8:1 AS AN ASIAN CHINESE

Elaine W. F. Goh

The Bible has been said to portray women negatively. Ecclesiastes 7:23–8:1 (particularly 7:26–28), according to Jennifer L. Koosed (2006, 77–78), is a text that "categorically condemns all women."[1] For contemporary readers, this passage is controversial in regard to gender. It is sometimes taken as Qoheleth's misogynistic view of women (Shepherd 2008, 325). Moreover, Ellen F. Davis (2000, 205) has described the relationship between Qoheleth and "the woman" in 7:26 as "an embittering romantic relationship" because Qoheleth never found a life partner to share his enjoyment of life. This chapter contributes an interpretation from an Asian Chinese perspective, arguing that Eccl 7:23–8:1 should be read in the light of Prov 1–9 if one embarks on a metaphorical interpretation. This chapter will also argue that, if one wishes to take its literal meaning, one should read this passage within the context of how males, and humanity in general, are depicted in the book of Ecclesiastes.

A Cultural Dimension of An Asian Chinese Understanding

Since ancient times, Chinese have employed rich imagery in their literature. Similes are often used to assert a point. From the animal world, foxes are used to illustrate seductive women in Chinese folklore. Snakes are used to express people with harmful intentions and are also associated with immoral and dangerous women. These images are part of the vocabulary and figures of speech in Chinese language, as reflected in musical plays, classical literature, and daily dialogues. For instance, the phrase "bewitched by a fox" (狐狸精, *hulijing*) is actually an idiom to express the type of woman who is as crafty as a fox. The Chinese idiom

---

[1] I use *Qoheleth* to refer to the person who speaks (as "I") in the book, and *Ecclesiastes* as referring to the book."

for *femme fatale* is made up from the words for snakes, scorpions, and beautiful women (蛇蝎美人, *shexiemeiren*). Etymologically, the word for a monster or a demon (妖, *yao*) has the radical for woman (女, *nv*) in its form. Similarly, the word for evil (奸, *jian*), traitor (奸人, *jianren*), and rape (姦, *jian*) all have the radical for woman (女, *nv*) in their etymology. Furthermore, the word for prostitute (妓, *ji*) also contains the radical for woman, although sometimes the word is used to denote a male prostitute (男妓, *nanji*). It is a sad fact that most, if not all of these words render women in a negative sense. Apparently from ancient times, the understanding of women has a negative undertone translatable into the Chinese language.

Against this cultural background, one could easily accept the passage in Eccl 7:26–28 at face value. "The woman," as such, is easily taken negatively and generally referring to women who are believed to be dangerous and deadly by nature, culturally speaking. As a result, the common approach taken by Asian Chinese when reading this passage is that women in general is taken to mean as such in the passage. It is argued in this chapter, however, that the woman "who is more bitter than death" is not just any woman in general, but a particular type of woman who is seductive, harmful, and deadly. It is similar to the occasion when one reads about a certain destructive and wicked man in the biblical text, like a murderer, where the reference is usually not generic (man) but specific (the murderer).

Ecclesiastes 7:23–8:1

Many commentators have identified the elements of ambiguity in the text of Eccl 7:23–8:1. Doug Ingram (2013, 219) maintains that ambiguity is part of the design of Ecclesiastes.

Seeking Wisdom

The theme that runs through Eccl 7:23–8:1 is on seeking wisdom. A chiastic structure is discernible in this passage. It begins with testing wisdom (7:23–25) and ends with having wisdom (8:1). Sandwiched in between the frame is 7:26–29, which elaborates on avoiding folly.

| A | | 7:23–25 | Testing wisdom |
|---|---|---------|----------------|
| | B | 7:26–29 | Avoiding folly |
| A' | | 8:1 | Having Wisdom |

Though this passage has only eight verses, the verb *māṣā'* ("to seek") appears eight times (verses 24, 26, 27 [2x], 28 [3x], and 29), making nine occurrences in total together with Eccl 7:14 in the same chapter. The verb is translated in NRSV as "to find out" or "has found," as well as the negation "I have not found" and the rhetorical question "who can find?" In short, Qoheleth is trying to know or to make sense of something. The verb *māṣā'* is significant as it is the very word used in the wisdom circle to promote the idea of seeking wisdom (see for example, Prov 2:4–5; 3:13; 8:8, 18, 35; 19:8). Pursuing wisdom is likened to pursuing a woman of noble character (Prov 18:22; 31:10)—she is more prized than precious stones! A decent woman makes an ideal wife. Understandably, the recipients of the book of Proverbs were mainly young men who were still single.

A. Testing Wisdom (7:23–25)

Qoheleth has tested (*nāsâ*) his life with pleasure (2:1), and he has tested (*nāsâ*) "all" with wisdom (7:23). In view of the previous passage, the word "all" (*kol*) here includes Qoheleth's endeavor to make sense of righteousness and wickedness in 7:19–22. "All" also includes how he attempts to seek wisdom. He encounters a difficulty, however, because he finds that wisdom is far from him. In such a short verse, Qoheleth conveys a seemingly contradictory statement—he has tested all things with wisdom, yet wisdom is far from him. One would ask, how could it be possible that Qoheleth possesses wisdom and yet wisdom is far from him? Ecclesiastes 7:16 gives a pointer, where Qoheleth has warned people of "acting too wise." Wisdom does not promise definite advantages to one who has it. Perhaps the problem that confronts all the sages is that, though they have learned some knowledge, they can never learn it all. Humans err, and the sages err as well. Even though Qoheleth is a sage, wisdom is a stranger to him at times, as 7:23 suggests.

And so, Qoheleth challenges anyone to find out the things which are far off and very deep (7:24). The expression "very, very deep" is repeated in Hebrew, *wĕ'āmōq 'āmōq*, conveying a superlative which means utterly or completely deep. Logically, no one can possibly comprehend it, therefore the rhetorical question, "who can find it out (*māṣā'*)?"

Qoheleth has nevertheless attempted to find it out, and in 7:25 he compounds his search with recurring infinitives like "knowing" (twice), "searching" and "seeking." These infinitives recall the motive in the book of Proverbs, where they are used repeatedly in order to convey the sages' intent for people to gain knowledge and understanding (Prov 1:2–6). Here in 7:25, Qoheleth aims at the "sum" (*mešbôn*), that is, the "payoff." It is after the very meaning of life that Qoheleth has been seeking, albeit rendered in an economical term. The payoff invites one to ponder, "is life meaningful after all?"

The next four nouns in 7:25 are the opposites of wisdom: "wickedness" (*reša'*), "folly" (*kesel*), "foolishness" (*hassiklût*), and "madness" (*hôlēlôṯ*). Among these, only "foolishness" (*hassiklût*) has a definite article. This definite article is significant as it will affect how one understands "the woman" (*hā'iššâ*) in the next verse, which also comes with a definite article. It is important to note that Qoheleth warns of wisdom's opposites and that one who seeks wisdom must know the differences between wisdom and folly. In the following verses, Qoheleth illustrates the real struggles one has to wrestle with in order to stay away from folly.

B. Avoiding Folly (7:26–29)

Avoiding folly is challenging. Qoheleth asserts that one would encounter the woman and that "she is more bitter than death" (7:26). Why would Qoheleth abruptly bring up a subject on woman, especially one that is preceded by the definite article (*hā'iššâ*)? R. Norman Whybray (1989, 125) pointed out that this unexpected subject matter has puzzled many commentators. There is no earlier mention of woman in the book, though the phrase is twice mentioned after (7:28 and 9:9). Qoheleth seems to expect the readers to know who the woman is. It appears then, that the wisdom circle has a common understanding with regards to the epistemology of wisdom and folly which includes the usage of rhetoric and imageries.

The female embodiment of wisdom is common in the book of Proverbs. The sages employ the metaphor of a good woman to illustrate wisdom, as the word "wisdom" is a feminine noun (e.g., Prov 1:20–33; 3:13–18; and 4:6–9). The sages also use the metaphor of a wicked woman to illustrate folly (e.g., 5:1–6; 7:6–27; 9:13–18). Understandably, Qoheleth and his audience were familiar with this wisdom etymology. In Eccl 7:26–29, Qoheleth warns about the reality of folly. *Hā'iššâ* (the woman) connects to *hassiklût* (foolishness), the only noun with a definite article in 7:25. Therefore, the woman here is not just any woman or even a specific woman in reality. The woman who is more bitter than death is wisdom's opposite. She is Lady Folly.

Qoheleth asserts that Lady Folly is more bitter than death (*mar mimmāwet*). Choon-Leong Seow (1997, 261) pointed out that the adjective "bitter" (*mar*) is problematic, given that with a feminine subject one expects the feminine adjective *marâ* rather than the masculine *mar*.[2] Nevertheless, scholars have noted some grammatical peculiarities in the book of Ecclesiastes. Examples include the demonstrative *zōh* taking place instead of *zō't*, *'ănî* occurs (29x) rather than *'ānōkî*, and *'ăšer* (89x) alternates with *še* (68x).[3] Hence the use of *mar* instead of *marâ* represents yet another peculiarity.

---

[2] See also Dahood (1958, 308–18; 1966, 275–76), who emends the word to *mrr*, meaning "strong" in Phoenician; hence one reads "she is stronger than death." Though such emendation is attested in Aramaic and Ugaritic, the notion that "Lady Folly is stronger than death" creates more questions. The book of Proverbs records that her feet go down to death (Prov 5:5) and her house is going down to the chambers of death (Prov 7:27); it would make no sense that she could be stronger than death.

[3] Besides, the numerous occurrences of Aramaic and Persian words, *hapax legomena* and peculiar Hebrew grammatical usage in Ecclesiastes point to a late period composition (see Schoors 1992, 221–24; Barton 1908, 52–53; and Seow 1997, 17–18).

Besides being described as bitter than death, Lady Folly is further said to be a trap (*hî' měṣôdîm*), her heart is snares and nets, and her hands are fetters (7:26). The heart in the human body represents one's motive which is hidden, and the hand denotes one's action that is visible. Therefore, the passage describes Lady Folly as dangerous inside and out. A trap, nets, and fetters are used by a hunter to entrap animals; here they become imageries that tell of Lady Folly's hunt for her prey. Lady Folly is depicted as a *femme fatale*. Consistent with the teaching of the sages, one should keep away from Lady Folly, and Qoheleth relates this avoidance with an intent to please God. In retrospect, Eccl 2:26 has mentioned about God who gives wisdom to the one who pleases him. Hence, one who has wisdom is one who pleases God, and is also one who escapes from Lady Folly. Conversely, the one who does not possess wisdom (the sinner) is entrapped in her nets and fetters.

It is noteworthy, nevertheless, that the proposition of Michael Fox (1999, 267–72) on this passage is indicative for an alternate reading. Fox maintains that the woman in this passage is an actual woman, and the passage is inevitably misogynistic. In spite of this, Qoheleth may not intend his remarks here to be taken with too much gravity. Fox is certain that Qoheleth does not defend the honor of women, yet Qoheleth does not think too highly of men either. Further, Qoheleth's comments on womankind in 7:26 resemble what is advocated in the book of Proverbs about the adulterous strange woman (e.g., Prov 22:14). Fox's suggestion, in my opinion, points to one who prefers to take the woman literally (not metaphorically) to read it in line with Proverbs, on the one hand, and in the light of how men and humanity are described in Ecclesiastes, on the other. Fox himself concludes that Qoheleth is "speaking of a flaw common to humanity generally."

Returning to the passage, there is a pause after Eccl 7:26, as Qoheleth is referred to in the third person in 7:27 (so in 1:2 and 12:8). The imperative for people to see implies a change of subject. Nevertheless, the subject matter that continues on is the motif of finding, and the verb (*māṣā'*) occurs twice in this verse. Qoheleth attempts to find the sum (*Hešbôn*) from one thing to another (7:27), as if calculating an account from another, sparing no effort in his pursuit of wisdom. In the next verse when Qoheleth further emphasizes that his mind has sought repeatedly, the verb *māṣā'* occurs another three times. This verse, however, poses at least three difficulties in its interpretation.

First, "I found [*māṣā'tî*] ... yet I have not found [*lō' māṣā'tî*]" is in 7:27 and in the first half of 7:28. It is repeated in the second half of 7:28: "One man among a thousand I found, but a woman among all these I have not found." The connection of 7:28b with 7:28a is not obvious. It is an abrupt comparison between a man and a woman, where one would expect a comparison between wisdom and folly instead: "One foolish person among a thousand I found, but a wise among all these I have not found." To remove its ambiguity, this verse is better posited as Qoheleth seeking Lady Wisdom, believing that she can deliver him from the traps and snares of Lady Folly, yet he has not found Lady Wisdom (Seow 1997, 68–69). Her elusive presence apparently troubled Qohelet.

Second, there is a perplexing gender issue in 7:27. The verb "says" (*'āmrâ*) is in the feminine form, as if Qoheleth the subject is female. The same verb nevertheless appears in the masculine form (*'āmar*) in 1:2 and 12:8. All three verses present the voice of the narrator in the book, who is both female (7:27) and male (1:2 and 12:8).

Third, a greater difficulty lies in the word "man" (*'ādām*) in 7:28b. If a male is meant by the *'ādām* in 7:28b, Qoheleth could have used *'iš* instead. Yet Qoheleth uses *'ādām*, and this usage refers to humanity (not just male) throughout the whole book. Further, when *'ādām* recurs in the next verse (7:29), clearly humanity is meant in "God made *human beings* upright, yet they have sought for many schemes." Therefore, as it stands, the comparison in this verse should be between a human and a woman, not between a man and woman. However, the comparison between humanity and woman is bizarre, because humanity and woman are not of equal standing. It appears more likely that humanity is compared to someone larger than a woman, for example, the personified wisdom. In short, 7:28b poses interpretive difficulties in a close reading. Taken at face value, it creates a gender-related misunderstanding. Therefore, Seow argues that 7:28b represents an insertion by the narrator, just as the third person's "Qoheleth says" in 7:27. According to Seow (1997, 265), the insertion may be a personal opinion or the narrator's interpretation of 7:28a, and as such, 7:29 continues the sequence of thought from 7:28a.

In my opinion, the phrase "among all these" (*bĕkol-'ēllê*) is most telling of how 7:28b should be understood. Ecclesiastes 7:28b does not say "a woman among all the other women," but it states "a woman among *all these*." To what could "all these" possibly refer? I suggest, in the continuation of the theme on seeking wisdom, Qoheleth is saying he has not found wisdom despite all of his efforts spent in its pursuit. "A woman" (wisdom) in 7:28b is set in opposite to "the woman" (folly) in 7:26. Qoheleth has already said that wisdom is far from him in 7:23 and here in 7:28b he once again asserts, "among all these efforts of seeking, I have not found wisdom." Taken as a whole, I suggest that 7:28 be translated as "A person among a thousand I found, but wisdom among all these (seeking) I have not found," wherein "a person" is set in view of "a thousand people" while "wisdom" is set in view of "all of his pursuit."

This perspective is significant for one to understand 7:27–29. Basically, it solves the difficulties with the use of *'ādām*. At best, it corrects a notorious misinterpretation of this text—that the teachings of Qoheleth, the male chauvinistic sage, devalue females. I have encountered people who use this passage to support gender-biases, and they promote that an upright woman is impossible to find because God has made only men upright. The woman mentioned in 7:26 and the images of a trap, nets, and fetters related to her could further be used to enhance such a view.

Qoheleth has finally found (*māṣā'*) a conclusion in 7:29, that "God made humans upright, yet they have sought for many schemes." The ninth occurrence of the verb *māṣā'* recollects what Qoheleth has been seeking—wisdom to understand certain truths in life. Qoheleth realizes two things: First, God has made humans upright, and this answers what he has asked rhetorically in 7:13, "See the work of God: who is able to straighten what he has made crooked?" Second, humanity has made things crooked by many "schemes" (*Hiššĕḇōnôt*). This word has appeared in 7:25 and 7:27 in singular form (*Hešbôn*); its meaning lies in an economical sense of counting. Elsewhere in 9:10, *Hešbôn* involves thinking and planning. Therefore, this verse suggests that humanity gives thoughts to the plans that are aimed at perverting God's initial intention. They attempt to straighten what God has made crooked and attempt to make crooked what God has straightened (Seow 1997, 276). Qoheleth points out the problem with humanity in 7:29, that is, the tendency to oppose God's will. In the words of Craig Bartholomew (2009, 175), "it is not the world that is crooked but humans," and humanity's quest for autonomy opposes their dependence on God. Seeking truth and meaning in life away from God is foolish. This caused Qoheleth to utter his sense of vanity in life many times in Ecclesiastes. In the pursuit of wisdom, humanity, including Qoheleth himself, has fallen into foolishness instead. Wisdom is elusive indeed, just as Qoheleth has been wrestling to comprehend it fully.

A'. Having Wisdom (8:1)

The theme of seeking wisdom runs through to 8:1, where Qoheleth presents two rhetorical questions to end this passage. Qoheleth did not begin by asking, "Who is the wise?" Since wisdom is difficult to hold on to (7:29), the question instead is, "Who is *like* the wise?" And further, "Who knows the solution of a matter?" These questions are rhetorical as Qoheleth expects "no one" as the answer.

The word for "solution" is *pēšer*, and it occurs only here in the whole of the Old Testament. It exemplifies Qoheleth's deliberate search for a way to attain wisdom. Wisdom's benefits come next: it makes one's face shine and changes the hardness of one's countenance. Numbers 6:25 speaks of God's countenance bringing forth grace and peace upon people; thus, in Eccl 8:1 a shining face conveys a kind of divine blessedness. Such blessedness reflects what is inside one's heart, and that translates into a person's countenance. Wisdom, after all, can make a difference to a person's life. It transforms a person's attitude and makes a person more amiable—if only one can have it!

## Folly as Feminine

The biblical wisdom tradition often uses personification as a literary device to articulate theology. Wisdom can be an abstract idea for common people, yet the sages were able to make it understandable through a construct of feminine imagery. Wisdom comes alive in the teaching of the sages. Wisdom incarnates as a noble female character and is highly advocated for the young and learning men to pursue wholeheartedly. Lady Wisdom will lead the seeking ones to the path of blessing and longevity. Conversely, folly is characterized as a seductive woman. Lady Folly is poised to take young men in the opposite direction, on the path of self-destruction. A good wife is a metaphor for wisdom and a seductress a metaphor for foolishness.

This construction of female embodiment stems from wisdom's *sitz im leben*. The learners were mainly young men in their formative years. Behind the likely postexilic compilation of Israel's wisdom literature, the sages promote the idea of obedience and the fear of the Lord in their teaching, hoping that the younger generation would dwell in the land continually.[4] Character building, choice of lifestyle, and how to cope with life challenges therefore became the emphases of their teaching.

The wisdom tradition disseminates wisdom through a moral construct, Lady Wisdom. Wisdom's embodiment is in feminine form. She is an ideal wife, and her value is far more precious than jewels. Therefore, Lady Wisdom is worth pursuing wholeheartedly. For dialectic purposes, the sages also create a metaphor of wisdom's opposite, Lady Folly. She conversely is an embodiment of an immoral and seductive woman. The sages warn against her deception and the danger that will lead to grievous harm, indicating a common ground of prophetic literature and wisdom literature. Both literature employ gender-related images in a negative sense to accentuate the importance of faith in God. While the prophets rebuke Israel's infidelity through images of adultery, the sages dwell on the images of *femme fatale*. Both types of writing nevertheless have a common goal: to guide the people of God to live a life of obedience, and to walk on the path of righteousness.

There are four wisdom poems in Prov 1–9 that advocate and extol personified wisdom. In Prov 1:20–33 Lady Wisdom speaks in the streets, in the squares, at the busiest corner, and at the entrance of the city gates. She rebukes the scoffers, the fools, and the simple ones. Proverbs 3:13–20 records that Lady Wisdom is better than silver and gold. She has long life in her right hand, and in her left hand are riches and honor. Her paths are pleasant and peaceful as she is the tree of life. The third wisdom poem, Prov 8:1–36, is packed with rich descriptions of her value. She does not merely appear in the royal court where kings and princes prize her, but also back in time at creation, where she is the architect at work. The fourth wisdom poem, Prov 9:1–18, depicts Lady Wisdom as the host of a sumptuous banquet who extends an invitation through her maidservant. Those who partake from her will have wisdom and life. This wisdom poem illustrates Lady Folly

---

[4] The collection of the book of Proverbs could have come about over a few hundred years, the final stage being in the postexilic period. On its postexilic compilation, see, for example, Camp 1985, 179–206; Fox 2000, 6; Lucas 2015, 6–8.

also, who hosts another meal with stolen bread and drink. Those who accept her invitation will face disaster. The theological message of these poems is clear: the one who chooses Lady Wisdom will get life; the one who follows Lady Folly will face death.

The female metaphors in the book of Proverbs are compelling. Wisdom and folly come alive, and they engage the readers to make a choice in life. If one were to read Eccl 7:23–8:1 in the light of the book of Proverbs, one would not miss the metaphorical meaning of the woman in 7:26, whom Qoheleth avers as "she is more bitter than death." This comes from frustration after Qoheleth has launched a desperate grasp for wisdom, yet here he is still wanting. In the words of Bartholomew (2009, 265–66), "Clearly these images are intended to evoke the inaccessibility of wisdom." And as Peter Enns (2011, 88–89) also suggests, the concluding section of this passage indicates Qoheleth's appeal to the sages who wrote Prov 1–9, "Show me, because I have not found her."

## Interpreting Ecclesiastes 7:23–8:1 as an Asian Chinese

Ecclesiastes 7:23–8:1 generated multiple and diverse interpretations. Though the passage contains ambiguities for which scholars do not agree on a solution, one should nevertheless begin with the best-informed interpretation. The parameter that this chapter undertakes has two considerations (so Kato 2012, 273–87). First, consistent in the depiction of the personified wisdom in the wisdom literature, Eccl 7:23–8:1 must be read in light of Prov 1–9. The woman intended in the passage, Lady Wisdom, is thus metaphorical. Second, even if an actual woman is meant in Eccl 7:23–8:1, the passage should be read alongside passages in Ecclesiastes on how a man (male) is described and thus on how humanity is being depicted at large.

The word for "man" (*'iš*) appears ten times in Ecclesiastes, most of which carry the sense of humanity (1:8; 4:4; 6:2 [2x], 6:3; 7:5; 9:14, 15 [2x, the second time with a definite article]; 12:3). Based on the occurrences of the word *'iš* in Ecclesiastes, it is highly unlikely that Qoheleth is targeting women in 7:26–29. Rather, he is rendering a self-critique as a sage and as a human, highlighting the elusiveness of wisdom and the unreliability of humankind. In sum, the passage can be read in two ways, metaphorically or literally. The metaphorical interpretation is favored in this chapter. The woman who is more bitter than death is none other than Lady Folly.

The interpretation of this passage among Asian Chinese generally reflect these two positions: metaphorical and literal. Archie Lee (1990, 98), for example, has taken "the woman" (*hā'iššâ*) in its definite form in 7:26 as personified folly. Lee rules out the possibility of *hā'iššâ* as referring to all women in general. Disagreeing with the *Studium Biblicum Version* (the Catholic Chinese translation), Lee opines that it is not possible that all women are more bitter than death in light of the positive undertone in Eccl 9:9, where Qoheleth instructs one to enjoy life with the woman they love. The reading of personified folly is more probable according to Lee, as in the wisdom literature folly is personified as a seductress and wisdom as a good wife. In Lee's reading (1990, 98), the passage conveys the message of wisdom's limitation, that wisdom does not guarantee a wise person's escape from the snares of the woman, that is, folly.

The interpretation of Lady Folly is also undertaken by Lo Hing Choi (2009, 110–11), who places stress on the feminine form of the Hebrew noun for folly and the presence of the definite article in *hā'iššâ*. Based on textual considerations, Lo also reads in light of the preceding verse where wickedness is associated with folly (7:25), and from Prov 5:3–5 where bitterness and death are connected to an adulteress. Therefore, according to Lo, Qoheleth's depiction of *hā'iššâ* in 7:26 should not be taken as misogynic, as Qoheleth merely emphasizes the attraction and the deadly consequences that come along with wickedness and foolishness. Thus, when Lady Folly is looking for her prey with weapons in her hands, only the sinner is captured by her.

The other position with regards to this passage takes the gender references literally. For instance, Philip Chia (1996, 94) opines that Qoheleth points out three enigmas on gender relations: first, women in general are corrupted according to 7:26; second, men are not better off than women, as both are equally corrupted according to 7:28–29; and third, humanity in general is corrupted in 7:29. In a more recent publication, Tse Wai-yi (2005, 238–39) avers that the presence of the definite article in *hā'iššâ* points to a specific kind of woman but not women in a general sense. Her reference comes from Prov 5:3–5, where an adulteress—the kind of woman meant in Eccl 7:26—is also connected to bitterness and death. Tse maintains that *hā'iššâ* in Eccl 7:26 is none other than the immoral type of woman who seduces men with her charm and deception, but a righteous man can get away from such a woman. The readings of both Chia and Tse rule out the possibility of the personification of folly.

Understandably, due to the varied textual considerations, Asian Chinese readers have not reached a consensus on the interpretation of Eccl 7:23–8:1. The perspective on personified folly is valid, however, as Asian Chinese are generally informed by recent scholarship on the wisdom literature. One cannot miss the vast research on rhetorical criticism and the studies of biblical images, which include metaphors and personifications. Yet the cultural dimension of Chinese interpreters, as mentioned in the beginning of this chapter, should not be sidelined either.

In my opinion, Eccl 7:23–8:1 can also be an echo of Prov 31:10–31. The book of Ecclesiastes often widens a reader's perspective to wisdom literature, especially to the prescriptive type of wisdom in the book of Proverbs. Just as the capable woman in Prov 31:10–31 is hard to find, wisdom is likewise beyond grasp in Eccl 7:23–8:1. While Lady Wisdom is more precious than jewels in Proverbs, Lady Folly is more bitter than death in Ecclesiastes. The connection between this woman in Eccl 7:26–29 and the woman in Prov 31 has long been suggested (see, for example, Wolters 2001, 93). One can put it more ironically: that Qoheleth is unable to find wisdom despite all his seeking, and Qoheleth's quest of Lady Wisdom has poignantly led him into the arms of Lady Folly (Bartholomew 2009, 268).

## Conclusion

Ecclesiastes 7:23–8:1 should not be taken as Qoheleth's misogynous statement. With the book of Proverbs in the background, wisdom is given a negative illustration in the book of Ecclesiastes—wisdom is beyond grasp, despite repeated effort. The common thread before Eccl 7:23–8:1 is Qoheleth's seeking wisdom. The passage follows the same theme of finding wisdom. The woman who is more bitter than death is none other than personified folly. She is Lady Folly, wisdom's opposite, consistent with the metaphorical portrayal of folly in the book of Proverbs. Reading the passage as a whole, Qoheleth's failure in his quest of wisdom, therefore, lies in the foolishness of human schemes to go against God's intention.

## Works Cited

Bartholomew, Craig G. 2009. *Ecclesiastes*. Baker Commentary on the Old Testament Wisdom and Psalms. Grand Rapids: Baker Academic.
Barton, George A. 1908. *The Book of Ecclesiastes*. ICC. Edinburgh: T&T Clark.
Camp, Claudia. 1985. *Wisdom and the Feminine in the Book of Proverbs*. Bible and Literature Series 11. Sheffield: JSOT Press; Almond.
Chia, Philip P. 1996. *Truth and Absurdity: On the Thought of Qoheleth*. Jian Dao Supplement Series 2. Hong Kong: Alliance Bible Seminary.
Dahood, Mitchell. 1958. "Qoheleth and Recent Discoveries." *Bib* 39:302–18.
———. 1966. "The Phoenician Background of Qoheleth." *Bib* 47:264–82.
Davis, Ellen F. 2000. *Proverbs, Ecclesiastes, and the Song of Songs*. Westminster Bible Companion. Louisville: Westminster John Knox.
Enns, Peter. 2011. *Ecclesiastes*. The Two Horizons Old Testament Commentary. Grand Rapids: Eerdmans.
Fox, Michael V. 1999. *A Time to Tear Down and a Time to Build Up: A Rereading of Ecclesiastes*. Grand Rapids: Eerdmans.
———. 2000. *Proverbs 1–9*. Anchor Bible. New York: Doubleday.
Ingram, Doug. 2013. "'Riddled with Ambiguity': Ecclesiastes 7:23–8:1 as an Example." Pages 219–40 in *The Words of the Wise Are Like Goads*. Edited by Mark J. Boda, Tremper Longman III, and Cristian G. Rata. Winona Lake: Eisenbrauns.
Kato, Kumiko. 2012. "Qoheleth (Ecclesiastes): Man Alone, without Woman." Pages 273–87 in *Feminist Biblical Interpretation: A Compendium of Critical Commentary on the Books of the Bible and Related Literature*. Edited by Luise Schottroff and Marie-Theres Wacker. Grand Rapids: Eerdmans.
Koosed, Jennifer L. 2006. *(Per)Mutations of Qohelet: Reading the Body in the Book*. LHBOTS 429. New York: T&T Clark.

Lee, Archie Chi Chung, and Chow Lien Hwa. 1990. *The Book of Ecclesiastes and The Song of Songs*. Edited by Chow Lien Hwa and Andrew Chiu. Chinese Bible Commentary 17. Hong Kong: Chinese Christian Literature Council.

Lo, Hing Choi. 2009. *From Vanity to Enrichment: Ecclesiastes and Life*. Hong Kong: Chinese Baptist Press.

Lucas, Ernest C. *Proverbs*. 2015. The Two Horizons Old Testament Commentary. Grand Rapids: Eerdmans.

Schoors, Antoon. 1992. *The Preacher Sought to Find Pleasing Words: A Study of the Language of Qoheleth*. Orientalia Lovaniensia Analecta 41. Leuven: Peeters.

Seow, Choon-Leong. 1997. *Ecclesiastes*. AB. New York: Doubleday.

Shepherd, Jerry E. 2008. "Ecclesiastes." Pages 253–365 in *the Expositor's Bible Commentary*. Edited by Tremper Longman III and D. E. Garland. Grand Rapids: Zondervan.

Tse, Mary Wai-yi. 2005. *Ecclesiastes: A Contemplation on Life*. Hong Kong: Ming Dao.

Whybray, R. Norman. 1989. *Ecclesiastes*. Grand Rapids: Eerdmans.

Wolters, A. M. 2001. *The Song of the Valiant Woman: Studies in the Interpretation of Proverbs 31:10–31*. Carlisle, UK: Paternoster.

# A READING OF ECCLESIASTES 8:1–9 IN MALAYSIA

Peter H. W. Lau

Since Christians are a minority in Malaysia, with Islam the official and dominant religion, as reflected in those holding power in government positions, there are divergent opinions about how Christians should approach human authorities. Approaches range from uncritical obedience to critical resistance. I will provide some insight on this issue from Ecclesiastes.

The approach in this chapter is as follows: I examine Qoheleth's advice for approaching a king in Eccl 8:1–9 to derive some general principles.[1] Old Testament examples of those who serve under a foreign king, such as Joseph, Daniel and Esther, will be adduced to support these principles. Then, since I write as a Christian for Christian readers, I will consider the difference that Jesus and the New Testament authors might make to these principles. This is based on the understanding that an Old Testament passage needs to read within its contexts: literary, historical-cultural, and canonical.[2] For Christians, this canonical context includes the New Testament. Indeed, Jesus asserts that the Old Testament anticipates and is fulfilled in him (e.g., Luke 24:25–27, 44–45; John 5:39; 2 Cor 1:20). A sketch of the sociopolitical situation in Malaysia will follow, so we can determine how the modified principles fit into the local context. Finally, this chapter concludes with some reflections on how to deal wisely with government authorities in Malaysia.[3] Although this chapter generally moves linearly, from the original text (Eccl 8:1–9) to the New Testament to the local context (Malaysia),

---

[1] I use *Qoheleth* to refer to the speaker of the majority of the book (1:2–12:8) and *Ecclesiastes* to refer to the book itself.

[2] For the different contexts that must be considered in biblical interpretation, see Duvall and Hays 2012, 115–62; Fuhr and Köstenberger 2016, 180–212.

[3] Although the hermeneutical method followed in this chapter is avowedly Christian, this does not mean that the product of this method is only applicable to Christians. Rather, many of the findings in this chapter will be applicable to other religious minorities in Malaysia and in differing degrees to Christians and religious minorities in other countries.

my local and theological contexts shape how I view the original text. My Christian Malaysian lens highlights aspects of the Ecclesiastes text that might not be so prominent if I was reading the same text within other contexts. That is, the method in this chapter contains more of a hermeneutical spiral than might meet the eye.[4]

### Wisdom in Dealing with the King (Eccl 8:1–9)

Ecclesiastes contains at least eight passages that describe the sociopolitical reality and/or give instructions about how to act wisely in such a situation.[5] I focus on Eccl 8:1–9 because it provides the most detail about how to approach a person in a place of authority. Some commentators prefer to read 8:1 with the previous section, especially because the theme of wisdom is also found in 7:19, 23, and 25. The verse is connected to the previous section; however, the catchwords in 8:1–9 bind it more tightly with the following verses.[6] Although there is debate about the coherence of this passage, in the following I seek to show how a dominant theme can be read from it.[7]

This passage outlines how a wise person in general, and a court official in particular, should respond to a king. There is no consensus about the structure of this passage, but Thomas Krüger (2004, 157) suggests that the first section (8:1–5) is "critically examined" by the second section (8: 6–9). He argues that the "internal contradictions" in this passage function to challenge readers to repeated reading. I prefer to view the second section as qualifying what Qoheleth says in the first, instead of as "contradictions" (cf. Schoors 2013, 619). Nonetheless, the general gist of Krüger's suggestion will be applied here. Wherever relevant, I will point out which interpretation is more likely on a first reading and which is more likely on subsequent readings, keeping in mind that there will of course be overlap.

Qoheleth begins in verse 1 by issuing a challenge: who is like the wise? Within the literary context, who is like the wise courtier with the ability to "interpret" (pēšer) a difficult "word" (dābār; 1b). On first reading, it would most likely refer to interpreting Qoheleth's following advice; on subsequent readings interpreting difficult matters or situations becomes more prominent.

---

[4] In relation to biblical hermeneutics, see especially Osborne 1991.
[5] These passages are 3:16–17; 4:1–3, 13–16; 5:8–9; 8:1–9; 9:13–18; 10:4–7, 16–20. For a discussion of these passages, see Garrett 1987, 159–77.
[6] These are listed by Krüger (2004, 151, fn. 2): mî (vv. 1a, 4b, 7b); ḥākām (1a, 5b); yāda' (1a, 5a, 5b, 7a); dābār (1a, 3a, 4a, 5a); 'ādām (1b, 6b, 8a, 9b).
[7] For instance, Murphy 1992, 82 sees a "dialectic pattern," with vv. 2–4 modifying v. 1, vv. 6–12a modifying v. 5 and vv. 14–15 in opposition to vv. 12b–13.

First, the courtier will have the correct outward appearance (8:1c). His face is to "shine," which has the idea of being gracious or to be pleasant.[8] The wise courtier is to change the "hardness of his face," that is, to remove a scowling face, which betrays his impudence (cf. Deut 28:50). Thus, as Michael Fox (1999, 276) comments, a wise official affects "a cheerful demeanor so as to ingratiate himself with whoever is in power and disarm his suspicions."

Second, the wise official will keep the command of the king "in the manner of [ʿal dibrat] an oath to God" (8:2b).[9] Since the king is God's vice-regent on earth, the wise courtier should remain loyal to the king.

What keeping the king's command might involve is outlined in 8:3. Due to semantic ambiguity, Qoheleth's first piece of advice has at least two possible meanings. On the one hand, a person might respond with "terror" (bāhal) to the power of the king, but Qoheleth advises discretion (NRSV: "Do not be terrified; go from his presence").[10] A restrained response would allow a person to leave the king's presence immediately if need be; for instance, to follow the king's command (8:2). On the other hand, taking bāhal as "hurry," Qoheleth advises a courtier to remain in the king's presence (ESV: "Be not hasty to go from his presence").[11] Perhaps continued access to the king will afford a courtier the best position to interpret a situation. This second option is more likely on subsequent reading, especially if read again after reading Eccl 10:4, "If the anger of the ruler rises against you, do not leave your place, for calmness will lay great offences to rest."

Qoheleth's second piece of advice about keeping the king's command is to "not persist in dābār rā ʿ" (8:3b). In 8:5 it probably refers to harm or punishment from the king. Thus, in 8:3 it could refer to at least two things that could bring harm to a courtier. On first reading it would most likely refer to any verbal challenge to the king's authority. Tremper Longman (1998, 322) suggests that dābār rāʿ is a "bad idea," any idea that the king dislikes. On subsequent reading, the interpretation of dābār rāʿ as seditious activity or rebellious talk against authorities gains more prominence in light of Eccl 10:20, "Even in your thought do not curse a king ... for a bird of the air will carry your voice, or some winged creature tell the matter."

---

[8] This is especially in reference to God's gracious response to humans (Num 6:25; Pss 31:18; 67:2; 80:4, 8, 20; 119:135; Dan 9:17); cf. Seow 1997, 277. One can also identify a fool by his appearance and behavior (Eccl 10:3).
[9] There is debate about whether šəbûʿat ʾĕlōhîm refers to God's oath to the king or a person's oath to the king made before God. For discussions, see Bartholomew 2009, 278; Fredericks and Estes 2010, 189; Seow 1997, 278.
[10] The meaning "stupefied" or "terrified" translates tibbāhēl (niphal), as pointed in the MT.
[11] This meaning would require repointing to the piel form. For further discussion of the two interpretations of bāhal see Schoors (2013, 600–1), who prefers the latter.

Reading 8:3 as a whole, it is possible to interpret 8:3a in opposition to 8:3b. Stay in the king's presence, followed by do not stay. James Crenshaw (1988, 150–51) suggests a harmonization: a courtier can stay long enough to assess a situation then leave when it is determined that "the matter will lead to royal recrimination." This interpretation is possible; nonetheless, the inherent semantic ambiguity allows for two opposite words of advice. Since ambiguity is found elsewhere in Ecclesiastes and wisdom literature in general, it is possible that it is deliberate here also, as well as the rest of this passage.[12] An advantage of the openness of the command allows it to be applied in a variety of situations. In a sense, the need to interpret the two situations in 8:3 are concrete applications of the principle in 8:1, namely, that it takes wisdom to interpret a *dābār* (8:1a). The need for wisdom to interpret each particular situation is thus reinforced by the wordplays in 8:3.

The common factor in Qoheleth's advice in 8:3 is the need for a measured response. At times, a wise courtier needs to hide their true feelings in a monarch's presence because his word is authoritative and no one can question him (3b–4). Yet the question challenging the king in 8:4 raises the possibility that a wise person might disagree with a king.

This becomes clearer in 8:5. For 8:5a, there are again two main interpretive options. On first reading, understood within the immediate context, *miṣwâ* refers to the king's "command" (cf. *pî-melek* [2]; *dəbar melek* [4]).[13] That is, this verse reinforces Qoheleth's advice to obey the king (8:1–4). On subsequent reading in light of 8:5b–9, along with the lack of a pronominal suffix on *miṣwâ*, it is possible that *miṣwâ* also alludes to God's "commandment." Drawing on Prov 24:21–22, Craig G. Bartholomew (2009, 282) suggests that the lack of a pronominal suffix is deliberate, as Qoheleth advises obedience to God and king only when they are in harmony. That is, Qoheleth advocates discerning obedience to a king, obedience when it does not contravene God's commandments.

Verse 8:5b affirms that the wise courtier will "know the proper time and *mišpāṭ*." On first reading, *mišpāṭ* is best understood as God's judgement, especially if we read within the literary context up to 8:5a, where in 3:17–18 *mišpāṭ* refers to God's judicial judgements (Seow 1997, 281). Verses 8:5b–7 would then reinforce the motif in Ecclesiastes of humankind's lack of control of the future, yet within God's timing there will be a judgement for all. On subsequent reading, however, 8:9 casts an interpretive shadow on the meaning of *mišpāṭ*. If 8:9 is a summary of the preceding instruction,[14] then it is a veiled "critique of

---

[12] In Ecclesiastes, see, e.g., Wilson 1998, 357–65. Cf. Prov 26:4–5, where two opposite responses are given to a similar situation; see the recent discussion in Schwáb 2016, 31–50.

[13] For royal command, see, e.g. 1 Kgs 2:43; 2 Kgs 18:36; 2 Chr 8:15; Esth 3:3; Neh 11:23.

[14] "All this" (*kol zeh*) refers to what precedes; so, e.g., Longman 1998, 215; Whybray 1989, 134. Others view this verse as an introduction to 8:9–15, esp. 8:9b, e.g., Fredericks and

contemporary government" (Krüger 2004, 157). With this understanding, *mišpāṭ* is taken as humanity making judgements; that is, because of the specter of abuse of power by the king, a wise courtier needs to have the discernment to know the proper time and procedure in specific circumstances.[15] This is consistent with the idea of the appropriate time for all human actions in 3:1–8, including when to speak and when to keep silent (Eccl 3:7).[16] Understood within the context of 8:1–5a, Daniel C. Fredericks and Daniel J. Estes (2010, 193) comment that there will be an opportune time and way to "challenge discreetly the king's command; but if the time is not right, the wise will know."

Nonetheless, a courtier must discern the wise course of action within constraints. Qoheleth observes that all humanity has a lack of control over the present and the future (8:6b–8). The rhetorical question in 8:7 highlights that fact: the wise person makes decisions based on finite knowledge (cf. 6:12; 8:17). Only God views the whole sweep of time, including the future (3:11, 14). God alone controls a person's days of life and day of death (8:8, 15). This reminds the reader that although the king might seem sovereign (8:4), the reality is that his power is limited. This restricted power of a king would be more prominent on subsequent readings. Strictly speaking, *hā'ādām* (8:9) could refer to anyone who is in authority.[17] But if it is read within the context of the previous verses, it would be natural to consider the referent to be the king. Thus, on subsequent reading, if a monarch is given to wickedness, they will find that they will be enslaved to it (8:8b). He may have power to perpetrate evil against others, but in the end the king will hurt others, and on subsequent reading it becomes clear that he will also end up hurting himself (8:9; cf. 8:8b).[18]

A summary of a first reading and subsequent readings are tabulated below:

---

Estes 2010, 194. Still others view 8:9 as a transition, e.g., Eaton 1983, 120–21; Seow 1997, 293.

[15] In this sense, *mišpāṭ* parallels *pēšer* (v. 1); cf. Ogden 2007, 141–42.

[16] Provan (2001, 165) suggests that a "wise heart" knows the appropriate action at the right time (8:5b) *and so* avoids any "harmful thing" (8:5a).

[17] *Hā'ādām* can be translated with a particularizing sense (e.g., NIV/NASB, "a man"; NRSV, "one person") or collective sense (e.g., ESV, "man"; JPS, "men"; NLT "people").

[18] Seow (1997, 284), notes that the ambiguity may be intentional: "oppression is harmful to humanity, oppressor and oppressed alike." In 8:5b–8, neither courtier nor king knows when trouble will come, and a courtier does not know when a king might make a poor decision. Thus, as Fredericks and Estes (2010, 194) comments, a wise person will "rely on the imperfect but structurally more secure government institutions rather than going it alone." This is more consistent with a first reading, in which loyalty to a king is especially enjoined. But on subsequent readings, a critical stance is more prominent.

| Verse | First reading | Subsequent reading(s) |
|---|---|---|
| 1a | Who is like the wise? And who knows the interpretation (*pēšer*) of a *word* (*dābār*)? | Who is like the wise? And who knows the interpretation of a *matter/thing (situation)*? |
| 1b | A person's wisdom enlightens his countenance, and his harsh face is changed. | Cf. 10:3, "Even when the fool walks on the road, he lacks sense, and he shows everyone he is a fool." |
| 2 | I (say,) "Keep the command of a king (*pî-melek*), yes in the manner of an oath to God. | |
| 3a | Do not be terrified (*tibbāhēl*) by his presence. *Leave!* | *Be not hasty to go* from his presence (cf. 10:4). |
| 3b | Do not take your stand in *a bad idea* (*dābār rā'*), for he does everything he wishes. | Do not take your stand in *seditious activity* (cf. 10:20), for he does everything he wishes. |
| 4a | Inasmuch as the word of a king (*dəbar melek*) is power, | |
| 4b | so who can say to him, 'What are you doing?' | |
| 5a | The one who keeps *a command* (*miṣwâ*; a king's) will not experience a bad thing (*dābār rā'*). | The one who keeps *God's commandment* will not experience a bad thing. |
| 5b | As for a time and (God's) *judgement* (*mišpāṭ*), a wise heart knows: | As for the proper time and *procedure*, a wise heart knows: |
| 6a | that for every matter there is a time and *judgement* | that for every matter there is a proper time and *procedure* |
| 6b | that the trouble of *a person* (*hā'ādām*) is heavy upon *him* | that the trouble of *a king* is heavy upon *him* [*the victim*] |
| 7a | that there is *no one* who knows what will happen | that there is *no one* [*neither courtier nor king*] who knows what will happen |
| 7b | that when it will happen, who can tell? | [*neither courtier nor king*] |
| 8a | There is no human who has authority over the life-breath (*rûaḥ*) to restrain the life-breath | [including the king] |
| 8b | and there is no authority over the day of death. | [including the king] |
| 8c | There is no discharge during a war, | [even for a king] |
| 8d | and wickedness will not save its master." | [including the king] |
| 9a | All this I saw when I set my heart to every deed that has been done under the sun | |

| 9b | in a time when *man* (*hā'ādām*) exercises authority (*šālat*) over another *to his hurt*. | in a time when *the king* exercises authority over another *to the hurt of his victim and himself*. |

Thus, this passage functions on two levels: (1) on the surface, as official advice to remain loyal to the king and (2) on a deeper level, as a subtle critique calling for discerning obedience.[19] Most Christian readers in Malaysia are particularly sensitized to the second level of reading.

To summarize the overall advice of Qoheleth in this passage: a wise courtier will be gracious in appearance and discerning in obedience, while keeping in mind the reality of the twin constraints of their lack of control of the future and of unjust government.

## Dealing with Authorities Wisely in the Malaysian Context

We will now consider how the principles from Eccl 8:1–9 could be applied in Malaysia. First, we will consider the provenance of Ecclesiastes so that we can identify areas of similarity and difference between the original context(s) and our contemporary context. Then, since the application of the passage is directed at Christians, we will briefly consider if Jesus and the New Testament modify the principles found in Ecclesiastes. Finally, we will make some specific applications of the modified principles to Christians in Malaysia.

The two main proposals for the provenance of Ecclesiastes dovetail nicely with the socioreligious background of Malaysia. Traditionally, Solomon was viewed as the author of Ecclesiastes, hence a date was set for it during the Israelite monarchy (late tenth century BCE). The recent consensus, however, is that the author of Ecclesiastes used a Solomon persona.[20] Due to the perceived Persian and Greek influences on the language and worldview respectively, the date of the book has been pushed to the post-exilic period.[21] In the traditional view, we read Eccl 8:1–9 as applying to an Israelite king. In the recent view, we read Eccl 8:1–9 as applying to a foreign king who ruled over God's people.

Unlike other Asian countries that abolished monarchy after becoming a republic, such as India and Indonesia, a monarchy was constitutionalized in

---

[19] Cf. Jones (2006, 228), who also suggests that Qoheleth speaks "indirectly through word-plays, and his subtle critique is veiled in ambiguity."
[20] E.g., Fox 2004, x. A few commentators still hold to Solomonic authorship, e.g., Fredericks and Estes 2010, 31; Garrett 1993.
[21] For an argument for a Persian provenance, see Seow 1996, 643–66. For an argument for the Greek influence, see Bartholomew 2009, 58–59. The latest possible dating of the book is about 180 BCE, as Ben Sira quoted and rephrased Ecclesiastes around this date.

Malaysia after gaining independence from the British Empire in 1957.[22] Malaysia was formed as a federal constitutional monarchy, with the head of state the Yang di-Pertuan Agong, a monarch elected by the nine hereditary Malay Rulers.[23] Malaysia also practices parliamentary democracy, with the prime minister as the head of government. Within this system, the king is accorded ultimate ceremonial authority but in practice yields little executive power.[24] In actuality, the executive authority lies with the prime minister and his cabinet.[25] Although it is conceivable for Christians to approach the king, on a day-to-day basis, they interact with government authorities, not royalty. Hence, the following discussion will focus on government authorities. Nonetheless, not only do the principles from Eccl 8:1–9 apply to those attending a royal court; they also apply to everyone living under a government. Thus, the Malaysian situation can be broadly understood to be similar to the traditional provenance of Ecclesiastes. However, the major difference is the system of parliamentary democracy along with the monarchy.

There are also similarities between the later provenance of Ecclesiastes and the Malaysian situation. Although Malaysia is not under the power of a foreign empire, Malaysian Christians live under the specter of an Islamic government. Christians are a minority group in Malaysia, comprising only 9.2 percent of the population, with Islam the majority at 61.3 percent.[26] Under the Federal

---

[22] In Southeast Asia the other two countries with monarchies are Cambodia and Thailand. Like Malaysia, Cambodia's monarchs are elected from royal families, while Thailand has a single hereditary ruling family.

[23] The Federal Constitution stipulates that the king rules for five years, then he vacates the throne. He is replaced by another ruler in a rotation system. The rulers eligible to be elected include the Yang Dipertuan Besar of Negeri Sembilan, the Sultan of Selangor, the Raja of Perlis, the Sultan of Terengganu, the Sultan of Kedah, the Sultan of Kelantan, the Sultan of Pahang, the Sultan of Johor, and the Sultan of Perak. At the state level, the head of state is either the Sultan, Raja, Yang di-Pertuan Besar, or the Yang di-Pertua Negeri. The chief ministers (Menteri Besar/Ketua Menteri) are the heads of state government.

[24] Cf. Article 40(1) of the Federal Constitution: "the executive authority of the Federation shall be vested in the Yang di-Pertuan Agong and exercisable, subject to the provisions of any federal law and of the Second Schedule by him or by the Cabinet or any Minister authorized by the Cabinet, *but Parliament may by law confer executive function on other persons*" (emphasis added). Recently, the members of royal families have been involved in politics; see Hamid and Ismail 2013.

[25] Nonetheless, the king is also given discretionary power, including the appointment of a prime minister and the withholding of consent to a request for the dissolution of Parliament; see Article 40(2) of the Federal Constitution. The king is also given "Special Emergency Powers," including the power to act as a legislature in place of Parliament; see Articles 149–151.

[26] According to the 2010 Population and Housing Census, 61.3 percent practices Islam, 19.8 percent Buddhism, 9.2 percent Christianity, 6.3 percent Hinduism, and 1.3 percent

Constitution, Malaysia was founded as a secular state, with Islam as the official religion. Since independence, the ruling political party has been Malay, which by default means that it is Islamic.[27] An Islamic resurgence in the 1980s culminated in the former prime minister, Dr. Mahathir Mohammad, declaring Malaysia an Islamic state in September 2001. Islamic influence is not only found in the government; it is also prevalent in many areas of society, including law, education, finance, and healthcare. Christians in Malaysia face political and religious oppression by government authorities, who primarily derive from the majority religion. Those who convert to Christianity from Islam face the most intense persecution, but the Christian church in Malaysia also faces restrictions in its religious practices.

Reading the Christian scripture pan-canonically, we find that the principles for dealing with authorities in Eccl 8:1–9 are reinforced and generalized in the New Testament. Submission to the state is also encouraged, since human authority is derived from God's authority (esp. Rom 13:1–7; Tit 3:1; 1 Pet 2:13–17).[28] Nonetheless, discerning obedience to the state is required (e.g., Matt 10:16; 22:2), since governing authorities are prone to abusing their power (e.g., Matt 10:16–24). When the demands of the state clash with the demands of God, Christians should obey God (e.g., Acts 5:27–29).[29]

With the Malaysian socioreligious background and New Testament modifications in mind, we will now apply Eccl 8:1–9 to the local context. Following the two levels of reading in the passage, there are two main ways for Malaysian Christians to apply it.

First, obey the government when their law does not contradict the law of God. It is possible to be a member of a minority group and still work within the sociopolitical structure of the time. Indeed, it is possible to remain loyal to a government and promote its interests; for instance, in the Old Testament some examples include Joseph (Gen 37–50), Daniel and his friends, and Esther. Hence, Malaysians can work with the democratic political system.[30] They might consider

---

traditional Chinese religions. See https://www.statistics.gov.my. Islam in Malaysia has changed over the decades; see Ng 2008, 3–4.

[27] Article 160 of the Constitution of Malaysia defines Malay as person "who professes the religion of Islam, habitually speaks the Malay language, conforms to Malay custom and (a) was before Merdeka Day born in the Federation or in Singapore or born of parents one of whom was born in the Federation or in Singapore, or is on that day domiciled in the Federation or in Singapore; or (b) is the issue of such a person." Thus, Malays who convert out of Islam are no longer considered Malay under the law.

[28] For a reading of Rom 13:1–7 within the Malaysian context, see Lim 2014, 37–47.

[29] Cf. the response of Daniel and his friends to the king's edict to worship a golden image (Dan 3).

[30] For an analysis of constitutional problems through the lens of pluralism in Malaysia, see Harding 2012.

entering politics to work for justice. They could follow the lead of Esther, who was able to change a decision of the king by working within the Persian legal framework; she did not seek to incite her people to rebel against the state.[31] Christians who are in government (either as government servants or in a position of power) should work wisely to bring about change for the common good. Despite often facing a lack of career advancement in Malaysia, Christians might choose to work in government as their area of ministry. Other Christians not working in government are enjoined to pray for kings and all who are in authority (1 Tim 2:1–2), including Christians in government.[32]

Moreover, in a gracious manner, much can be done to strengthen the Malaysian democratic political system. Some vital actions that Christians can be involved in include:

- Promoting freedom of the press, which makes possible the exposure of corruption, malpractice, and incompetence;
- Agitating for good governance and robust checks and balances in the political system;
- Pushing for electoral reform. In Malaysia, the Coalition for Clean and Fair Elections (better known as Bersih, meaning "clean" in Bahasa Malaysia) has been pushing for a reform of the electoral process since 2005. Relating to electoral reform, Bersih calls for five items: (1) Revise and update the electoral roll, removing deceased persons and multiple persons registered under a single address, so-called phantom voters; (2) Reform the postal ballot system to allow all citizens to vote; (3) The use of indelible ink for all elections in order to reduce voter fraud; (4) A campaigning of no less than twenty-one days for national elections; (5) Free and fair access to media coverage for all political parties, especially at state-funded media agencies;[33]
- Encouraging a strong opposition and an independent judiciary. Monarchs in Malaysia previously were literally able to live without anyone questioning what they did. But an amendment to the Constitution of Malaysia in 1993 removed legal immunity for royalty. In light of the reality of unjust government (see esp. Eccl 8:8b–9), a strong opposition is required to question the government, to pose the question: "What are you doing?" (Eccl 8:4). Although the prime minister (and to a lesser extent the king) of

---

[31] Similarly, Daniel served in the king's court under four kings from two different empires for sixty years (Dan 1:18–21).
[32] Some of these include Ong Kian Ming, Steven Sim, Datuk Paul Low, and Hannah Yeoh; for the story of the latter, see Yeoh 2014. For the story of a Christian East Malaysian State politician, see Bian 2014.
[33] Bersih also calls for three other items are not directly related to electoral reform. See http://www.bersih.org/about/8demands/.

Malaysia has been entrusted by God with much power, he cannot do whatever he pleases (8:3); he needs to be answerable to someone.

Second, in the face of injustice and abuse of power and oppression, discerning obedience is required. Qoheleth observes that these are part of life in this world (esp. 3:16–17; 4:1–3; 5:8–9; 8:8–9; see Meek 2013, 69–72). Although Islam is the official religion, freedom of religion is enshrined in the Federal Constitution of Malaysia (Articles 3 and 11). This has caused much contention among religious groups. Some issues against which Malaysian Christians might voice their dissatisfaction include:

- The difficulties faced by Muslims who convert to Christianity. The high-profile case of Lina Joy, who in 2007 was not allowed to remove the designation "Muslim" from her national identity card, highlights the restriction of freedom of religion and the obstacles faced by converts in Malaysia. Hilmy Noor (1999) too faced persecution when he converted from Islam to Christianity, including his detention under the Internal Security Act of Malaysia.
- Restriction of religious practices. For instance, it is very difficult to gain building licenses for Christian places of worship. There was also tension when the government banned the use of "Allah" by Christians. In relation to this issue, Islamic authorities seized Bibles in the Malay language (Alkitab). The Christian minority must remain vigilant, and critically resistant against such injustices.
- The growing influence of Islamic law. Many political observers view the Hudud Bill, read in Malaysian Parliament on 24 November 2016, as a further sign of the growing influence of Islam in Malaysia. The bill aims at expanding the powers of the Syariah court. Although the bill specifies that the increased penalties only apply to Muslims, critics of the bill are concerned about the effects of the bill for the whole of Malaysian society, especially non-Muslims.

In these situations, defying or even breaking the law of the land may be necessary. Malaysian Christians can follow the advice of Eccl 8:1–6a and, with a deferential tone and nonconfrontational rhetoric, petition the government through channels such as: writing letters to the local parliamentary member, signing petitions, and protesting at public rallies. One example of the last channel is the Bersih rallies, calling for clean and fair elections in Malaysia. The rallies began in Kuala Lumpur then spread to other cities around the world.[34]

---

[34] The fifth and latest rally was on 19 November, 2016, calling for: (1) clean elections; (2) a clean government; (3) strengthening of parliamentary democracy; (4) the right to dissent; and (5) empowering of the East Malaysian states, Sabah and Sarawak. See http://www.bersih.org/press-statement-17-november-2016-bersih-2-0-calls-on-malaysians-to-come-

## Conclusion

In this chapter I have shown that there is much wisdom to be gained from a close reading of Eccl 8:1–9 sensitive to the local context of Malaysia. For the Christian minority (and, to an extent, other religious minorities), both obedience and critical resistance will be required at different times, depending on the situation. A challenge is to provide constructive criticism: not only to criticize the government but also to offer possible solutions.[35] For we, as citizens, are to work for the peace and prosperity whichever nation we live in (cf. Jer 29:7). Despite our best efforts, however, we will find that injustice and oppression will always be found in any society because of the pervasive influence of sin (e.g., Eccl 7:20, 29). Yet we live in hope of another reality: God will bring justice for the oppressed—if not in this world, then in the next (Eccl 3:17; 11:9; 12:14).

## Works Cited

Bartholomew, Craig G. 2009. *Ecclesiastes*. Baker Commentary on the Old Testament Wisdom and Psalms. Grand Rapids: Baker Academic.

Bian, Baru. 2014. *The Long Awakening*. Kuching: Baru Bian.

Crenshaw, James L. 1988. *Ecclesiastes*. OTL. London: SCM.

Duvall, J. Scott, and J. Daniel Hays. 2012. *Grasping God's Word: A Hands-On Approach to Reading, Interpreting, and Applying the Bible*. 3rd ed. Grand Rapids: Zondervan.

Eaton, Michael A. 1983. *Ecclesiastes: An Introduction and Commentary*. TOTC. Leicester: InterVarsity Press.

Fox, Michael V. 1999. *A Time to Tear Down and a Time to Build Up: A Rereading of Ecclesiastes*. Grand Rapids: Eerdmans.

———. 2004. *Ecclesiastes*. The JPS Bible Commentary. Philadelphia: Jewish Publication Society.

Fredericks, Daniel C., and Daniel J. Estes. 2010. *Ecclesiastes and the Song of Songs*. Nottingham: Inter-Varsity Press.

Fuhr, Richard A., and Andreas J. Köstenberger. 2016. *Inductive Bible Study: Observation, Interpretation, and Application through the Lenses of History, Literature, and Theology*. Nashville: B&H Academic.

Garrett, Duane A. 1987. "Qoheleth on the Use and Abuse of Political Power." *TrinJ* n.s. 8:159–77.

---

down-to-the-streets-for-bersih-5-and-stand-united-for-a-new-malaysia/. The international *Bersih* site can be accessed here: https://www.globalbersih.org.

[35] Cf. Datuk Paul Low, Christian and member of the Malaysian Cabinet as the Lead Minister for Governance and Integrity, as quoted in Lum (15 September 2013), http://christianitymalaysia.com/wp/ways-higher-ways-yb-senator-datuk-paul/.

Garrett, Duane A. 1993. *Proverbs; Ecclesiastes; Song of Songs*. NAC. Nashville: Broadman Press.
Hamid, Ahmad Fauzi Abdul, and Muhamad Takiyuddin Ismail. 2013. "The Monarchy in Malaysia: Struggling for Legitimacy." *Kyoto Review of Southeast Asia: Monarchies in Southeast Asia* 13.
Harding, Andrew. 2012. *The Constitution of Malaysia: A Contextual Analysis*. Constitutional Systems of the World. Oxford: Hart Publishing.
Jones, Scott C. 2006. "Qohelet's Courtly Wisdom: Ecclesiastes 8:1–9." *CBQ* 68:211–28.
Krüger, Thomas. 2004. *Qoheleth: A Commentary*. Hermeneia. Minneapolis: Augsburg Fortress.
Lim, Kar Yong. 2014. "Reading Romans 13:1–7 in a Multi-Faith Context: Some Reflections from Malaysia." Pages 37–47 in *What Young Asian Theologians Are Thinking*. Edited by T. H. Leow. Singapore: Trinity Theological College.
Longman, Tremper. 1998. *The Book of Ecclesiastes*. NICOT. Grand Rapids: Eerdmans.
Lum, Adeline. 2013. "His Ways Are Higher Than Our Ways—Datuk Paul Low." *Christianity Malaysia* (15 September): http://christianitymalaysia.com/wp/ways-higher-ways-yb-senator-datuk-paul/.
Meek, Russell L. 2013. "Amos and Ecclesiastes: Toward Developing a Theological Response to Oppression." *SBET* 31:61–74.
Murphy, Roland E. 1992. *Ecclesiastes*. WBC 23A. Dallas: Word.
Ng, Kam Weng. 2008. "Pluralist Democracy and Spheres of Justice: The Quest for 'Complex Equality' in an Islamist Context." Pages 1–40 in *The Quest for Covenant Community and Pluralist Democracy in an Islamic Context*. Edited by M. L. Y. Chan. Singapore: Trinity Theological College.
Nor, Hilmy. 1999. *Circumcised Heart*. Petaling Jaya: Kairos Research Centre.
Ogden, Graham S. 2007. *Qoheleth*. 2nd ed. Sheffield: Sheffield Phoenix.
Osborne, Grant R. 1991. *The Hermeneutical Spiral: A Comprehensive Introduction to Biblical Interpretation*. Downers Grove: InterVarsity Press.
Provan, Iain W. 2001. *Ecclesiastes; Song of Songs*. NIVAC. Grand Rapids: Zondervan.
Schoors, Antoon. 2013. *Ecclesiastes*. Leuven: Peeters.
Schwáb, Zoltán S. 2016. "I, the Fool: A 'Canonical' Reading of Proverbs 26:4–5." *JTI* 10:31–50.
Seow, C. L. 1996. "Linguistic Evidence and the Dating of Qohelet." *JBL* 115:643–66.
Seow, C. L. 1997. *Ecclesiastes*. AB 18C. New York: Doubleday.
Whybray, R. Norman. 1989. *Ecclesiastes*. NCBC. Grand Rapids: Eerdmans.
Wilson, Lindsay. 1998. "Artful Ambiguity in Ecclesiastes 1, 1–11: A Wisdom Technique?" Pages 357–65 in *Qohelet in the Context of Wisdom*. Edited by A. Schoors. Leuven: Leuven University/Peeters.

Yeoh, Hannah T. S. 2014. *Becoming Hannah: A Personal Journey*. Petaling Jaya: SIRD Centre.

# FISHING / EXILE FOR MEANING: A *FAKAHĒ* READING OF ECCLESIASTES 8:1–17

Tauʻalofa Angaʻaelangi

This chapter offers a *fakahē* reading of Eccl 8:1–17, a text that several critics question whether it has relevance for modern times. I beg to differ, under the influence of David Penchansky (2012, 9), who argues that wisdom literature is "worthy of our attention because the questions that they ask are human questions, ones that emerge from the depths of people's experience. Many wonder at the meaning of existence, the possibility for happiness, the inevitability of death." In wisdom literature, contradiction is part of our journey.

> An important feature of wisdom material is that it can never summarize human experience within one brief statement. Wisdom sayings have to be general enough to make good sense, but they may not be true in every situation. Wisdom writings speak to a given context and without knowing the proper context we may easily misunderstand them. (Ogden and Zogbo 1997, 1)

Wisdom plays a significant role in all aspects of life and in cultures. As Graham Goldsworthy (2011, 42) puts it, "Every culture, ancient and modern, has developed its own wisdom, and recorded it in literature. Such wisdom can be based on human experience from which people learn what is in life and how to deal with it."

Like other biblical texts, wisdom texts are open for readers to weave their experiences and stories into them. The outcome is that readers come to own the wisdom/biblical texts, and the texts are changed in the process. To appropriate the words of the Samoan literary critic Albert Wendt, "novels are about other novels, stories are about other stories, poems are about other poems. The changes come about in how you tell them" (Ellis 1997, 88). The act of interpretation involves adding stories onto (and about other) stories, and in the process the stories change. All cultures record their own wisdom, and a lot depends on the tellers and writers of those records. In this regard, the tellers and writers, as well as the hearers and readers, are capable of taking the texts and their meanings into exile (*fakahē*).

## *Fakahē*

The Tongan word *fakahē* refers to two activities: a type of fishing and the taking of people into exile. The term gained currency when men and women of the Wesleyan Church were forced to move first to smaller islands in the Tonga group and then to an island in Fiji because they did not accept the Church of Tonga, which was established by the native king, Tupou I.

### *Fakahē* as Fishing

The *fakahē* of *te'epupulu* and *lomu* (two types of sea cucumber) takes place during low tide. People go out to the reef looking for sea cucumbers, which they slit open at the belly with a sharp instrument in order to squeeze out the roe, a Pasifika island delicacy. The harvested sea cucumbers are put back so that their wounds close and heal, until the next person comes along to *fakahē* it. *Fakahē* as a type of fishing is life-giving for villagers in Tonga and the neighboring islands, especially the poorer families who cannot afford expensive fishing gear or a vessel so that they could venture beyond the reef.

Two concepts could be drawn from the process of *fakahē*. First, a sacrifice is involved in order to find food. In this case, the sea cucumber is sacrificed. Second, from the shore, it may appear that the fishers are lost or wandering aimlessly. But the fishers have a purpose, to feed their families. What they bring home, they also share with their neighbors. This happens at another level for the islanders who have migrated overseas. We *fakahē* (in other words, we work for wages) in order to participate and contribute to our communities in our host countries, as well as to remit assistance to our families at the home islands. We do not *fakahē* just for ourselves, but for our people in diaspora and at home. 'Epeli Hau'ofa (1994, 156) highlighted the capacity of Oceanic migrants to contribute to the local and global economies of their host countries:

> Everywhere they go, to Australia, New Zealand, Hawai'i, the mainland United States, Canada, Europe, and elsewhere, they strike roots in new resource areas, securing employment and overseas family property, expanding kinship networks through which they circulate themselves, their relatives, their material goods, and their stories all across their ocean, and the ocean is theirs because it has always been their home.... [The] resources of [Oceania] are no longer confined to their national boundaries. They are located wherever these people are living.... One can see this any day at seaports and airports throughout the central Pacific, where consignment of goods from homes abroad are unloaded as those of the homelands are loaded.

Drawing from the fishing ground, one could say that islanders in diaspora commit to *fakahē* (in both senses of the term) in order to feed their new communities, as well as those at home.

## *Fakahē* as Exile

The period 1870–1890 was significant in the life of the Methodist Church in Tonga. Major changes took place in the relationship of the church and the state. Some of the Methodist missionaries were advisors to King Tupou I, including Rev. Shirley Baker who was also the chairman of the district. Baker's affiliation with politics and trades landed him in disputes with his minister colleagues, leading to complaints and charges against him. He supported the king and joined forces with other members of the Methodist church who desired a self-governing church independent of the Methodist Conference in Australia. Alfred Harold Wood (1975, 136) noted that,

> The king and people of Tonga, with their national pride, had reached the point of desiring a self-governing Church and were anxious to achieve this before Fiji or any other islands. Their country was independent; why should not their Church have more responsibility they might well ask. They deserved to have these privileges, if only because Tonga was the first Wesleyan Mission in the South Pacific and the whole group had been evangelized years before this movement for self-government began.

In 1873, Baker attended the Methodist conference in New South Wales and submitted a request that the church in Tonga becomes independent from New South Wales and Queensland. Baker's proposal was rejected by the conference. His colleagues in Tonga were distressed by his actions. His rivalries with the conference in Australia and other ministers in the Methodist church back in Tonga continued on his return. He established the Free Church of Tonga on Sunday 4 January 1885 in Lifuka, Ha'apai. When he alerted King Tupou of the newly established church, Tupou

> was displeased with Baker taking the matter into his own hands ... after he had mollified Tupou it was publicly proclaimed that all Wesleyans were expected to join the new Church. Everyone in Vava'u expressed compliance, and almost the same unanimity appeared in Ha'apai.... No one gave heed to the guarantee of freedom of worship in the 1875 constitution. (Wood 1975, 179)

Baker viewed his establishment of the Free Church of Tong as a success, but this split the Wesleyan Church of Tonga, and it led to the persecution of those who chose to stay with the Wesleyan Church.

> All public servants and all village mayors were required to join or forfeit their positions.... For more than two years after the formation of the Free Church and with only a few intermissions, many Wesleyans suffered floggings, deprivation of office, damage to property, heavy fines, long terms of imprisonment, and banishment. It was incredible that such widespread and harsh persecution occurred within what was really the same religious denomination. (Wood 1975, 184)

Some of the people who remained in the Wesleyan church were taken into exile, the Tongan name for which is *fakahē*. In the Ha'apai group, Wesleyans from Ha'ano, Lofanga, Nomuka, and Felemea were taken to the house of their minister where they were under house arrest for three months. In this group were two ministers and Salote Mafile'o Pilolevu, the very daughter King Tupou I. They were beaten every day, pressuring them to change their membership to the new church.

Wesleyans from Lofanga and nearby islands in the Ha'apai group were taken to the uninhabited volcanic islands of Kao, Tofua, Tonumea, and 'Ata. There were limited resources in these islands, and the exiled people fed on coconuts, roots, birds, and shellfish.

The superintend of the northernmost island of Niua was taken with forty of his members to Tongatapu, and they were persecuted for not joining the new church. Baker's main opponent was Rev. James Egan Moulton who founded the Methodist boy's college and named it after the king—Tupou College. Moulton translated some of the letters for a small group of people (about ninety of them) who remained in the Wesleyan Church, asking that they be taken to another island where they would continue their worship. King Tupou accepted Moulton's petition: "They sailed on the 14th February 1887, not knowing their destination ... after they left it was announced they were heading for Fiji. They were taken to the island of Koro where they remained until 1890" (Wood 1975, 189). This *fakahē* is told in stories and hymns of the Wesleyan church, and in the rivalry between Tupou College (in which Moulton was principal) and Tonga College (which was established by the Tongan government). Conflicts in the Tongan church and community today appear to be due to unaddressed issues from the *fakahē* time.

In the case of the Wesleyan Church of Tonga, *fakahē* was both internal within the group and into foreign waters. To be forced out of one's preferred home is *fakahē*. The Tonga Wesleyans taken in *fakahē* fit the profile of forced migrants: "those who have been driven from home by wars, persecutions, and natural calamities" (Cruz 2014, 2). The Wesleyans had no other choice but to leave for their safety. If they had remained in the kingdom, they would have been beaten or killed.

It is likely that many of those who joined the Free Church did so not because of theology or conviction but in obedience and loyalty to Tupou (Wood 1975, 185). The forced conversion of people played a key role in the disunity of the Church in Tonga.

## *Fakahē* Reading of Ecclesiastes 8

The key hermeneutical questions in Eccl 8:1—"Who is like the wise person? Who knows the interpretation of a thing?"—have captured the attention of many critics. I am drawn, on the other hand, to something that, some might say, is vain—*countenance*.

### Countenance (8:1)

According to Qoheleth, "a person's wisdom illumines his countenance (*mar'eh*) and changes the hardness of his face" (8:1). The verse associates as well as distinguishes "countenance" from "face." The Hebrew *mar'eh* is not limited to facial expressions but includes the figure and body of a person. In the *fakahē*, the body is what encounters space, such as one's home and new (diaspora) countries. The body is the teller of its own stories—of grief, longing, love, violence, and so forth. As Sef Carroll (2010, 80) points out, "The body embodies the memories and stories of the spaces it has inhabited. When the bodies of guest and host meet, it opens up the opportunity to explore the stories of violence and welcome they embody as well as the stories and histories of the space." The body tells its own stories, in relation to other bodies, in ways that the face cannot.

In Tonga, it is common for the body to be used as a metaphor to lament one's story and longing. The late Queen Salote composed a lament titled *'Oketi* (orchet) for her late husband: "*This body* has become a thing of no worth, overcome by all-conquering love, for your image made of *precious stories*, I shall string them for my garland.... Ah, that this body, sweetened with praises is but poison to your mission, yet, gladiolus, this love of mine will never end" (translated and cited in Taumoefolau and Ellem-Wood 2004, 176; my italics). One could hear and feel the grief of the late queen in the metaphors that reference the body as having worth (but is not lost, with the death of her beloved) and endowed with stories.

Our bodies tell our stories in different places. This could be problematic because the telling and the stories are not in our control. Our skin (color) sets limits and reveals that we are foreigners, even before the people around us hear our stories. Our skin also makes our longing for our place of birth too obvious. This longing is for the relationships with family and place. As Jione Havea (2015, 148) notes,

> It is possible in the island worldview to be distanced (in space) and at the same time be connected (in relations). In other words, islanders are relational people, and isolation has to do with relations rather than with distance. Relations are woven in the interaction between people, obliging one to another.... Islanders attach to island roots and island homes, because the islands "contain" our ancestors, heritages, and customs.

The relations of one's body are tied to place and land, ancestors, and customs. The body of one who migrates belongs to the place of birth and to the community. Therefore, the body tells the story of the individual and at the same time represents its place of origin and its people. In this connection, countenance/body is not vain.

## The Word of the King Is Powerful (Eccl 8:2–5)

What is vain, according to 8:2–4, is any resistance against the king: "Keep the king's command because of your sacred oath. Do not be terrified; go from his presence, do not delay when the matter is unpleasant, for he does whatever he pleases. For the word of the king is powerful, and who can say to him, 'What are you doing?'"

Returning to the 1880s in Tonga, Eccl 8:2–4 contain words that would have been heard at meetings (*fono*) called in order to convince the villagers to join the newly formed church. Tongan islanders were expected to obey, and they knew the consequences of not following the orders of their king. I make this connection because "obedience, in many cases was due to the chiefs' intimidation. It was indeed a new thing in Tonga for anyone to resist the expressed will of the king" (Wood 1975, 185).

There is a warning in Eccl 8:3—"Do not be terrified; go from his presence, do not delay when the matter is unpleasant, for he does whatever he pleases." In the old days in Tonga, complete obedience was the rule and people avoided causing trouble with the king.

Qoheleth is aware of the power in the king's commands, and he does not expect resistance against the king's orders. The king will do what he likes; his words are powerful. People who follow the king's commands will be rewarded (8:5), and this is what happened to those who joined the new Church of Tonga. They were rewarded. For Qoheleth, as it was for Baker and those on his side, "one of the major themes is authority or who controls what" (Ogden and Zogbo 1997, 276). They would have been surprised, and annoyed, when they ordered the *fakahē* of the resisters first within Tonga and to the island of Koro (Fiji). This *fakahē* reading is attentive to the expressions of authority and control in the text and calls attention to situations in which the presuppositions of the text (e.g., that the king's words are always observed) are undermined.

## Time (Eccl 8:5b–9)

Authority and time intersect in verses 5b–9. As in the previous section, "we see how Qoheleth uses various means to make the point that people are very limited in the amount of power they have" (Ogden and Zogbo 1977, 291). Qoheleth has seen life under the sun and uses two strong Hebrew verbs to emphasize his expression, "I observed [and] while applying my mind" (Ogden and Zogbo 1997, 292). "If one understands v.9b as the temporal accusative of v.9a, then the formulation here is a sharp critique of contemporary government: they turn out to the detriment of the dominated ones" (Krüger 2004, 156).

In the context of *fakahē*, time is lived. Taungāpeau (2010, 41) describes the Tongan notion of time in this way:

> *Taimi* [time] is a movement, and we participate in that movement since we all have a slice of it in different time framing and we all get to our destination when the frame is completed. The force that cause this movement is something beyond our control, but we react and obey that force by moving along with it.

This notion of time rearranges our place under the sun and points to the place of humanity in the order of creation. This makes sense to the one doing *fakahē* fishing, for she or he fishes when the tide is low (and this varies from day to day). She or he listens to the rhythm of nature, for the right moment to go out in order to do *fakahē*.

Wickedness and Evil (Eccl 8:10–14)

There is emphasis on wickedness and evil in this section. It is not clear what Qoheleth understands to be evil. He speaks of the existence of evil people, and the desire of the human hearts to do evil. In this connection, I wonder what migrant readers consider as evil in their current society. In the case of Pasifika islanders, there are two types of migrants—the legal migrants, who have come through the proper immigration processes, and the so-called undocumented migrants, referring to those who "jumped ship" and those who have overstayed their permits or visas.

The legal migrants have access to privileges and services in the host country, in comparison to the undocumented people who could be arrested and deported back to their home country. The undocumented ones are often "dobbed in" (reported) by people from the same islands and even by their own relatives. When this happens, there are two kinds of wicked people. On the one hand, the undocumented people are wicked because they have broken the law of the adopted land. On the other hand, those who dob in the illegal migrants are wicked because they have prevented those people from providing for their families at home. In both cases, there is injustice. And Qoheleth identifies those who do not serve justice with those who do not "fear the Lord" (v. 12).

For those who are legal, we may see the undocumented people as wicked because we think that since we entered the country in the right way we are therefore law abiding citizens. This raises the question of how migrants (some legal, some illegal) live as relational people in our new context. How do we continue as life-giving people to our communities? Verse 11 highlights that evil works are not brought to justice or quickly dealt with. The next verse recollects that there is injustice and that some of those who committed evil deeds have never been brought to justice. The wicked will be dealt with because they are the opposite of those who fear God. In the *fakahē*, the ones who fear God will keep their relations with others instead of using their legal status to elevate themselves in their relationship with the illegal others.

"Fear of the Lord" is usually translated into Tongan as *'apasia ki he 'Eiki*. Futa Helu explains *'apasia* in terms of the two words that have been joined: *'apa* and *sia*. *'Apa* comes from the word *'a'apa*, which means to reach out or up to something. This is also the root of the word *faka'apa'apa*, which means respect. *Sia* means different things depending on the context. For instance, in the word *moko-sia* it refers to a feeling of being cold. *Sia* also refers to a mount that has been raised (with rocks and soil), used for two primary purposes—for the residence of the king or chief and/or for the snaring of *lupe* (native pigeon) (Helu 2006, 29). When this second notion of *sia* is joined with *'apa*, the Tongan sense of *'apasia* (fear) is about reaching toward to serve (as in the case of the king) or reaching in order to catch (as in the case of the *lupe*) the Lord. A *fakahē* reading holds both meanings of *'apasia ki he 'Eiki* together.

*'Apasia ki he 'Eiki* assumes that one is in awe of the relationship with God, and within that overwhelming feeling she or he comes to respect God. So the one who is in *fakahē* will face injustices with reverence for, and expectations upon, her or his Lord/*'Eiki* (present at the *sia*). This is the expectation but not always the reality. The reality, according to Qoheleth, is very insulting: "there are righteous people who are treated according to the conduct of the wicked, and there are wicked people who are treated according to the conduct of the righteous" (8:14). The response to this kind of reality, in the *fakahē* setting, is *mapuhoi* (sigh).

*Mapuhoi* (*Hebel*; 8:10b, 8:14)

The Hebrew *hebel* is usually translated as "vanity" but also "frustration" (in NJPS). *Hebel* comes from "the sound a breath makes.... Then by extension, it means 'breath' or 'vapor', having the sense of something in substantial and occasionally something 'not real'" (Penchansky 2012, 51–52). The Tongan translation uses the word *muna*, meaning insignificant or irrelevant, as translation for *hebel*. Like vanity, *muna* has a negative connotation as if Qoheleth is only pessimistic. Penchansky writes: "Pessimistic Qoheleth uses *hebel* as his repeating chorus.... This repeated phrase functions as a motto or thesis statement to summarize how Pessimistic Qoheleth wants the book to be read" (51). Penchansky also observes that "in Ecclesiastes we cannot nail down a definitive meaning or translation for *hebel*.... It means different things in different places" (52).

In my *fakahē* reading, the Tongan word *mapuhoi* is a more appropriate choice for translating *hebel*. *Mapuhoi* refers to when someone takes a deep breath after hard work, just before resting she or he gives *mapuhoi* (exhales, with a sigh). It is about tiredness, and some frustration, but not resignation. For someone in *fakahē* (whether fishing or in exile), *mapuhoi* would be meaningful. She or he is tired from hard work, and from separation, and she or he exhales and sighs. *Mapuhoi* gives *hebel* a positive nuance as compared to *muna* and vanity. This word ties in well with the subject of the next section, labor.

Enjoyment (Eccl 8:15–17)

Qoheleth instructs people who work hard to enjoy themselves with what they have worked for because those are gifts from God. What they gain from their labor are the fruits of their fear of the Lord and of keeping their relations.

The *fakahē* reader may start by asking what is rewarding for the one who fishes and makes sacrifices? Qoheleth commands everyone to enjoy all that God has provided. The *fakahē* reader will associate enjoyment with the delight in catching or sacrificing something. Building personal wealth is not the aim of one in *fakahē*, but rather for the benefit of family and communities. This attitude is based on what Tongans call *fatongia*. The closest English translation for *fatongia* is duty or obligation, except that *fatongia* is more of a way of life. Kuli Fisi'iahi (2015, 1) explains that *fatongia* "carries the idea of the relationship by keeping the allocating task, duty or obligation which was specifically bestowed on a particular individual or group." Fisi'iahi adds, "Fatongia ... gives the kainga [people, relatives] some sort of selfworth.... They feel a fulfilment when they have done their fatongia. The fatongia then becomes the dynamic of ... relationships. Fatongia comes with great affections and it becomes a valuable asset to the Tongan culture" (1). In this regard, the fulfilling of *fatongia* or task (compared to the results of labor) is the enjoyment.

Enjoyment comes after *mapuhoi*. This delightful feeling is in exchange for wealth. The catch of the *fakahē* are to do with activities that sustains life for all. Graham Ogden and Lynell Zogbo (1997, 48) assert this to be divine bounty: "Eating and drinking are vital to the sustaining of life.... God provides us with what is basic to our survival.... Therefore to eat, drink and take pleasure in these activities, as well as in the rewards which are additionally part of the divine bounty." All of creation is God's gift, and humans are to enjoy the divine bounty.

Limits of *Fakahē* Reading

I propose *fakahē* reading as an option for Pasifika islanders at home as well as in the diaspora who daily face the challenges of, and struggles with, oppression and marginalization. This hermeneutical approach, of course, has limits. In the first instance, much depends on whether one (at home or in diaspora) finds appealing to cultural principles to be useful and advantageous or not. This concern is critical given that, in my case, "Tongan culture, like any other, is neither pure nor innocent" (Vaka'uta 2010, 152). If the reader is a *tu'a* (commoner) than the *fakahē* approach will put her/him in a critical position. Nāsili Vaka'uta (2010, 151–52) describes the status and role of the *tu'a* in the following terms:

> As a tu'a, I am viewed by my own as an outsider. I belong to the largest, group in the Tongan socio–religious hierarchy. My identity is fabricated in relation to my sacred other, the *'eiki* (insider/chief).... The *'eiki* occupies the top or the centre of society; I, the *tu'a*, am (dis)(mis)placed at the underside and the periphery. Culturally speaking, I do not belong in the society in which I was born and bred. I, the *tu'a*, am worthless (*kainanga–e–fonua*), ignorant (*me'avale*), and predestined to serve the *'eiki*.

The challenge for the *tu'a* reader, which includes the *fakahē* reader, is why should she or he maintain culture if the culture disadvantages her or him? It is critical that *fakahē* reading does not perpetuate dis/misplacement of the reader, especially the *tu'a*. In this regard, the *fakahē* reading invites the individual to look into the place of mis/displacement and engage in the struggle for life.

In Tonga's *fakahē* era, people were dropped off with limited resources. And they managed to find food and to survive. Somewhat related to this, *fakahē* fishing is not a way of work that will make someone wealthy. The catch is limited, and so are those who nowadays prefer that delicacy. It is nonetheless an island way of life, where the family benefits from the reaping and hard work of the *fakahē* mother and father. Despite the "demoralizing and humiliating [of the tu'a]" (Vaka'uta 2010, 152) the *fakahē* reading is hopeful because it reminds the reader of the process of "wandering around" to find sustenance for oneself and for one's family.

*Fakahē* as fishing is time consuming, and one wanders around "under the sun." One has to keep a close eye for when the tide comes in, to get out of the water in time. It is also painful especially for the *te'epupulu* and *lomu* as their bodies are pierced, cut and emptied out. Then thrown back to the sea to heal and to be a source of life for the next *fakahē*.

*Fakahē* reading is obviously not for everyone, not for every Pasifika islander, and not for every Tongan. Migrants from other countries and contexts will have other influences on their reading practices, so the hermeneutical approach and the interpretations will be different for Koreans, Rotumans, Tokelauans, and Fijians because of ethnicity, age, gender, religion, and so forth. Even among my Tongan people, our locations, whether in Tonga or in diaspora, determine how we read. For those of us in diaspora, context and culture for ones who migrated to New Zealand are different for the context and culture for those who migrated to other Pasifika islands, Australia, United States, and other lands. Nonetheless, despite the differences, there are also links and commonalities. As we learn from African Americans, "Although there is no one African American perspective, the operative assumption of African American biblical interpretation is that sociocultural space (esp. race) matters; that it determines in large measure how and what one think, not only about scripture but also about oneself" (Soulen 2011, 1).

## Conclusion

A difficult and ambiguous text such as Eccl 8 invites us to open up new meanings to terms such as vanity and labor, which have been used as excuse for reading the text negatively. Ecclesiastes 8 does not focus only on the intellectual capacity of the individual, but it also allows readers to look into the wisdom of the community. That wisdom can illustrate a life-giving experience for people in *fakahē*, whether at home or in diaspora. The *fakahē* reading also creates space for readers in diaspora to question the dis/advantage of grasping on to their home (past) culture. In diaspora, there is room for many choices. But when we want to bring change to our home countries, we need to be aware that those back home do not have the choices we do. Regardless of the choices we have in our host countries, some in diaspora choose to be connected to their home (is)lands. Their choice is their *fatongia*, which gives one enjoyment.

## Works Cited

Carroll, Sef. 2010. "Being a Stranger at Home and Away." Pages 80–97 in *Talanoa Ripples: Across Borders, Cultures, Disciplines*. Edited by Jione Havea. Massey, New Zealand: Massey University.

Crenshaw, James L. 1998. *Ecclesiastes: A Commentary*. London: SCM.

Cruz, Gemma T. 2014. *Toward a Theology of Migration: Social Justice and Religious Experience*. New York: Palgrave.

Ellis, Juniper. 1997. "'The Techniques of Storytelling': An Interview with Albert Wendt." *Ariel* 28.3:79–94.

Fisi'iahi, Kuli. 2015. "Theology Begins with Humanity: Most Important Thing We Can't Live Without Is Love." Paper presented at the biannual meeting of the Oceania Biblical Studies Association. Piula Theological College, Samoa. 11 September.

Goldsworthy, Graham. 2016. *The Southern Baptism Theological School*. 24 November. http://www.sbts.edu/wp–content/uploads/sites/5/2012/02/pages–from–sbjt–v15–n3_goldsworthy.pdf.

Hau'ofa, 'Epeli. 1994. "Our Sea of Islands." *The Contemporary Pacific* 6.1: 148–61.

Havea, Jione. 2015. "Sea–ing Ruth with Joseph's Mistress." Pages 147–61 in *Islands, Islanders and the Bible*. Edited by Jione Havea, Margaret Aymer and Steed Vernyl Davidson. Atlanta: SBL Press.

Helu, Futa. 2006. *Koe Heilala tangitangi 'o Salote Pilolevu*. Nukualofa: Atenisi Press.

Krüger, Thomas. 2004. *Qoheleth*. Minneapolis: Fortress.

Ogden, Graham, and Lynell Zogbo 1997. *A Handbook on Ecclesiastes*. New York: United Bible Societies.

Penchansky, David. 2012. *Understanding Wisdom Literature.* Grand Rapids: Eerdmans.

Soulen, Richard. 2011. *Biblical Criticism.* Louisville: Westminster John Knox.

Taungāpeau, 'Epeli. 2010. "Can I Be Tongan in a Strange Promised Land?" Pages 40–46 in *Talanoa Ripples: Across Borders, Cultures, Disciplines.* Edited by Jione Havea. Massey, New Zealand: Massey University.

Taumoefolau, Melenaite, and Elizabeth Ellem-Wood, eds. 2004. *Songs and Poems of Queen Salote.* Nuku'alofa: Vava'u.

Vaka'uta, Nāsili. 2010. "Tālanga: A Tongan Mode of Interpretation." Pages 149–65 in *Talanoa ripples: Across Borders, Cultures, Disciplines.* Edited by Jione Havea. Massey, New Zealand: Massey University.

Wood, Alfred. Harold. 1975. *Overseas Missions of the Australian Methodist Church: Tonga and Samoa.* Melbourne: Aldersgate.

# A TIME TO JUDGE: SEEKING JUSTICE WITH QOHELETH AND ANCIENT TAMIL WISDOM

D. Gnanaraj

Living is an arduous business for the deprived, made even more unbearable by the enduring presence of oppression. For Tamils in Sri Lanka, an ethnic minority, repressions at the hands of the Sinhalese majority have been a bitter reality since independence in 1948. The sporadic, unchecked cases of violence culminated in a ghastly genocidal finale in 2009, with as many as 40,000 Tamils dead from indiscriminate shelling and as many as 300,000 Tamils displaced in the northern and eastern regions of Sri Lanka (Lynch 2011). The Tamils' voice has been systematically silenced within Sri Lanka as well as in the international arena, despite the efforts of Tamils around the globe. Justice remains elusive, trapped within the firm grasp of global power structures that protect their self-interests.

Qoheleth[1] championed the cause of the silenced in a similar social milieu. He engages the oppressed in his comprehensive universal quest and earnestly grapples with their desperation, anguish, and fear. His candid analysis draws out significant insights concerning the nexus between oppression and abuse of political power. God, for him, seems to be uninterested in the affairs of the world. Yet, he ironically refuses to disbelieve in the fairness of divine justice and its eventual certainty.

---

I would like to gratefully acknowledge the generous assistance from friends, for reading the manuscripts and offering valuable suggestions: Dr. G.S. Prabin, Assistant Professor of Tamil at Muthayammal College of Arts and Science in Tamilnadu, critically read and commented on the translation and interpretation of Tamil poetry; Sanath Kumara, a doctoral candidate at Torch Trinity Graduate University, clarified crucial points from a Sinhalese perspective; and Joshua Isaiah, a Faculty at Lanka Bible College, Sri Lanka, made important suggestions from a Tamil perspective.

[1] In this essay, *Qoheleth* refers to the speaker in the book of Ecclesiastes.

Similarly, ancient Tamil wisdom writings, particularly *Tirukural* and *Silapathikaram*, deliberate on the issue of injustice emanating from the seats of power and its devastating effect among the common folks. These works capture the attitudes and values of the Tamil society during the *Sangam* or classical period (ca. 300 BCE–300 CE). In this chapter, I read Qoheleth with these two classical Tamil works in view of the present conditions of Tamils in Sri Lanka. The present study strives to empower their muted aspirations for justice and desire for reconciliation towards building a peaceful egalitarian community.

Tamils in Sri Lanka and the Emergence of the Ethnic Conflict

The Sri Lankan civil war is conventionally dated between July 1983 and May 2009 (when armed resistance ended). However, the origin of Tamil-Sinhalese conflict can be traced way back in the history of Sri Lanka and surreptitiously continues even today. At the heart of the conflict stand the issues of land, language, and religion. The Sinhalese ethnic majority claims the right of ownership to the land and views Tamils as "a foreign" ethnic community (Ross and Savada 2002, 145–47). In fact, considering the geographical proximity of Tamil homeland in South India with the northern part of Sri Lanka, there were many political as well as cultural exchanges in the centuries before the advent of the British on the island. The strong historical evidence for the presence of Tamils in Sri Lanka much before the British era or even before the arrival of the Sinhalese themselves has been at best downplayed (Chattopadhyaya 1994, 3–4).[2] During the British era, a large number of Indian Tamils were settled in the tea plantations as laborers. At the time of independence, the Tamil population of Sri Lanka stood at around 12 percent and Sinhalese at around 70 percent. At least three major reasons are behind the conflicts between these two ethnic groups: repercussion of colonial policies, the rise of Sinhalese nationalism, and the ideology of politicized Sinhalese Buddhism.

First, many former European colonies today trace the origin of problems back to their colonial experience, and Sri Lankan is no exception. The British began to take over the smaller nation states in Sri Lanka in an attempt to form a unified British Ceylon. In 1818, with the annexation of the last great kingdom of Kandy, a Hindu Tamil kingdom, they achieved it.[3] For the first time, Sri Lanka was ruled

---

[2] According to a legend in *Mahavamsa*, Prince Vijaya, the eponymous ancestor of the Sinhalese, landed with his group on the shores of Sri Lanka to find it inhabited by a thriving indigenous population. He married a Tamil *Pandiya* princess from the mainland India. Sri Lanka was invaded several times by the *Cholas* in the tenth and eleventh century CE. Tamil traders also frequented the shores of Sri Lanka. Thus, the presence of Tamils in Sri Lanka in the pre-British era is a well-established fact.

[3] Having accepted British supremacy, the Sinhalese chieftains worked alongside the invading British to ensure the fall of Kandyan kingdom. Initially following the *Kandyan*

from a centralized bureaucracy from Colombo, a Sinhalese-Buddhist dominated area in the southern part of the island. Primarily, the British established the capital in Colombo for administrative convenience. Once they gave independence to Sri Lanka in 1948, they left the country without sharing powers among the nation states they annexed or properly installing measures to safeguard the rights of the minorities. Even this would not have been problematic had not the nationalists hijacked the broader collective national vision for a much narrower majority-dominated ethnic idea.

Second, the rise of Sinhalese nationalism in the nineteenth century had much stronger effect on the post-independence politics of Sri Lanka. In the same year after independence (15 November 1948), the Sinhalese-dominated parliament of Sri Lanka passed the *Ceylon Citizenship Act* that endangered the citizenship status of 700,000 Tamils. Kanapathipillai (2009, 70) observes that "the year 1948 was a significant year for Sri Lanka. Not only was it the year of independence, but it also marked the exclusion of a significant minority from the polity of Sri Lanka." Several Indian Tamils lost their citizenship and were repatriated to India. Later, the *Sinhala Only Bill* (1956) made Sinhalese the only official language of the country and further marginalized the Tamil language and its speakers. There was a growing sense of alienation resulting from other government policies such as "reduced quotas of university places for Tamils and ban on the importation of Tamil books and films" (Bouma, Ling, and Pratt 2010, 110). Gradually, the discontent brewed further when the democratic appeals to redress these issues were blatantly ignored. Tamils began to strongly feel that the crisis of their disenfranchisement could only be rectified by the creation of a separate state for Tamils. At this point, the sixth amendment of 1983 outlawed any aspirations for a separate state even by peaceful means, thus pushing the debate out of the democratic arena into militant territory.[4]

---

*Convention* (1815), Kandyan Kingdom was allowed to exist as a protectorate, but later in 1818 absorbed into the British Ceylon.

[4] As a Tamil myself, I identify with the nonviolent democratic political process and neither subscribe nor support violent political ideology. Violence can neither beget peace nor consensus, but only silence. In fact, Tamils under S. J. V. Chelvanayakam chose nonviolent approach which largely proved to be ineffective. He entered into pacts with Sinhala politicians such as S. W. R. D. Bandaranaike (1957), Dudley Senanayake (1965), but they were later abrogated due to pressure from Sinhala nationalists. Few years after his death, the burning of Jaffna Library in 1981—containing important cultural artifacts of immense historical value—became a watershed moment for the Sri Lankan Tamils. Their distrust in the democratic political process reached a tipping point, tilting public sentiments in favor of armed resistance. The Liberation Tigers of Tamil Eelam (LTTE) emerged as the face of Tamil armed resistance and came to represent the Tamil aspirations for fair governance when the democratic voices of Tamils were largely suppressed by the majority.

Third, the political ideology of Sinhalese Buddhism also contributed to the crisis.[5] Gordon Weiss, a former United Nations official who documented the final phase of the war, argues that one of the major problems that he perceived was the disproportionate influence of "a violently nationalist coterie of Buddhist monks" in the political arena. On the political-religious nexus of Sri Lanka, he perceptively observes:

> The relatively recent political gestation of ideas that have given these monks an influence beyond their numbers includes a toxic mixture of religion, nationalism and xenophobia, as well as a blood-and-soil claim to territory based on obscure two thousand year old Buddhist texts. (Weiss 2010, xxi)

The major political parties of Sri Lanka—United National Party (UNP) and Sri Lanka Freedom Party (SLFP)—sought to gain political mileage by aligning with the Sinhalese-Buddhist majority, excluding Tamils who are largely Hindus or Christians. Nationalist Buddhist monks have consistently opposed a two-state solution or concession of any territory to the Tamils through different political lobby groups until now (Bouma, Ling, and Pratt 2010, 111; Ridge 2007; Mohan 2015).

Along with these, a combination of factors contributed to the escalation of conflict into a bloody insurgency that resulted in the loss of at least 100,000 lives. 40,000 of these reportedly were killed during the final phase of the civil war. Another 300,000 were internally displaced, held against their will in government camps in frugal conditions. The horrendous violence, atrocities, and human rights violations committed against the minority Tamil community left a deep scar on Tamils in Sri Lanka and elsewhere. Tamils in Sri Lanka await justice for the oppressions they have endured for the last seven decades. Their bitter tears still remain unwiped as justice is yet to be realized.

## Qoheleth on Oppression and Justice

While we hold that every text is a product of its time and draws its strength from the world it seeks to espouse, Ecclesiastes lacks any direct historical reference or allusions to any of the events or persons in the known history of Israel. It seems Qoheleth took enormous measures not to restrict the work to any specific time period. This intentional ambiguity has infused a timeless dimension to the reading of Ecclesiastes. In fact, it is important not to be dogmatic about the vexing issue of dating Qoheleth. The scenarios envisaged by Qoheleth readily fit into any period, be it Solomonic, Persian, Ptolemaic, or even ours (Gnanaraj 2012, 1–21).

---

[5] The Buddhist revival of Anagarika Dharmapala (1864–1933) gave the vision for a Sinhala-Buddhist nation state. Alvappillai Veluppillai (2006, 98) explains his dark side, "He was a champion of Sinhalese nationalism and had attacked vehemently Tamil and Muslim minorities in his writings."

Reading Qoheleth within the social backdrop of any of these periods would do justice to its message. On the one hand, he describes a situation of increasing foreign trade, a thriving economy and fairly peaceful times; on the other hand, he describes rampant bureaucratic abuses, unbridled greed, abuse of power against the poor, and indifference to the deprivations of the weak.

At best, Qoheleth presents two contrasting views: *a high view from above*, which exalts the grandiose achievements of the royal elite, and *a low view from below* that critiques such a lofty attitude by pointing out the very oppression such strivings create in the fragmented world of the powerless, the oppressed, the *hā'ăšuqūîm*. Such bipolar perspectives are to be anticipated as Qoheleth announced at the outset (1:3) that the scope of his quest would encompass a search beyond the comfort of his royal precincts into the sweltering surroundings *under the sun*. It is highly likely that this book was a pre-exilic royal composition, befitting to be read as a royal self-criticism bemoaning the vexation of human attempts for glory through accomplishments and political control (Gnanaraj 2017, 161–63; Shields 2006, 24–27; Young 1993, 147–48).

Ecclesiastes 3:16–17; 4:1–3; and 5:17–18

In the first two chapters, Qoheleth derives his conclusions from his personal experiences of pleasure, wealth, and wisdom. From chapter 3 on, he conducts himself as an outside investigator—who did not engage in acts of oppression, was not being oppressed, and did not initiate any counter measures to address oppression. He intends *to observe all the oppressions* that are done *under the sun*. Of the three passages related to this theme, the first two are based on his observation ("I saw"—3:16; 4:1), and the third is a preemptive instruction ("if you see"—5:17) to those about to witness or experience oppression in its various forms.

*Ecclesiastes 3:16–17*

> [16] And I saw something else under the sun: In the place of justice—wickedness was there, in the place of righteousness—wickedness was there. [17] I said in my heart, "God will judge the righteous and the wicked, for there is a time for every activity, and for every deed." (Author's translation)

This rather appalling observation of injustice is presented in the climatic section that contains the poem on time and forms an *inclusio* with 3:1.[6] He witnesses the dethronement of justice and the reversal of just order in the world. The place of justice and of judgment refer to the center of sociojudicial activity in ancient Israel "where righteousness ought to triumph and rights of the poor are to be protected"

---

[6] 3:1 *lakkōl zəmān wə'ēt ləkāl-ḥēpeṣ taḥat haššāmāyim*; 3:17b *kî-'ēt ləkāl-ḥēpeṣ wə'al kāl-hamma'ăśê šāmi*.

(Garrett 1987, 162). The repeated *šāmmâ hāreša'* is emphatic: at the very heart of the system, there was wickedness (Goh 2016, 30–47).[7] The role of sociopolitical leadership to address the problem of injustice is under serious question, as Qoheleth saw wickedness in the very seats of justice. How could the wicked cleanse a nation of wickedness? How could anyone rely upon the unjust for justice? In Qoheleth's assessment, the situation is rather grim.

Yet, Qoheleth does not perceive this appalling situation as entirely hopeless; rather, he calls his readers to turn from their corrupt leaders to the sole divine deliverer. The closing refrain in verse 17a positively picks up the theme of time in 3:1–8 and asserts that there will be a time for judgement that will once for all resolve the problem of injustice. The judgment for injustice is certain, but the time of its execution is frustratingly indeterminate (Seow 1997, 166). Garrett (1987, 163) explains, "The time and place of this judgment is uncertain, but it is related to the idea of death and the grave. Beyond that, this 'eschatological hope' is remarkably undefined.... Qoheleth does not speculate about what type of punishment the wicked will receive." So in his estimation, this could be well in the near future or in an eschatological future in the economy of God, the knowledge of which is well beyond human grasp. Meeks (2013, 70) concurs that "Ecclesiastes does not offer an *immediate* solution to the problem, but it does give hope of a time in which injustice is righted and suffering alleviated, not unlike the New Testament (cf. Rev 21:3–4)." To sum up, verses 16–17 acknowledge the ubiquity of oppression but offer hope of divine vindication in its time.

*Ecclesiastes 4:1–3*

> Again I looked and saw all the oppression that was taking place under the sun: I saw the tears of the oppressed—and they have no comforter; power was on the hand of their oppressors—and they have no comforter. And I said that the dead, who had already died, are happier than the living, who are still alive. But better than both is the unborn, who has not seen any evil under the sun. (Author's translation)

Qoheleth continues to unravel the theme of power abuse in 4:1–3. Here his rhetoric reaches its emotional high as he graphically presents the case of the oppressed. The three-fold repetition of the root *'šq* in 4:1 might well refer to a variety of abusive socioeconomic practices including extortion, political oppression, violence, and other wrongs committed against the defenseless (Mazzinghi

---

[7] "The place of justice—there wickedness! The place of righteousness—there wickedness!" The Hebrew word *hāreša'* is translated as "injustice/evil" (Bartholomew 2009, 176–77), "iniquity" (KJV), "wickedness" (NIV, ESV, NRSV). The threefold repetitions of the root *rš'* and "there" (twice as *šāmmâ*, once as *šām*) in 3:16–17 seem to imply the pervasiveness of wickedness *in* the place of justice.

2009, 546). The poignant image of flowing tears on the face of the oppressed announces a bleak situation—no comforters, advocates, or defenders. The oppressed battle it all alone with their waning strength. This explains their lack of strength to even lift their own hands to wipe their tears. In reality, power is in the hands of the oppressors, which denies any respite for the oppressed. The juxtaposition of "tears of the oppressed" (*dim ʿat hā ʿăšuqîm*) and "hand of the oppressors" (*miyyad ʿōšqêhem*) in 4:1 is striking: it is normal human tendency to extend one's hands to wipe the tears of the suffering people. But the hands of oppressors do not extend mercy, rather they intensify oppression. There is another point to note: from the *hands of God* come the joy of eating and drinking, and from the *hands of the oppressors* come oppressions, which do not allow people to enjoy the blessings of God in peace. And God does not seem to do anything about it!

Qoheleth generally affirms life and holds that life is better than death at any given moment (cf. 9:4). But in the context of overwhelming oppression he acknowledges death as a better option over life and being unborn as the best of all. The oppressed are able to identify themselves with Qoheleth in his dismal assessment. These words of Qoheleth should not be taken as supportive of suicide. He is just expressing his personal turmoil (Garrett 1987, 163). He identifies well with the groaning of the oppressed and their wish that they were never born (cf. Job 3:3–5; Jer 20:18): "Who, in looking on the misery of the poor and oppressed, has not sometime felt what Qoheleth felt?" (Garrett 1987, 163).

To sum up, power is in the wrong hands, and it has become coercive, abusive, and oppressive. No one seems to protect the defenseless from it. The oppressed can take solace in the certainty that God will judge evil (cf. 3:17) and that they will not always be afflicted. There will be a time for the restoration of the just order. Overall, it is this hope, however fragile it might be, that characterizes Qoheleth's outlook.

*Ecclesiastes 5:8–9 [Heb. 5:7–8]*

> If you see the oppression of the poor and the violation of justice and righteousness in a province, do not be surprised at the matter; for, one official[8] watches over another; and higher officials are over them. And the profit from the land is for all; even the king is served from the fields.[9] (Author's translation)

---

[8] The translation of the Hebrew *gābōah* is disputed. It literally means "high one" without bureaucratic connotation. Seow, following Kugel, translates it as "arrogant one," implying persons with "higher socioeconomic-political status, but not necessarily a bureaucrat" (Seow 1997, 203–4). While this translation is correct in principle, the context of 4:8 with references to justice and righteousness, "the domains of government" demands the translation "higher official" with bureaucratic overtone (Bartholomew 2009, 216).

[9] Verse 8 [Eng. verse 9] has several translational difficulties: *bakkōl* (translated here "for all"), *neʿĕbād* (Niphal perfect, translated as "is served"). Several alternative translations

In these verses, Qoheleth returns to ponder the issue of oppression as an instructor ("If you see"). Earlier he perceived the constant presence of oppression "due to the corruption inherent in bureaucracy" (cf. 3:16) and its devastating effect on the weak (4:1–3; Meeks 2013, 71). Now he affirms the reality that the oppression of the poor and denial of their rights are to be expected in every age and every place. Qoheleth does not restrict the presence of injustice geographically ("in a province"); rather he points out that it occurs in places where justice should reign (Seow 1997, 202).

Here, Qoheleth helps the oppressed to have a reasonable expectation from the oppressive power structures. Tremper Longman (1998, 156–57) notes here that "while the previous passage simply urged caution before divine authority (5:1–7), the present one urges resignation before human authority." Such a reading results from Longman's frame-narrative presuppositions and is unwarranted. Qoheleth's initial astonishment at the absence of advocates for the oppressed (4:1) now turns instructive as he exhorts readers not to be surprised at oppression. There might be many bureaucrats, each one of them having their superiors in the hierarchy, within a system actually made to enforce justice. Yet they remain too preoccupied to watch out for justice. Instead, they only protect each other's self-interest: "One crow does not peck out the eyes of another" (Delitzsch 1975, 293). If one takes time to trace the strands of oppression in a remote province, they may be startled to discover king at the other end of the strand. Such a revelation of the inherent flaw of the bureaucratic system should not shock us as we are already informed.

Qoheleth's Observations and Recommendations

Qoheleth focuses his attention *above*, on the seats of power in 3:16–17, providing assessment of those at the top of bureaucratic hierarchy—be it in a local community, in a province or in a country. His finding, that wickedness masquerades and occupies the seats of justice, reveals the reason for the difficulty of accessing justice through the muddied sociojudicial system.

His focus turns *below* to the oppressed commoners in 4:1–3, empathizing with their miserable lot. This is emotionally gripping for Qoheleth as he feels the weight of oppression in all its destructive force. His musing, that being unborn is

---

are suggested: "a king for a plowed field" (Bartholomew 2009, 218); "a king is subject to the land" (Koh, 56), "a king over cultivated land" (Eaton, *Ecclesiastes*, 101-102), "a king committed to cultivated fields" (ESV), "even the king benefits from the field" (Longman 1998, 157), and Seow altogether omits reference to king and takes *ne'ĕbād* with the field (Seow 1997, 204). When taken together with 4:8, the chain of officials leading from the low to high should reach the king, who is the highest official of all in a government. Thus, I prefer the translation: "Even the king is served by the fields." By extension, it means that the oppressed poor working in the field in a province will have to bear with the extortions not just from the officials, but from the king himself.

the best option in the face of such an oppressive situation, reveals the despondency of the situation and can be considered a suggestion born out of his vexing helplessness.

Finally, he *recommends* that the poor be prepared to face unjust situations. Even kings might be complicit, as the seats of power are hand in glove with the oppressors. The only hope is divine justice, which is at best ambiguous and indefinite. Though it is unclear when God will dispense justice, he will certainly judge. While appealing to higher authorities for justice, Qoheleth encourages the readers to be realistic about the oppressive realities of their surroundings and to be confident of divine justice in due time. In a world unredeemed, this is the best solution Qoheleth could offer for the oppressed.

## Oppression and Justice in Ancient Tamil Wisdom

Tamils have been known for their literary activity and business prowess from ancient times. The ancient Tamil literary corpus known as *Sangam* literature contains a staggering collection of indigenous epic poetry and wisdom maxims. *Tirukural* and *Silapathikaram*—two of the *Sangam* literatures dated 300 BCE to 300 CE—are selected for our study (Pandiyan 1987, 40). Two chapters of *Tirukural* that reflect on justice and injustice are selected: *Sengonmai* (Just Rule, ch. 55) and *Kodungonmai* (Unjust Rule, ch. 56). Sections of a Tamil epic *Silapahtikaram* (lit., "An Epic of Anklet") that address an oppressive situation and the response of the oppressed are also taken together. While *Tirukural* addresses and advises primarily the rulers/kings, *Silapahtikaram* illustrates the fury of the oppressed that refuse to be silenced before overwhelming social odds.

### *Tirukural* on Oppressive and Just Rule

*Tirukural* is a nonreligious wisdom composition, containing 1330 highly structured *kural* (couplets), arranged under 133 chapters and three major categories: *Aram* (virtue; chapters 1–38), *Porul* (wealth and politics; chapters 39–108), *Inbam* (love; chapters 109–133).[10] The writer, *Tiruvalluvar*, explored every aspect of human life in his terse poetic innovations (Culter 1992, 550). His reflection on justice and injustice in chapters 55 and 56 are found within the larger category of wealth and politics. His tone is straightforward and honest, based on his observations and his ideal aspirations. Recently, Tirukural has been compared with the book of Proverbs in the South Asia Bible Commentary.

---

[10] Each couplet contains exactly seven words, four in the first line and three in the second. This arrangement is uniformly present in all of its 1330 couplets. Also, each of the seven words in a couplet is further governed by Tamil poetic syllabic rules, known as *sir*. This is an unparalleled intellectual accomplishment of the Classical Tamil period, providing valuable insights about the culture, values, and life in the ancient Tamil country.

In chapter 55 *Tiruvalluvar* begins with his definition of justice and goes on to espouse the benefits of just rule for the people and the king himself. He defines justice as fair treatment of all under a ruler's scepter (*Kural* 541). He refers directly to a king and/or his scepter in nine couplets in this chapter. The scepter is symbolic and alludes to the presence of justice. He compares a just rule to benevolent rain (*Kural* 542) and a just king as the one clearing a field of weeds (*Kural* 550). He points out that people adore a just ruler and will be loyal to him (*Kural* 544), but the one who fails to dispense it will be destroyed by his own (mis)deeds (*Kural* 548). Justice not only benefits the people, but also shields the rulers themselves (*Kural* 547). In his estimation, it is not the spear that gives long-term victory for a ruler but the unbent scepter (*Kural* 546). These wisdom maxims aim to primarily encourage the rulers to value justice and restrain them from the unfair treatment of their subjects.

In chapter 56 the descriptions of unjust or tyrannical rule are laid out using evocative imagery. An unjust ruler is compared to a paid assassin, an extortionist, a robber, and a drought. When injustice increases, *Tiruvalluvar* warns that there will be no rain and the monsoons will fail (*Kural* 559), cows' milk will dry up, and the learned will forget their books (*Kural* 560). These images paint an impoverished dreary landscape and cultural deterioration resulting from the injustices of a king. Most relevant to our present study is *Kural* 555, which focuses on the *tears of the oppressed*:

*Allarpat tatraa thaluthakan neerantae*
*Selvathai thaikkum padai.*[11]

Tears of those oppressed with unbearable grief
Are the weapons that erode an unjust rulers' wealth

Tears of the oppressed, in the imagination of the Tamil sage, are transformed into mighty weapons (lit., "army") that pull down unjust kingdoms. What seems innocuous and feeble is potentially formidable and a mighty force. He cautions that rulers ignore the grievances of the weak to their own detriment. Eventually, the tears will defeat the spears and the unjust scepter will be held accountable before the aggrieved. This brings forth the issue of where real power is: though power seems to reside with and wielded by kings, in reality power is with the lowly subjects. This is an important lesson *Tiruvalluvar* wanted the royalty to remember.

To sum up, by presenting two contrasting portraits of a just and tyrannical rule in the consecutive chapters, the Tamil sage goads the rulers to pursue justice, fairness, and equality. Elsewhere, he offers them a path to be remembered like a *deity*, revered by their subjects (*Kural* 388). His aim was to cultivate and ingrain a greater cultural sensitivity towards justice. For he knew that when justice

---

[11] All the translations of Tamil poetry are mine.

becomes the habit of the rulers, people can live in peace. His insights greatly shaped the aspirations for justice in the ancient Tamil country and it continues to exert significant influence even today on the quest of Tamils.

*Silapathikaram* on the Oppressed and Injustice

*Silapathikaram* is one of the five celebrated classical Tamil epics comprising of 5,762 lines of narrative poetry, composed by a *Chera* Prince Ilangoadigal towards the end of the *Sangam* era. The three major episodes of the story are set across the three ancient Tamil kingdoms. The story revolves around the lead pair, Kanngi and Kovalan, and the vicissitudes of their life. Following is a summary of the epic:

> Kovalan and Kannagi lived in the city of *Poompuhar*, the capital of the *Chola* kingdom. In the course of time, Kovalan fell for a Courtesan named Madhavi. He spent all his wealth and fortunes on his illicit affair. Later, he realized his error and returned to his wife who forgave her remorseful husband. They move on to Madurai, the capital of the neighboring *Pandiya* kingdom, to restart their lives together. On reaching Madurai, Kannagi gave one of her two anklets (*silambu*) to be sold as capital for her husband's new business venture. While Kovalan was trying to find a suitable buyer, he was arrested and charged with robbery. Earlier, one of the queen's anklets was stolen by a royal goldsmith. Seeing Kovalan with a similar anklet in the marketplace, he seized the opportunity to blame Kovalan for thievery. Kovalan was immediately arrested and beheaded for stealing the queen's ornament. The news of this misfortune reached Kannagi. She ran to see her murdered husband. Her inconsolable tears turned into rage. With fire in her teary eyes, she rose up with the remaining anklet in her hand, and stormed into the royal court demanding justice for her slain husband. She proved Kovalan's innocence by breaking her anklet before the king. Her anklet contained precious stones, whereas pearls adorned the queen's ornament. The king realized his misjudgment and immediately died of a broken heart. Kannagi's rage then burned the entire city of Madurai. At last, she ascended to the skies to be reunited with her husband from the *Chera* country.

There are few poignant scenes which are worth exploring. First is the lament of Kannagi holding her slain husband in her breast, asking those around why no one stepped in to stop this heinous injustice:

*Pendirum undukol pendirum undukol*
*Konda koluna rukurai thanguruvum*
*Pendirum undukol pendirum undukol*

*Santorum undukol santorum undukol*
*Eentra kulavi eduthu valarkuuruvum*
*Santorum undukol santorum undukol*

*Theivamum undukol theivamum undukol*
*Vaivaalil thappiya mannavan kuudalil*
*Theivamum undukol theivamum undukol*
(*Mathurai Kandam, Ursul vari*, 51–59)

Are there women? Are there women?
Who could bear such wrong to their wedded husband?
Are there women? Are there women?

Are there good men? Are there good men?
Those [who] care for their own young and guard them—
Are there good men? Are there good men?

Is there a god? Is there a god?
In this city where an innocent is slain by the king's sword
Is there a god? Is there a god?
(2.19.51–59)

In fact, there was no one to comfort her! First, she appealed to the virtuous women, then good men, and finally to the deity. All were present, yet all were silent in the hour of injustice. For Kannagi, their silence made them complicit in the reckless royal action.

Her transformation from a wailing woman who lost her beloved into a vigorous seeker of justice is rather dramatic. She refused to succumb to self-pity and sorrow; rather, she resolved not to die without seeing justice being done. She resolved to take the fight to the king:

Kaichinan thaninthantri kanavanai kaikudaen
Theevaenthan thanaikandi thirankaetpal yaanentaal
Entaal ezhuntal idarutra theekanaa
Nintaal ninainthaal nedungayarkan neersoora
Nintaal ninainthaal nedungayarkan neerthudaiyaa
Sentaal arasan selunkoyil vaayilmun.
(*Mathurai Kandam, Ursul vari*, 70–75)

Till my great wrath is appeased, I will not join my husband
I will see the cruel king and ask for his explanation
Saying this, she stood up with sorrow and fury
She stood ruing, her large eyes full of tears
She stood ruing, her large eyes full of unwiped tears
She went to the gates of the palace of the king.
(2.19.70–75)

Again, the poet captures the emotions of Kannagi very powerfully as an embodiment of a woman still laden with sorrow, yet with a raging longing for the justice that has been denied. Her unwiped flowing tears would in due course spell doom to the kingdom where the scepter is bent and justice corrupted.

Her confrontation with the king is rather dramatic and intense. The king asked her who she was. She proudly recollected that she hailed from *Puhar*, from the land of a legendary Tamil king who even dispensed fair justice to a bereaved cow.

> Vaayir kadaimani nadunaa nadunga
> Aavin kadaimani uguneer nenjusuda thaanthan
> Arumperar puthalvanai aazhiyin madithon
> Perumpeyar puharen pathiyae…
> (*Mathurai Kandam, Vazakurai Kaathai*, 53–56)

> Ringing the bell at the palace gate in intolerable grief
> The flowing tears of the cow paining his heart
> His own son, he allowed to be killed on chariot wheels
> That's my great town, *Puhar* its name.
> (2.20.53–56)

This story gave Kannagi the moral courage to challenge the injustice that was done to her. She held her composure till the end as she broke open her anklet that revealed the precious stones. The scattered pieces of precious stones from Kannagi's anklet hit the king on his face. He realized his grave error and confessed: "Am I the king? I am but a thief who stole justice from an innocent" (2.20.75–77). With his confession he fainted and fell down from the throne dead. The king atoned for his misdeed with his own life, exiting the scene with dignity.

To sum up, the female protagonist transforms from a passive person to an ideal seeker of justice. She had to overcome enormous disadvantages in her search for justice: she was a woman, a widow, an immigrant; she had to overcome the stigma of being the wife of an accused; she was poor and unknown. Eric Miller calls Kannagi "a global symbol of justice, and of the dignity of the individual" (Miller 2006). This epic affirms the ancient Tamils' vision for a just order where even a person of no means, if wronged, could challenge the most powerful king.

Observations and Recommendations

Tamil *Sangam* literatures address the problem of oppression and injustice with a two-pronged approach. While admonishing the rulers to dispense justice and the self-injurious consequences at the face of its deferral or denial, it also encourages the common folk to actively seek justice regardless of the odds. In fact, when the power structures fail to uphold the very function for which they are established and become exploitive, it falls upon "those below" to stand up for and demand the restoration of the just order. *Silapathikaram* is a reminder that people should become active participants in the creation and defense of this just order, rather than being passive recipients of injustice. The powerful image of a widowed woman with teary eyes, and an anklet in her raised hand, demanding justice at the court of an unjust king, continues to inspire Tamils in their quest towards achieving justice and reconciliation.

## In Pursuit of Justice

After the bloody end of armed resistance in May 2009, there have been calls for an independent international enquiry into the war crimes committed at the final phase. The total secrecy with the entire area surrounding the final battle and the imposition of bans on international aid groups to enter conflict zones have given rise to the serious accusation of war crimes. The disturbing videos of Sri Lankan Army soldiers casually executing Tamil prisoners of war (Harrison 2013), the use of prohibited heavy weapons, and the rape and murder of several Tamil women reveal a disproportionate military response, parallel to the horrors Hitler's Nazis inflicted on German Jews (Roy 2017). In spite of the piling evidence, the government of Sri Lanka continues to deny such crimes and instead protect the perpetuators of heinous violence. Weiss (2011, xxiv) observes on this situation as follows, "I believe that the tactical choices the SLA was directed to make, and which contributed to the deaths of so many civilians, warrant a credible judicial investigation of the kind that the Sri Lankan state, in its current guise, is no longer capable of mounting." Furthermore, the diplomatic cover the Sri Lankan Government enjoys from China and India at the United Nations continues to frustrate the Tamils' ongoing struggle to attain justice.

The unprecedented oppression inflicted on Tamils in Sri Lanka since independence calls for a culturally sensitive biblical response. Qoheleth and the Tamil sages can offer insights that would inspire Tamils. They both observe the reality of oppression from the perspective of their own cultural and religious convictions.

Qoheleth documents the sorry state of the oppressed and their unmitigated misery; the Tamil sages, on the other hand, explore what the oppressed can do once they find a way to turn their sorrow into a reckoning force. While Qoheleth uses tears to show the despondency of the oppressed, the Tamil sages derive wisdom lessons for the rulers not to naively ignore the tears of the weak but to address it before they turn into weapons of destruction.

Qoheleth's forewarning prepares the weak to be unsurprised before cases of oppression. He asks the reader to accept their lot (cf. Eccl 10:20) and to wait for divine intervention in an *indefinite* future. This conviction that God will judge is central to his belief. Also, the solidaric presence of comforters, as Qoheleth seems to imply, might mitigate situations of injustice, though not rectify it. In the final stages of war in 2009, Singhalese churches and its leaders largely kept silent from addressing the violence against the Tamils, fearing public sentiments. This had left the suffering Tamils to fend for themselves in their hour of crisis. There were no comforters indeed!

Conversely, the Tamil sages remind people that a vision of a just world is a shared responsibility of both the ruler and the ruled. They perceived that any pessimistic outlook would strengthen the oppressive forces and further delay the realization of justice. In their estimation, a just king is considered to be *a god* by his subjects. This approach reveals their shrewd political pragmatism that encouraged rulers to aspire for greatness through just rule.

## Conclusion

Qoheleth and the Tamil sages, despite the prevalence of oppression in their respective communities, are realistically optimistic about achieving justice. They understand the uphill task that faces those seeking for it. Qoheleth's biggest problem was not the mere presence of oppressive realities, but the absence of comforters which makes it even more painful. Jesus Christ assured that he would send the *comforter*, the *paráklētos*, to be with the oppressed in this intermittent period till divine justice is ultimately realized (John 14:16). The Church of Christ, empowered by the power of this Spirit of justice, needs to stand with the oppressed in their aspiration for peaceful coexistence in their tattered habitat under the sun (Nesiah 2002, 79). Singhalese churches need to boldly join their Tamil counterparts in the pursuit of justice and promotion of reconciliation and positive peace in Sri Lanka.

As for the Tamil cause for justice in Sri Lanka, guns have fallen silent, but tears remain unaddressed and unwiped. That is a far greater weapon that would eventually erode the oppressor's might and bring injustice to its rightful end. In the words of Qoheleth, God will judge in his time, in an imminent time ushered in by the collective tear-filled voices of the oppressed.[12]

## Works Cited

Bartholomew, Craig. 2009. *Ecclesiastes*. BCOTWP. Grand Rapids: Baker Academic.
Bouma, Gary D., Rod Ling, and Douglas Pratt. 2010. *Religious Diversity in South East Asia and the Pacific*. National Case Studies. New York: Springer.
Chattopadhyaya, Haraprasad. 1994. *Ethnic Unrest in Modern Sri Lanka: An Account of Tamil-Sinhalese Race Relations*. New Delhi: M.D. Publications.
Culter, Norman. 1992. "Interpreting Tirukural: The Role of Commentary in the Creation of a Text." *JAOS* 112:549–66.

---

[12] I am very grateful to Palestinian theologians Rev. Dr. Mitri Raheb, President of Dar al-Kalima University College of Arts and Culture in Bethlehem, and Rev. Prof. Yohanna Katanacho, Academic Dean of Nazareth Evangelical College, for reading this chapter and offering valuable comments and suggestions.

Delitzsch, F. 1975. *Proverbs, Ecclesiastes and Song of Songs*. Translated by M. G. Easton. Grand Rapids: Eerdmans.

Eaton, Michael A. 1983. *Ecclesiastes: An Introduction and Commentary*. Downers Grove: InterVarsity Press.

Garrett, Duane A. 1987. "Qoheleth on the Use and Abuse of Political Power." *Trinity Journal* 8 (Fall): 159–77.

Gnanaraj, D. 2012. *The Language of Qoheleth: An Evaluation of the Recent Scholarly Studies*. New Delhi: ISPCK.

———. 2017. "Royal Autobiography and the 'Anti-Royal' Passages in Qoheleth: Some Observations." *Torch Trinity Journal* 20.2:155–67.

Goh, Elaine W. F. 2016. "Political Wisdom in the Book of Ecclesiastes." *The Asia Journal of Theology* 30:30–47.

Harrison, Frances. 2013. "Witnesses Support Claim that Sri Lanka Army Shot Prisoners." *Independent*. 24 February. http://www.independent.co.uk/news/world/asia/witnesses-support-claim-that-sri-lanka-army-shot-prisoners-8508617.html.

Koh, Y. V. 2006. *Royal Autobiography in Qoheleth*. Berlin: de Gruyter.

Kanapathipillai, Valli. 2009. *Citizenship and Statelessness in Sri Lanka: The Case of the Tamil Estate Workers*. Delhi: Anthem Press.

Longman III, Tremper. 1998. *Ecclesiastes*. NICOT. Grand Rapids: Eerdmans.

Lynch, Colum. 2011. "UN: Sri Lanka's Crushing of Tamil Tigers May Have Killed 40,000 Civilians." *The Washington Post*. 21 April. http://www.washingtonpost.com/pb/world/un-sri-lankas-crushing-of-tamil-tigers-may-have-killed-40000-civilians/2011/04/21/AFU14hJE_story.html.

Mazzinghi, Luca. 2009. "The Divine Violence in the Book of Qoheleth." *Bib* 90:545–58.

Miller, Eric. 2006. "In Praise of Kannagi." *The Hindu*. 16 June. http://www.thehindu.com/todays-paper/tp-opinion/in-praise-of-citizen-kannagi/article18438651.ece

Mohan, Rohini. 2015. "Sri Lanka's Violent Buddhists." *The New York Times* 2 January. https://www.nytimes.com/2015/01/03/opinion/sri-lankas-violent-buddhists.html.

Nesiah, Anita. 2002. "The Challenge of Christian Responsibility in Times of War and Violence: The Case of Sri Lanka." *Feminist Theology* 11.1:71–81.

Pandian, Jacob. 1987. *Caste, Nationalism and Ethnicity: An Interpretation of Tamil Cultural History and Social Order*. Bombay: Sangam Books.

Ridge, Mian. 2007. "Sri Lanka's Buddhist Monks are Intent on War." *The Telegraph*. 17 June. http://www.telegraph.co.uk/news/worldnews/1554817/Sri-Lankas-Buddhist-monks-are-intent-on-war.html.

Ross, Russel R., and Andrea Matles Savada. 2002. "Sri Lanka: A Country Study." Pages 77–220 in *Sri Lanka: Current Issues and Historical Background*. Edited by Walter Nubin. New York: Nova Science Publishers.

Roy, Arundhati. 2009. "This Is Not a War on Terror. It Is a Racist War on All Tamils." *The Guardian*. 1 April. https://www.theguardian.com/commentisfree/2009/apr/01/sri-lanka-india-tamil-tigers.

Seow, C. Leong. 1997. *Ecclesiastes*. AB. London: Yale University Press.

"Sri Lankan Forces 'Raped' Tamils in Custody, Study Says." 2013. *BBC News* 26 February. http://www.bbc.com/news/world-asia-21577866.

Veluppillai, Alvappillai. 2006. "Sinhala Fears of Tamil Demands." Pages 93–113 in *Buddhism, Conflict and Violence in Modern Sri Lanka*. Edited by Mahinda Deegalle. London: Routledge.

Weiss, Gordon. 2011. *The Cage: The Fight for Sri Lanka and the Last Days of the Tamil Tigers*. London: The Bodley Head.

Wintle, Brian, Havilah Dharamraj, J. B. Jeyaraj. 2015. *South Asia Bible Commentary: A One Volume Commentary on the Whole Bible*. Rajasthan: Open Door Publications.

# READING ECCLESIASTES IN THE LIGHT OF TAMIL SANGAM LITERATURE

M. Alroy Mascrenghe

Tamil is one of the classical languages in the world, with a rich literature that spans over 2500 years (Varatharasan 1989, 25). Among Tamil literature, *Sangam*[1] literature is the oldest and has a well-documented manual of grammar—*Thol-kappiyam*—which lays the rules for poetics and prosody as well as details how a poetic scene should be composed (Subramanian 1982, 13). In the section on content, the ancient Tamils looked at the world in terms of *thinai* (திணை). Everything in their primordial world corresponded to *akam thinai*—inside, and *puram thinai*—outside.[2] This categorization formed their worldview, which in turn formed their literature.

---

An different version of this work was presented at the 2019 Annual Meeting of the Society of Biblical Literature.

[1] The Pandyan kings who ruled in Mathurai formed Tamil Academies (Sangam). The Sangam literature is generally believed to be written in the Third Sangam.

[2] For *akam-puram* classifications see Subrahmanian 1977, 365–67; Jesudasan and Jesudasan 1961; Kailasapathy 1968; Sivatham 1974, 20–37; Devadevan 2006, 199–218; Norman Cutler 1987, 61. Clark-Deces (2005, 122–23) traces the same categorization in the modern-day Tamil dirges and funeral petitions. A similar approach is taken to rituals by Isabelle Nabokov (2000, 8–9). A work on love in Tamil families starts with this ancient classification (Margaret Trawick 1990, 25–26). In a recent article based on archaeological evidence, Iravatham Mahadevan (2010) demonstrated how *akam* and *puram* served in the ancient days as address signs. Etiologically *akam* was the inside (or inner) city and *puram* was the area outside the (or the outer) city. *Akam* became associated with things happening inside the city (mainly love), and *puram* was associated with things happening outside (mainly war).

## *Akam—Puram*

*Akam* poetry focused mainly on love and family, life viewed from inside, while *puram* poetry focused mainly on war, life viewed from outside. *Akam* poetry is about inner experience (Ramanujam 2006, 12). It is mostly imaginary, and women dominate *akam* poetry in which the subject is pre-, post-, and extramarital love. "Love in all its variety—love in separation and in union, before and after marriage, in chastity and betrayal—is the theme of *akam*" (Ramanujan 2014, 10). *Puram* is a person's "interactions in society" (Hart 1975, 7). Heroism in all its variety—actions before and after the battle—is the theme of *puram*. *Puram* poetry in general is about action and is largely history (Varatharasan 1989, 30). Men dominate *puram* poetry because it celebrates victories and war heroes (Parthasarathy 1994, 72).[3] As the man who wins the war captures the land, the one who wins in love acquires the woman and her body. *Akam* and *puram* correspond broadly to eroticism and heroism (Varatharasan 1989, 29). Thus, the whole range of human experience—"sentiments and exploits"—are covered in the classical Tamil literature (Zvelebil 1974, 10).

The *akam-puram* tradition predates Sangam literature in oral folklore. The Sangam poets followed the same tradition and documented the rules pertaining to them (Varatharasan 1989, 31):

- No proper names can be mentioned in *akam* poetry (Tholkappiyam 57). The subject matter of love was considered taboo in most Tamil communities, so mentioning names of the lovers reveal their identity and threaten their day-to-day life. A twelfth century CE work on grammar, *Akaporul Vilakkam* (அகப்பொருள் விளக்கம், 48), defines how an affair should be communicated to the family: The girl cannot convey her affair to the father directly. She must first talk to her friend (*pangi*), the friend then talks to her own mother (foster mother of the girl), the foster mother then talks to the girl's mother, and the girl's mother carries the news to the father. This gives an insight into the tradition that must be followed when writing romantic narrative poetry.
- The persons depicted in the *akam* poetry are idealized types rather than historical persons. Because *akam* is the inner world, it has neither history nor geography.
- The realm of *puram* poetry, on the other hand, is the real world and the events depicted happens in a specific geographic location and a specific time in history. Names are mentioned in *puram* poetry (so Nambiayakkaporul).

---

[3] However, the few women in *puram* poetry are there to celebrate their fallen war heroes (husband or sons).

Tamil Bhakthi literature, which originated around the eighth century CE, contains devotional songs by Hindu poets to their gods and goddesses. They are among the richest and most poignant poems ever written. Bhakthi poetry is a fusion between *akam* and *puram* categories (Shulman 2001, 73, 310). The experience of human beings was transposed onto the divine being. Women sang to the gods as their lover. The genre of the hymns sung to wake up the kings was applied to the divine king and was called *Thirupalliyelluchhi*. Thirupalliyelluchhi later evolved to denote the poems that were written to wake up the gods.[4]

## *Thinai*—Poetics

Both *akam* and *puram* have categories of *thinai*'s.[5] *Akam* has five *thinai*'s, each corresponding to a landscape: *Kurinchi* is the mountainous region; *Mullai* is the forest; *Marutham* is the field; *Neithal* is the sea and coastal area; *Paalai* is the arid area.[6] Each *thinai* also describes the time (*muthal porul*), fauna and flora (*karu porul*), and the behavior or stages in one's love life (*uri porul*). Behavior (*uri porul*) can be divided into two: union and separation (Mariaselvam 1988, 111). Union is described in *kurinchi thinai*. It is the meeting of lovers, their falling in love, and their sexual union. Separation for different reasons is described in the other *thinai*'s (Selby and Peterson 2008, 26). These indicate that "the poetic world of ancient Tamils is the correspondence between time, place, and human experience" (Murali 1998, 157).

There is a natural relationship between *thinai* and the associated behavior. For example, since *kurinchi thinai* is used to narrate the meeting and union of lovers, it is set in the mountains under the cover of midnight. The mountain affords the much-needed privacy for lovers. In the course of time, this would have become the dominating behavior pattern in this *thinai*. Similarly, the *marutham thinai* is characteristic of agricultural and civilized lifestyle. The wealth in the region gives rise to the "institution of public women," creating mayhem in the family (Meenakshisundaran 1965, 19).

---

[4] Peter Craigie (1979, 172) and Chaim Rabin (1973, 216–17) both have seen a parallel between this transformative tradition and the interpretation history of Song of Songs. The allegorical interpretation looked at Song of Songs as the love between God (bridegroom) and his people (bride). It took something of the human experience and transposed it onto the divine, a parallel to what Bhakthi poetry does. (I acknowledge the assistance by Saundra Lipton from the University of Calgary on acquiring the articles by Chaim Rabin and Peter Craigie.)

[5] This does not mean that all poems can be fitted into a strict taxonomy. There is room for overlap of *thinai*'s—Tinaimayakkam (Ramanujan 2006, 214).

[6] Two more *thinai*'s added later—*kaikilai* (one sided love) and *perunthinai* (love between unequal people) (Varatharasan 1989, 34).

The five landscapes distinguish a man's lifestyle and behavior. The food, profession, and culture are all dependent on the landscape in which he lives (Kaviarasu 2017, 79).[7] As K. Kaviarasu aptly put it, "the mindscape of the man is conditioned by the landscape in which he lives" (79).

*Puram* has seven *thinai*'s. Since *puram* deals with war, most of its *thinai*'s are related to this subject. Capturing the cows of the enemy country to signal the beginning of the war is *vethci*, camping in the enemy country is *vanchi*, attacking the enemy's wall is *ulinchai*, the actual battle is *thumbai*, achieving victory is *vakai*, praise of the victorious king is *paadan*, and describing the transitoriness of life is *kanchi*. When written from a didactic perspective, *kanchi thinai* (the focus of the current study) poems instruct the king about the ephemerality and the uncertainty of life.

*Thinai* is thus related to ecocriticism (study of how nature and the natural world are used in literature). The division of *akam* and *puram*, and their corresponding *thinai*, is based on anthropo-geography[8] and consequently on the behavioral pattern of the inhabitants. A. K. Ramanujan (2011, 241), applying Saussure's semiotic theory of the signified and the signifier to these traditions (see Saussure 2011), concluded that in the "Tamil system of correspondences, a whole language of signs is created by relating the landscapes as signifiers to the *uri porul* or appropriate human feelings."

*Kanchi Thinai*

*Kanchi thinai* expresses the impermanence of life.[9] As the ancient grammar manual Tholkappiyam (76) describes it:

> The corresponding *thinai* for *kanchi* in *akam* is *perunthinai*. *Kanchi thinai* expresses the transitoriness of the world. Impermanence is expressed in terms of Youth, Wealth and Body. (Kesigan 1964, 283)

It is appropriate that this *thinai* is under *puram* (poetry mostly about war). However, it is not described here as a way of encouraging a man to give his life in battle. Rather, it is meant as a bridle on man's desire to conquer the world through war. The world is transitory and so are human beings, including the great kings

---

[7] Since the landscape determines the profession of the person, Nirmal Selvamony (2001) has concluded that this helped to create the Aryan Varna concept—the concept of creating a caste hierarchy based on one's profession.

[8] Thani Nayagam (1953, xv) uses this term in relation to *thinai*-poetics.

[9] *Kanchi thinai*, according to Puraporul Venpaa Maalai, is related to war. Nevertheless, according to Tholkappiyam it relates to the transitoriness of life. The latter work talks about warfare in *kanchi thinai* and moves what Tholkappiyam calls as *kanchi* into Potuvial (Subramanian 1982, 21). However, since Mathurai Kanchi is a much earlier work it adheres to the rules specified in Tholkappiyam and has been classified as such.

on earth. Qoheleth, who claims that he was king in Jerusalem, sees life as meaningless. The meaninglessness is expressed in many aspects of life, which can be interpreted through *puram thinai* categories.

Reading Ecclesiastes as *Kanchi Thinai*

For Ecclesiastes to be read in the light of *akam-puram* conventions, we must not rely on literary devices or even genre, but rather on the subject matter, as *thinai* is part of *porul* in Tamil grammar.[10] The subject matter of Ecclesiastes signals that it pertains to the *kanchi thinai*. Right from the beginning, Qoheleth talks about the transitoriness of life.[11] He goes to great lengths to show that every aspect of life (*puram* life) is meaningless. Because of the "cyclic nature of human existence on the macroscopic level, Qoheleth's world is uniform (1:4–8), unchanging (1:9–10), and therefore predictable" (Frydrych 2002, 15).

Qoheleth does not talk about the *akam* life in the way that the author of Song of Songs does.[12] He occasionally advises the youth to be happy with their wives (9:9). But beyond that, no description of the *akam* life is found in Ecclesiastes.[13]

The tradition of *akam-puram* can be seen in the gender dominance in Song of Songs and Ecclesiastes. In Songs of Songs the unnamed Shulamite woman dominates the scene, and even when the man talks, he talks of her or on her behalf (e.g., Song 4; Longman 2001, 15). In Ecclesiastes, only the voice of the man is heard. The woman is silent.

If Ecclesiastes is to be read in the light of *puram* poetry, a criterion to be satisfied is that there should be proper names. While the name Solomon or any

---

[10] After a detailed analysis of linguistic evidence and literary parallels, Chaim Rabin (1973, 216) suggested that the author of Song of Songs had travelled to South India and was familiar with Tamil poetry. If that indeed was the case, then it is further possible to suggest that the Hebrew poetry was influenced by the *akam-puram* classification, *thinai*-poetics. Songs of Songs may very well pertain to the *akam thinai* and Ecclesiastes to the *puram thinai*. While not excluding this possibility, the scope of the present study is limited to reading Ecclesiastes in the light of Tamil *thinai*-poetics. We apply the classical Tamil *akam-puram* classification, its concepts, and its themes to Ecclesiastes for greater appreciation and analysis of the latter. While Chaim Rabin used a diachronic method, what we have used here is reader-response criticism. Whether the biblical authors were familiar with the classical Tamil poetry is beyond the scope of our present study.
[11] I use *Qoheleth* for the preacher and *Ecclesiastes* for the text.
[12] For a comparison of Song of Songs and Tamil poetry, see the seminal article by Chaim Rabin (1973). See also Peter C. Craigie (1979) and Abraham Mariaselvam (1988).
[13] There are seemingly sinister statements about women (Eccl 7:26, 28), which have led Longman (1998, 206) to conclude that Qoheleth is a misogynist. However, Qoheleth's statements are not made in the context of family, like the ones in Prov 21:9; 27:15; cf. 31:10.

other specific names are not present, the author gives strong indications about who he is or who he is pretending to be:[14]

| | |
|---|---|
| 1:1 | the son of David (*ben-Dawid*), king in Jerusalem. |
| 1:12 | I, the Preacher, have been king over Israel in Jerusalem. |
| 1:16 | I have acquired great wisdom, surpassing all who were over Jerusalem before me. |
| 2:7 | I had also great possessions of herds and flocks, more than any who had been before me in Jerusalem (cf. 2:9). |

These are specific indications of who the author might be. Associating Jerusalem with his identity, the author speaks about a period in which the son of David was the king in Jerusalem. So there is a person, a place, and a period. The presence of these satisfies the condition for it to be analyzed through *puram thinai* categories.

As per the Tholkappiyam formula (76) given above, Qoheleth talks about the transitoriness of life in terms of youth, body, and wealth, making our interpretation more appropriate.

Transitoriness of Youth and Body

Qoheleth talks about the transitoriness of youth and the body (12:1–7). The instruction to remember the creator in the days of youth is vivid and graphic. The images of strong men, grinders, windows, each connoting backbone, teeth and eyes, respectively, are unparalleled in biblical poetry.

Transitoriness of Wealth

Since Qoheleth sees wealth as a result of toil, he expresses their meaninglessness based on four reasons. First, he does not know what kind of man will inherit his wealth, whether a wise man or a fool (2:18). Second, he contrasts someone who has no one to leave anything behind, someone who has neither a son nor a brother (4:8). Third, money is transitory, so he cannot take anything with him (5:15). Here we hear an echo of Job: "naked I came … naked I shall return" (Job 1:21). Fourth, Qoheleth explains that money is meaningless because it never really satisfies (5:11).[15]

---

[14] While the scholars in the precritical era and the early church fathers (e.g., Origen) identified Solomon as the author of Ecclesiastes, modern scholarship has questioned his role. For a discussion, see Bartholomew (2014, 44).

[15] This verse has been interpreted variously, but Longman's explanation as the increase in bills suits the context. As the wealth increases so does the expenses. Therefore, the wealthy person has no real enjoyment in his wealth than to see it pass through his hands (Longman 1998, 165).

## Mathurai Kanchi

The text selected for the present comparison is *Mathurai Kanchi*, which is part of the Sangam anthology *Pathu pattu*.[16] The name derives from its belonging to the *kanchi thinai* (which describes the transitoriness of life). Written by the king's good friend Mankudi Maruthanar, it praises King Pandyan Neduncheliyan and his capital Mathurai, hence the name *Mathurai Kanchi*. It describes the activities of the city during both day and night and serves as a window to life in ancient Tamil Nadu. Containing 782 lines, it is the longest poem in *Pathu pattu*.

The poem starts by portraying the glories of the Pandyan King and his capital. It then elucidates the immortality of life by narrating the life of the kings who ruled in a much older period but who have now perished. It then provides a detailed description of the city during the day and night. The structure of the poem is as follows (Chellia 1985, 277):

| Lines | |
|---|---|
| 1–205 | The glories of King Neduncheliyan and his ancestors |
| 206–237 | Transitoriness of life |
| 238–326 | Description of the fivefold lands |
| 238–270 | Description of *marutham* tract |
| 271–285 | Description of *mullai* tract |
| 286–301 | Description of *kurinchi* tract |
| 302–314 | Description of *paalai* tract |
| 315–326 | Description of *neithal* tract |
| 327–724 | Description of the capital city Mathurai |
| 725–752 | Soldiers' praise of the king |
| 753–782 | The poet's praise of the king and conclusion |

### Ecclesiastes—*Marthurai Kanchi*

The obvious difference between the two texts is the approach in getting the message across. Speaking in first person singular and addressing no one in particular, Qoheleth is outspoken about the meaninglessness of life. He pronounces almost every aspect of life, including the grandeur of a king's life, as meaningless. On the other hand, speaking in third person singular and addressing the king, the Tamil poet has reasons to be subtle. He may fall out of favor with the king if he pronounces the king's pleasure pursuits as pointless. The king's craving for victory must be curbed; however, it can only be done without offending his pride. Thus, the poet takes a very indirect approach.

---

[16] *Pathu pattu* is an anthology of ten ancient poems dating roughly from 500 BCE to 200 CE. Nedunel vadai, another poem in the same *Pathu pattu* anthology, is also about Pandyan Neduncheliyan. Readers may access the present text at https://learnsangamtamil.com/maduraikanchi/.

The Tamil poet sings the glories of the king (lines 1–205). Similarly, Qoheleth proclaims his own achievements (1:1, 12, 16, and 2:7). When a man who has enjoyed everything claims, "it is meaningless," there is more credibility to his claim than that of someone without such an experience. The Tamil poet is well aware that the king has also experienced everything in life. So he talks about the only experience he has not had—death—very subtly by referring to the demise of the great kings of the past (lines 210–237).

Under the Sun and Surrounded by the Sea

The beginning lines describe the land of Mathurai using the sea as the boundary marker: "In this large world, pounded by the large, long and tall waves." The roaring waves make a stunning similarity to the momentariness of life. So much noise but all gone in the very next second. Later in the poem, the poet describes the kings of old who lived life with such grandeur but who are no more, just like the waves. Though the city is magnificent, the sea with waves is a constant reminder that life, even with all its glory, will soon end.

While the Tamil poet demarcates the land as surrounded by the sea, Qoheleth demarcates the land with his oft-repeated phrase "under the sun" (*taḥat hašomeš*). This is the realm in which his observations about life take place. For Qoheleth, the sun is part of the natural cycle that indicates the repetitiveness of life—there is nothing new. The sun is seen as a "marker of time" and a reminder that life is running out (Crenshaw 2013, 70). It is a supreme irony that while the world under the sun is full of light, humans remain in darkness with perplexing questions about the meaning of life (Lohfink 2003, 37).[17] The sun literally pants (*šā'ap*) back to its place (Eccl 1:5), giving the image of an old sun and making a contrast to the youthful sun portrayed in the Psalms (Brown 2000, 45): "The sun, which comes out like a bridegroom leaving his chamber, and, like a strong man, runs its course with joy" (Ps 19:4–6). Overall, the sun signals a life that will soon end, making a parallel to the waves in the Tamil poem.

While the Middle Eastern life is lived under the sun, the south Indian life is lived in the land surrounded by the sea.[18] If the sun indicates the cyclic nature of life, the sea indicates the transitive nature of life. Both speak about the temporal and transitive nature of life.

---

[17] Tomas Frydrych (2002, 45) has seen three spheres in Qoheleth: the sphere of God, the sphere of the living, and the sphere of the dead.

[18] The sea plays a vital role in Tamil thinking, and the land mass is often defined in terms of the sea. This idea is further attested in the same poem in lines 69–70 and 199. As mentioned previously, there is even an *akam thinai* called *neithal*, which narrates life in and around the sea. There is also a legend about the sea engulfing part of Mathurai in prehistoric times.

## A Hedonistic Life

The Tamil poet gives a vivid description about Neduncheliyan's sex life in lines 710–713. The poet describes how the king slept in his palace embracing women who were like peacocks. Their faces were like the lotus flowers found in the ponds of gods, their bodies were like mango tree leaves, and their ears were sagging because of the weight of their gold earrings.

This is the same path of pleasure pursued by Qoheleth: "I got ... many concubines, the delight of the sons of man" (Eccl 2:8). While Qoheleth does not describe the beauty of women because he proclaims the meaninglessness of life directly, the Tamil poet describes them in detail because his approach is indirect and the description of women does not dilute his message.

Qoheleth refers to drinking wine—"I searched with my heart how to cheer my body with wine" (Eccl 2:3; 9:7; 10:19)—and the Tamil poet also refers to drinking liquor many times:

> They (the kings of the ancient times) did not cease drinking toddy (213).
> They emptied huge leather bags of liquor (228).
> In every field, they made toddy
>     under every tree, they slaughtered goats (751).

## Being Happy with One's Wife

Qoheleth instructs young men to be happy with their own wives (9:9). But he does not explain how it is to be done. Proverbs 5:19 may shed further light on Qoheleth's imperative: "Let her breasts fill you at all times with delight; be intoxicated always in her love." How can a woman's breasts fill a man? Another anthology from Sangam literature *Kaliththogai* (*akam thinai*) sheds light on this (Arasu 2012, 167):

> Man has wounds caused by the horns of a killer bull.
> A woman pressed her nipples on the wounds
> And the warmth of the breasts healed the wounds. (106)

However, in *Mathurai Kanchi* it is different: "The prostitutes embrace the men so tightly that the jewels they wear on their bosom causes wounds on the man's chest" (569). Whereas in *akam* poetry the lover's embrace heals the wound, in *Mathurai Kanchi*, written in *puram thinai*, a prostitute's embrace wounds.

The final advice of the Tamil poet (lines 778–782) to drink liquor served in gold cups by women wearing gold jewels, makes a striking parallel to Qoheleth's advice: "Enjoy life with the wife whom you love" (9:9) and "drink your wine with a merry heart" (9:7).

## Preparing for Advice

In preparation for giving advice, the poet shows how the king destroyed the countries that refused to be subject to him. A graphic and gruesome description of war and its aftermath are narrated:

> Countries became forests
> Where there were once cattle
> Now there are wild animals
> Where there was a town
> Now it is all in ruins
> Women with bangles forgot the *Thumangai* dance
> Where there were once halls
> Now demons are dancing
> Where there were young women
> Now widows are crying. (lines 156–166)

While not directly asking the king to give up his quest for war, the poet tries to dissuade the king by showing the negative effects of war. The picture of the city with its crying women will evoke sympathy in the king's mind.

## The Transitive Nature of Life

Following a long praise of the king, the poet comes to the core of *kanchi thinai* in lines 210–237: he describes the glories of the ancient kings who have now perished. By implication, the poet hints that King Neduncheliyan will also perish like his ancestors. Lest King Neduncheliyan think that these were kings of no worth, the poet goes to great lengths to show they were indeed great kings too: the abundance of their food and wealth, the abundance of their generosity (giving gifts to poets was an ancient custom), and how they took tributes from the vassal kings and how they occupied enemy lands, similar to what Pandyan Neduncheliyan had done.

By first narrating the glories of King Neduncheliyan (lines 1–205) and then describing the glories of the bygone kings (lines 206–237), the poet helps the king to identify himself with the celebrated kings of the past. King Neduncheliyan is great and glorious, and so were the kings of the past. They are dead and gone now, and the implication is clear—so will he be. This will therefore teach the transitive nature of life to the king.

The concluding line in this section is probably the most important line linking this poem to *kanchi thinai*: "sand brought to the shores by the ocean waves." The poet makes another reference to the sea to illustrate his point about the transitoriness of life. He describes the number of kings who ruled in the past as greater than the sand brought to the shore by the sea. The poet implies that similar to the sea washing away the sand, time has washed away these kings. Neither the greatness of their life nor their glory enabled them to stay on this earth forever. They are gone and forgotten. This is exactly what is going to happen to Pandyan Neduncheliyan too. Qoheleth has the same message:

> But the dead know nothing, and they have no more reward, for the memory of them is forgotten. Their love and their hate and their envy have already perished, and forever they have no more share in all that is done under the sun. (Eccl 9:5–6)

While not talking particularly about kings, Qoheleth's message is similar to the Tamil poem. The reference to their love, hate, and envy indicates the kind of lives they lived on earth and resembles the description of the greatness of the ancient kings by the Tamil poet. They, the dead, have no share with the living and are forgotten forever.

## Conclusion

Qoheleth and the Tamil poet (through the pursuits of Pandyan Neduncheliyan) have seen the pleasures of life. They come to the same conclusion: it is meaningless, and the world is transitory. The difference is what they do with this knowledge. The concluding lines of the Tamil poem address this concern:

> May you enjoy this good life that has been given to you,
> being served liquor in gold cups by young women
> with glittering ornaments![19]

The poem pertaining to *kanchi thinai*, the purpose of which is to remind the impermanence and the meaninglessness of life, ends by advising the king to enjoy life to the full! This is the supreme irony of the text: it instructs the king to live with the very things it claims are transitory. This is similar to the ideology of Qoheleth as expressed in verses 5:8, 9:7, 9:9, and 11:9.

The transitoriness of life has not caused either of them to endorse an ascetic way of life. Their philosophy seems to be, "life is short, so enjoy as much as you can." However, a stark difference in terms of the Hebraic monotheistic value system must be noted. Ecclesiastes ends with the following note:

> The end of the matter; all has been heard. Fear God and keep his commandments, for this is the whole duty of man. For God will bring every deed into judgment, with every secret thing, whether good or evil. (12:13–14)

Qoheleth brings God into the equation. It is in this light that life's meaning can be found—by living in the presence of a God who expects people to fear and obey

---

[19] "Maduraikanchi," https://learnsangamtamil.com/maduraikanchi/.

him. There are many references to God in Ecclesiastes: creator (3:11), judge (3:17; 11:9; 12:14), giver of life (8:15), transcendent (5:2), someone who gives food and wealth (3:13; 5:19; 6:2), someone to be feared (3:14; 5:7; 8:12–13) and someone to heed (5:1). God is closely associated with humans, rewarding good behavior and punishing bad behavior (2:26; 5:2–6; 8:12–13; 11:9; 12:14). These characteristics of God are meant to mold the behavior of the people. The presence of God makes life meaningful in Ecclesiastes. Without God, life is meaningless. Without holy characteristics, God becomes an idol and human endeavors become idol worship, and Qoheleth labels idols as meaningless: toil, wealth, victory, and liquor. Because God is our creator, the answer to the question of who we are lies in who God is. Biblical ethics is based on theology.

Without such a theology, the Tamil poet resorts to the pleasures of this life. He ends the poem with women, gold, and liquor. There is no presence of a God who demands people to be holy as he is holy (Lev 11:45). While there is similarity in the concluding verse of the Tamil poem and Eccl 9:9, there is also a difference. The Tamil poem ends by asking the king to enjoy life with liquor and *women*, while the Hebrew text ends by asking the young man to enjoy life with his *wife* (9:9). Qoheleth adheres to the biblical system of morals.[20]

In this study we looked at Ecclesiastes in the light of *puram thinai*. Though the *akam-puram thinai*'s were not explicit in Qoheleth's thinking, we have seen his dissatisfaction with the elements that constitute the *puram* life. As we have seen, Qoheleth was describing the *puram* life in most of Ecclesiastes—what happens on the outside. He pronounced almost every area of *puram* life as meaningless. But he hardly spoke anything about the *akam*, family life. The only place Qoheleth refers to the *akam* life, he speaks well of it (9:9). The meaning of life is also to be sought in the *akam* life, in living with and loving one's spouse. The meaning of life is not in seeking glory in the war field, but living with the woman one loves.

## Works Cited

Arasu, V. 2012. *Sangam Literature—Different Reading* [Tamil]. Chennai: Maartu Veliyittagam.

---

[20] Scholars disagree on whether the advice is for a promiscuous or for a family-oriented life, i.e., whether Qoheleth's advice is to be happy with any woman one loves (*'išoh 'ăšer-'āhabtā*) or with one's wife. The absence of the definite article before the word *'išoh* is the strongest argument in favor of the former. However, as Seow (1997, 301) and Bartholomew (2014, 304) both point out, *'išoh* by itself may refer to one's wife—without the definite article—when the context demands it (Gen 30:4, 9; 1 Sam 25:43; Deut 22:22). Moreover, within the context it appears the reference is to a wife: (1) It is a woman one loves (*'āhab*) (2) God approves of it. Qoheleth would not dare to say that Elohim approved of a promiscuous lifestyle.

Bartholomew, Craig. 2014. *Ecclesiastes*. BECNT. Michigan: Baker Academic.
Brown, William. 2000. *Ecclesiastes*. IBC. Louisville: John Knox.
Chellia, J. V. 1985. *PattuPattu, Ten Tamil Idylls*. Tanjavur: Tamil University.
Clark-Decès, Isabelle. 2005. *No One Cries For the Dead: Tamil Dirges, Rowdy Songs, and Graveyard Petitions*. Berkeley: University of California Press.
Craigie, Peter C. 1979. "Biblical and Tamil Poetry: Some Further Reflections." *SR* 8:169–75.
Crenshaw, James. 2013. *Qoheleth: The Ironic Wink*. Columbia: The University of South Carolina Press.
Cutler, Norman. 1987. *Songs of Experience: The Poetics of Tamil Devotion*. Bloomington: Indiana University Press.
Devadevan, Manu V. 2006. "Lying on the Edge of the Burning Ground: Rethinking Tinais." *JESHO* 49: 199–218.
Frydrych, Tomas. 2002. *Living under the Sun*. Leiden: Brill.
Hart III, George L. 1975. *The Poems of Ancient Tamil*. Berkley: University of California Press.
Jesudasan, C., and H. Jesudasan. 1961. *A History of Tamil Literature*. Calcutta: YMCA Publishing House.
Kailasapathy, K. 1968. *Tamil Heroic Poetry*. Oxford: Oxford University Press.
Kaviarasu K. 2017. "Tinaipoetics: An Ecopoetics of South India." *Literary Studies* 30:76–82.
Kesigan, Puliyur. 1964. *Tolkappiyam Thelivurai* [Tamil]. Chennai: Paari Nelayyam.
Lohfink, Nobert. 2003. *Qoheleth*. Translated by Sean McEvenue. CC. Minneapolis: Fortress.
Longman, Tremper. 1998. *Ecclesiastes*. NICOT. Grand Rapids: Eerdmans.
———. 2001. *Song of Songs*. NICOT. Grand Rapids: Eerdmans.
Mahadevan, Iravatham. 2010. "'*Akam and Puram: 'Address' Signs of the Indus Script*." http://rmrl.in/?page_id=1044.
Mariaselvam, Abraham. 1988. *The Song of Songs and Ancient Tamil Love Poems: Poetry and Symbolism*. Rome: Pontifical Biblical Institute.
Meenakshisundaran, T. P. 1965. *History of Tamil Literature*. Annamalainagar: Annamalai University.
Murali, S. 1998. "Environmental Aesthetics Interpretation of Nature in 'Akam' and 'Puram' Poetry." *Indian Literature* 42.3:155–62.
Nabokov, Isabelle. 2000. *Religion against the Self: An Ethnography of Tamil Rituals*. Oxford: Oxford University Press.
Parthasarathy, R. 1994. "Classical Tamil Poetry and Tamil Poetics." Pages 66–77 in *Masterworks of Asian Literature in Comparative Perspective: A Guide for Teaching*. Edited by Barbara Stoler Miller. Columbia Project on Asia in the Core Curriculum. Armonk, N.Y: M.E. Sharpe.
Rabin, Chaim. 1973. "The Song of Songs and Tamil Poetry." *SR* 3:205–19.

Ramanujam, A. K. 2006. *The Collected Essays of A K Ramanujam*. Edited by Vinay Dharwadker. New Delhi: Oxford University Press.

———. *Poems of Love and War: From the Eight Anthologies and the Ten Long Poems of Classical Tamil*. New York: Columbia University Press, 2011.

———. 2014. *The Interior Landscape*. New York: NYRB.

Saminathaiyar, V. 1986. *Pathupattu Original and Commentary by Nachinarkiniyar* [Tamil]. Tanjavur: Tamil University.

Saussure, Ferdinand de. 2011. *Course in General Linguistics*. New York: Columbia University Press.

Selby, Martha Ann, and Indira Viswanathan Peterson, eds. 2008. *Tamil Geographies: Cultural Constructions of Space and Place in South India*. Albany: SUNY Press.

Selvamony, Nirmal. 2001. "Oikopoetics and Tamil Poetry." *Tinai 1*. Chennai: Persons for Alternative Social Order.

Seow, C. Leong. 1997. *Ecclesiastes*. AB. New Haven: Yale University Press.

Shulman, David. 2001. *The Wisdom of Poets*. Oxford: Oxford University Press.

Sivatham, K. 1974. "Early South Indian Society and Economy: The Tinai Concept." *Social Scientist* 3:20–37.

Subramanian, S. V. 1982. *Studies in Tamilology*. Madras: Tamil Patippakam.

Subrahmanian, K. 1977. "Love and Landscape Equation in Tamil Poetry." *The British Journal of Aesthetics* 17:365–67.

Thani Nayagam, X. S. 1953. *Nature in Ancient Tamil Poetry*. Tuticorin: Tamil Literature Society.

Trawick, Margaret. 1990. *Notes on Love in a Tamil Family*. Berkeley: University of California Press.

Varatharasan, M. 1989. *History of Tamil Literature* [Tamil]. Mumbai: Sakithya Academy.

Zvelebil, Kamil. 1974. *The Tamil Literature*. Wiesbaden: Otto Harrassowitz.

# A COMPARATIVE ANALYSIS OF THE PHILOSOPHIES OF QOHELETH AND CHUANG-TZU: SHARED THEMES IN WISDOM LITERATURE AND TAOIST PHILOSOPHY

Sehee Kim

In the book of Ecclesiastes, Qoheleth starts his teachings with the well-known utterance, "Vanity of vanities, all is vanity."[1] He repeats this phrase (with variations) throughout his teachings to imprint this motto on his readers. This overtone in Qoheleth's teachings might be somewhat confusing for readers who expect to learn how to live their daily lives wisely from the wisdom literature. However, Qoheleth's realistic approach could be soothing for readers who are either experiencing a disoriented period of any sort in their lives or who have ever thought about this world in a skeptical or pessimistic way.

Skepticism in wisdom literature had already been in existence long before Qoheleth's teachings in the ancient Near East and, in fact, seems to have existed universally in the Asian world as well.[2] This chapter compares the texts of

---

[1] *Hebel* has various connotations in the Hebrew Bible: "breath/vapour, idols, worthless/false, no purposes/useless, futile, nothing/empty, fleeting, deceptive in appearance" (Christianson 1998, 79-80). While this word can connote positive or negative meanings, in most of the occurrences *hebel* has a negative meaning (80). Michael V. Fox (1999, 27–50) translates *hebel* as "absurdity" because he believes that in Qoheleth's theology, the meaning of *hebel* is a literary device to challenge God about the irrationality of worldly affairs rather than simply a complaint about nothingness. I partially agree with his notion, especially when Qoheleth raises questions about the inequality, unfairness, and injustice in the world. This chapter uses the classic translation of "vanity" for *hebel* because it connotes the widest range of this Hebrew word, including Fox's concept of absurdity as one of the negative aspects of *hebel*.

[2] Recently, it has been debated whether wisdom literature is a valid category in the Hebrew Bible; some contend that the origin of this term is vague and uncertain (see, e.g., Kynes 2018). This chapter uses the traditional categorization of wisdom literature in which

Chuang-tzu, one of the most significant philosophers in ancient China, to Qoheleth's teachings. The two have strikingly similar, analogous concepts on many themes, such as living, working, wisdom, power, and death.

## Qoheleth in Wisdom Literature

*Ecclesiastes* is the Latinized version of the Greek translation of the original Hebrew name of this book in the Hebrew Bible. The original name of this text was Qoheleth, which is best translated as "collector or preacher" (BDB 875) in English. Due to its lack of basic theological elements that other parts of the Bible address, such as revelation, salvation, or divine teachings, it was disputed for some time whether this text should be considered orthodox.[3] However, Qoheleth was included in the biblical canons of both Judaism and Christianity, and scholars agree that this can be largely attributed to the appendix at the end of the book (12:9–14), whose general tone make the book of Ecclesiastes more orthodox.

The book of Ecclesiastes dates roughly from the second half of the fifth and the first half of the second centuries BCE in Palestine, based on linguistic grounds: two Persian loan words, "grove" (*pardēs* 2:5) and "sentence" (*pitgām* 8:11), indicate that the text dates after the postexilic period, and the terminal date for its composition is set by the reference to the text in Sirach, which was written in the first half of the second century BCE (Machinist 2004, 1605).[4]

The Hebrew noun *ḥokma* ("wisdom") occurs twenty-eight times in the book, and other nouns and verbs related to wisdom appear twenty-four times, showing that Qoheleth paid much attention to wisdom. This interest, however, is developed in unconventional ways in his teachings. He often gives a twofold evaluation of the themes he raises, such as life, wisdom, labor, power, judgment, and death. Looking into the dynamic that each theme has in the teachings is worthwhile because these tensions and contradictions are one of the key points that reveal Qoheleth's theology.

---

Ecclesiastes is a primary member of this genre, along with Proverbs and Job, without disregarding the significance of this recent debate. Examples of skeptical and pessimistic texts in ancient Near Eastern literature are "The Admonitions of Ipuwer," "The Instruction of King Amenemhet I," "The Complaints of Khakheperre-Sonb," "The Babylonian Theodicy," and "The Sumerian Job," which were composed from the third to the second millennia BCE (Sneed 2012, 44–45).

[3] The dispute regarding whether the text was orthodox continued for a while; for instance, Theodore of Mopsuestia, a bishop of Antioch in the fifth century CE, rejected the canonization of Qoheleth, insisting that the book was not inspired by the divine (Seow 1997, 4).

[4] It is impossible to assign exact dates to this book based on current evidence. It is now generally agreed that the date of Sirach is the *terminus ad quem* for this book and that nothing more can be determined. Scholars have suggested possible initial dates ranging from the second half of the third century BCE to the first half of the second century BCE, but all of these proposals are tenuous (see Krüger 2004, 19; Whitley 1979, 132–48).

## Chuang-tzu in Taoist Philosophy

Not much is known about the life of Chuang-tzu (莊周: ca. 369–286 BCE) except what is given in *The Grand Scribe's Records*, written by historian Ssu-ma Ch'ien (145 or 135 to 86 BCE). According to his account, Chuang-tzu was born into a poor family and served as a superintendent in a lacquer garden when he was young. One of the most famous anecdotes about Chuang-tzu is that he declined the offer by King Wei of Chu (370–319 BCE) to serve as prime minister (Sorajakool 2009, 17). Instead, he seems to have lived his life as a recluse, interacting with farmers, fishermen, woodsmen, and nature itself.

Chuang-tzu lived during the Warring States Period, which lasted from approximately 475 BCE to the unification of China under the Qin Dynasty in 221 BCE. It was a time of transition, uncertainty, and divergence because of ceaseless conflicts and wars in the country. In this time of confusion, the Hundred Schools of Philosophy (諸子百家) began to flourish in China; these schools sought to understand the ultimate structure of reality and bring about harmony in all spheres of human action amidst constant change. Chuang-tzu developed the philosophies of Taoism (道家), already established by Lao-tzu (老子: d. 531 BCE), in unconventional but profound ways. That is, Chuang-tzu focused on the equality and unity in nature and the universe, whereas Lao-tzu aimed at recovering and reforming social and moral rules. Their writing styles were also very different—Chuang-tzu used a number of allegorical and metaphorical devices to express his thoughts, but Lao-tzu employed brief but dense words to emphasize his main focuses (Höchsmann 2001, 4–8).

The present form of *The Complete Chuang-tzu* is regarded as having been compiled by Liu An in 122 BCE during the Han Dynasty and later edited by Kuo Hsiang, a neo-Taoist, around 300 CE. Kuo Hsiang divided the book into thirty-three chapters and grouped them into three categories. The first seven chapters are "inner chapters," which are believed to have been written by Chuang-tzu or his immediate followers. The next fifteen chapters, or "outer chapters," and the rest of the book, the "miscellaneous chapters," are believed to have been written by editors or commentators seeking to expand the compilation of Chuang-tzu's writings (Zhuangzi 1998, xv).

## Shared Themes in Qoheleth's and Chuang-tzu's Writings

### Attitude toward Life

Basically, both Qoheleth and Chuang-tzu argue that there are not many things that humans can control in their lives.[5] Instead, much of life is actually dependent on

---

[5] In this paper, the English translations of verses from Ecclesiastes are all from the ESV's 2016 translation. The English translations of Chuang-tzu's writings are from Watson's

heaven and the laws of nature.

> I have seen everything that is done under the sun, and behold, all is vanity and a striving after wind. What is crooked cannot be made straight, and what is lacking cannot be counted. I said in my heart, "I have acquired great wisdom, surpassing all who were over Jerusalem before me, and my heart has had great experience of wisdom and knowledge." (Eccl 1:14–16)

> Be not overly righteous, and do not make yourself too wise. Why should you destroy yourself? Be not overly wicked, neither be a fool. Why should you die before your time? (Eccl 7:16–17)

> To know what you can't do anything about and to be content with it as you would with fate—only a man of virtue can do that. (The Sign of Virtue Complete [Zhuangzi 2013, 36])

> Life and death are fated—constant as the succession of dark and dawn, a matter of Heaven. There are some things that man can do nothing about—all are a matter of the nature of creatures. (The Great and Venerable Teacher [Zhuangzi 2013, 44])

Beginning his teachings with deep laments on the vanity of human lives, Qoheleth supports this idea by explaining how incapable humans are in dealing with issues great and small over their lifetime. That is, we are only human, so we cannot make straight or subversively change what God has made crooked for any reason (see Eccl 7:13). Therefore, Qoheleth confidently gives his audience an insightful tip because he has already experienced all the issues in the world and has realized their emptiness and unfairness. The advice is to know one's limits and live within those boundaries. We do not have to be overly righteous or overly wicked because the former would make our lives too harsh and the latter too vulnerable. Living moderately, at least, will keep us safe—neither overly cautious nor overly risky.

Chuang-tzu expresses a similar general idea about the appropriate attitude toward life. Realizing that we cannot do anything in terms of various issues that come up in our lives is the first and foremost thing we can do to follow the Tao (道). Tao means "the way," and its Chinese character is a combination of the symbols for "head" (首) and "to go" (之), which leads to the meaning of "the direction" or "the prescribed way" (Höchsmann 2007, 29). The origin of Tao is uncertain, but it is considered the beginning of heaven and earth itself, which is the origin of all created beings. The Tao, too, is not obtained by human efforts—Taoism tells us that we should leave everything as it is because Tao means not

---

translation (Zhuangzi 2013) and Mair's translation (Chuang Tzu 1998). The Chinese characters in *Chuang-tzu* are from Kim's translation (Zhuangzi 2015).

doing anything. However, this does not mean that the Tao itself does not do anything because the Tao "does everything by doing nothing" (Chuang-tzu 1989, 8).

Wisdom

Both texts manifest a twofold attitude toward the evolution of wisdom. On the one hand, it is unnecessary for people to try to earn it with great effort because that also is vanity and like chasing the wind. On the other hand, Qoheleth and Chuang-tzu agree that wisdom is very much better than foolishness.

> For in much wisdom is much vexation, and he who increases knowledge increases sorrow. (Eccl 1:18)

> For what advantage has the wise man over the fool? And what does the poor man have who knows how to conduct himself before the living? (Eccl 6:8)

> Who is like the wise? And who knows the interpretation of a thing? A man's wisdom makes his face shine, and the hardness of his face is changed. (Eccl 8:1)

> Your life has a limit, but knowledge has none. If you use what is limited to pursue what has no limit, you will be in danger. If you understand this and still strive for knowledge, you will be in danger for certain! (The Secret Caring for Life [Zhuangzi 2013, 19])

> Great understanding is broad and unhurried; little understanding is cramped and busy. Great words are clear and limpid; little words are shrill and quarrelsome. (Discussion on Making All Things Equal [Zhuangzi 2013, 8])

Qoheleth's negative attitude toward wisdom (e.g., Eccl 1:13–18; 2:1–11) is new in the Hebrew Bible. Although wisdom literature emphasizes the extreme difficulty of achieving wisdom, it has always been considered a great virtue for humans to pursue throughout their lifetime. Biblical authors praise wisdom and describe it as more precious than jewels (e.g., Job 28; Pss 37; 49; 111; Prov 3:13–18; 8:1–21). Qoheleth's pessimistic view concerning the seeking of wisdom does not derive from the assumption that wisdom has no worth. He is well aware of the priceless value of wisdom, but some things that happen in our lives are beyond our ability to understand (Fox 1999, 88). In addition, no matter how much wisdom we possess, we still do not know what is to be, for nobody can tell us how it will be (Eccl 8:7). Because Qoheleth recognizes that wisdom is critical but is also "vanity," he inclines toward ignorance, although he both affirms and rejects the value of wisdom (Fox 1999, 93).

Chuang-tzu's notions about wisdom are similar to those of Qoheleth. To Chuang-tzu, wisdom is also far more precious than ignorance. However, he believes that the process involved in earning it is too long and painful to be accomplished in the short human life span. Although we may try hard to obtain it throughout our lifetime, it is almost impossible to attain the master level of wisdom. Wisdom has no limit, so we are sure to be overwhelmed by its limitless nature. Also, this becomes more complicated when we examine the quality of wisdom.

Both Qoheleth and Chuang-tzu have an extremely high standard for wisdom, and they argue that when we obtain a small amount of wisdom, not the level of a master, we are actually placing ourselves at risk. These two philosophers do not put wisdom in the category of the more, the better. In fact, if we do not achieve the master's level of wisdom, we will be in danger due to our incomplete knowledge.

Labor

Both of these great thinkers, Qoheleth and Chuang-tzu, hold an unfavorable view of labor. Perhaps most humans would agree with them on some of their points.

> And I applied my heart to seek and to search out by wisdom all that is done under heaven. It is an unhappy business that God has given to the children of man to be busy with. (Eccl 1:13)

> I hated all my toil in which I toil under the sun, seeing that I must leave it to the man who will come after me, and who knows whether he will be wise or a fool? Yet he will be master of all for which I toiled and used my wisdom under the sun. This also is vanity. (Eccl 2:18–19)

> What gain has the worker from his toil? I have seen the business that God has given to the children of man to be busy with. (Eccl 3:9–10)

> That which all under heaven [天下] respect is wealth, honor, longevity, and a good name; that which they take joy in is security for their persons, rich flavors, beautiful clothes, pretty sights, and agreeable sounds; that which they look down on is poverty, meanness, premature death, and a bad name; that which they find distasteful is getting no ease for their persons, no rich flavors for their mouths, no beautiful clothes for their bodies, no pretty sights for their eyes, and no agreeable sounds for their ears. If they do not get these things, they become greatly troubled and frightened. Is it not foolish how this is all for the body? (Ultimate Joy [Chuang Tzu 1998, 166–67])

> The Great Clod burdens me with form, labors me with life, eases me in old age, and rests me in death. So if I think well of my life, for the same reason I must think well of my death. (The Great and Venerable Teacher [Zhuangzi 2013, 44])

> Once a man receives this fixed bodily form, he holds on to it, waiting for the end. Sometimes clashing with things, sometimes bending before them, he runs his

course like a galloping steed, and nothing can stop him. Is he not pathetic? Sweating and laboring to the end of his days and never seeing his accomplishment, utterly exhausting himself and never knowing where to look for rest—can you help pitying him? I'm not dead yet! he says, but what good is that? His body decays, his mind follows it—can you deny that this is a great sorrow? Man's life has always been a muddle like this. How could I be the only muddled one, and other men not muddled? (Discussion on Making All Things Equal [Zhuangzi 2013, 9])

To Qoheleth, labor is comprised of obligation, pleasure, pain, frustration, and, once again, vanity. People should labor in any kind of format to sustain their daily lives. The motivation for labor that Qoheleth finds has two possibilities: one can undertake it under either one's own or God's initiative (Eccl 1:13). God has commissioned us to explore what our occupation should be under heaven (Krüger 2004, 63), and we can choose what to do to sustain our lives. Undoubtedly, toil is not always exciting, but Qoheleth finds it has some rewards: "everyone should eat and drink and take pleasure in all his toil—this is God's gift to man" (Eccl 3:13). What then is the problem? Why is labor also absurdity and vanity, like chasing the wind?

The problem occurs when the consequences are not rational or appropriate. For instance, some people may have to give to others the products of their labor, or some may be able take advantage of others unfairly (Eccl 8:14; 9:2). This irrationality is often not compensated for by one's sense of accomplishment or enjoyment of the task—that is not sufficient (Fox 1998, 228). In addition, Qoheleth distinguishes clearly between the "portion" (*ḥēleq*) and the "profit" (*yitrôn*) of labor. He defines eating, drinking, and pleasure (Eccl 5:18; 8:15) as the gifts of a benevolent God to human beings. The portion is the reasonable reward from above for humans' labor, which means it is not dependent on human ability (Krüger 2004, 3). Profit is in addition to the portion. It is the "surplus of a transaction, hence additional value" (Seow 1997, 103–4) that remains at a person's disposal. When Qoheleth thinks about the goodness of labor, the designated portion is not good enough—he desires that work should be profitable, although he accepts the portion as a gift from God.

Chuang-tzu's view of labor is even more pessimistic than Qoheleth's. To him, sweating and laboring are merely exhausting and rarely lead to remarkable results. Interestingly, when Chuang-tzu mentions labor, he uses the same expression, "under heaven" (天下), that Qoheleth uses (the three instances are Eccl 1:13; 2:3; 3:1). Qoheleth uses the idiom "under the sun" more often in his teachings, which has the same meaning as "under heaven." Seow (1997, 105) proposes that this term be interpreted as "this world or the realm of the living," which is opposed to "the netherworld or the resting place with the shades."

In this world, however, Chuang-tzu attempts again to transcend labor and its associated consequences. Instead, he chooses to be free from all earthly desires such as wealth, honor, good food, or beautiful clothes, which humans universally need for their comfort and entertainment. He argues that when we are obsessed with possessions, it is painful when we are not able to obtain what we want. If we are beyond desire and greed from the start, we may not have to deal with an inner struggle and will in the end attain peace of mind.

Power

Qoheleth and Chuang-tzu are consistently opposed to the human desire for power. If they did not care for work but longed for power, readers might have been greatly disappointed with their argument.

> Again I saw all the oppressions that are done under the sun. And behold, the tears of the oppressed, and they had no one to comfort them! On the side of their oppressors there was power, and there was no one to comfort them. (Eccl 4:1)

> Better was a poor and wise youth than an old and foolish king who no longer knew how to take advice. For he went from prison to the throne, though in his own kingdom he had been born poor. I saw all the living who move about under the sun, along with that youth who was to stand in the king's place. There was no end of all the people, all of whom he led. Yet those who come later will not rejoice in him. Surely this also is vanity and a striving after wind. (Eccl 4:13–16)

> All this I observed while applying my heart to all that is done under the sun, when man had power over man to his hurt. (Eccl 8:9)

> Once, when Zhuangzi was fishing in the Pu River, the king of Chu sent two officials to go and announce to him: "I would like to trouble you with the administration of my realm." Zhuangzi held on to the fishing pole and, without turning his head, said, "I have heard that there is a sacred tortoise in Chu that has been dead for three thousand years. The king keeps it wrapped in cloth and boxed, and stores it in the ancestral temple. Now would this tortoise rather be dead and have its bones left behind and honored? Or would it rather be alive and dragging its tail in the mud?" "It would rather be alive and dragging its tail in the mud," said the two officials. Zhuangzi said, "Go away! I'll drag my tail in the mud!" (Autumn Floods [Zhuangzi 2013, 137])

Qoheleth states that he had been a king and had obtained great power, wealth, and advantage (Eccl 1:1–2:9). At last, however, he realized that all sorts of authority cannot be redeemed from absurdity. His critical view of power and dominion is based on two phenomena. The first is that even a king may be foolish when compared with a wise but poor young man (Eccl 4:13). Although Qoheleth says that all that we pursue in life is vanity, without question he ranks wisdom highly among the virtues he introduces. For him, wisdom without power is better than power without wisdom, regardless how much power one has. The second phenomenon is that, in many cases, rulers do not care much about social justice or the welfare of their people (Eccl 4:1; 5:8; 10:16). They are more concerned with their own pleasure, which goes beyond what they need (Krüger 2014, 4). If men of power and influence do not pay attention to their people, do they make a contribution to God and God's people?

Chuang-tzu's story of his rejection of the offer to be an administrator in the Chu Dynasty illustrates very well his indifference to power and dominion. He instead chooses to pursue freedom by interacting with nature and following the Tao (道). The portrayal of a fisherman that he uses in this anecdote is noteworthy in its literary connotations and insights. Kirill Ole Thompson (1998, 15–16) describes why the metaphor of a fisherman is well suited to Chuang-tzu's philosophical purpose: "(1) their cultivation is not an artificial regimen, nor is it ascendant in nature—it consists in the very process of their apprenticeship and work as fishermen and proceeds as a gradual deepening of their experience of rivers, lakes, and seas; (2) their realization and insight occur out of their daily interaction with and contemplation of rivers, lakes, and seas—their realization arises spontaneously through their direct experience of these waters, as limpid manifestations of *dao*." Chuang-tzu's portrayal of fishermen has inspired Chinese poets, painters, and readers to recast their images over and over again, resonating with the deep meaning that the great philosopher had in his mind when he portrayed them (15).

Judgment

Both Qoheleth and Chuang-tzu point out that worldly issues are confusing and challenging to judge. Whether we want to or not, we often judge and are judged by each other, and the results are unfair and questionable.

> In my vain life I have seen everything. There is a righteous man who perishes in his righteousness, and there is a wicked man who prolongs his life in his evildoing. (Eccl 7:15)

> But all this I laid to heart, examining it all, how the righteous and the wise and their deeds are in the hand of God. Whether it is love or hate, man does not know; both are before him. It is the same for all, since the same event happens to the righteous and the wicked, to the good and the evil, to the clean and the unclean, to him who sacrifices and him who does not sacrifice. As the good one is, so is the sinner, and he who swears is as he who shuns an oath. (Eccl 9:1–2)

> Moreover, I saw under the sun that in the place of justice, even there was wickedness, and in the place of righteousness, even there was wickedness. I said in my heart, God will judge the righteous and the wicked, for there is a time for every matter and for every work. (Eccl 3:16–17)

> The end of the matter; all has been heard. Fear God and keep his commandments, for this is the whole duty of man. For God will bring every deed into judgment, with every secret thing, whether good or evil. (Eccl 12:13–14)

> Suppose that you and I have a dispute. If you beat me and I lose to you, does that mean you're really right and I'm really wrong? If I beat you and you lose to me, does that mean I'm really right and you're really wrong? Is one of us right and the other wrong? Or are both of us right and both of us wrong? Neither you nor I can know, and others are even more in the dark. Whom shall we have decide the matter? Shall we have someone who agrees with you decide it? Since he agrees with you, how can he decide fairly? Shall we have someone who agrees with me decide it? Since he agrees with me, how can he decide fairly? Shall we have someone who differs with both of us decide it? Since he differs with both of us, how can he make a decision? Shall we have someone who agrees with both of us decide it? Since he agrees with both of us, how can he make a decision? Given that neither you nor I, nor another person, can know how to decide, shall we wait for still another? (On the Equality of Things [Chuang Tzu 1998, 23])

> It is easy to keep from walking; the hard thing is to walk without touching the ground. It is easy to cheat when you work for men, but hard to cheat when you work for Heaven [天]. You have heard of flying with wings, but you have never heard of flying without wings. You have heard of the knowledge that knows, but you have never heard of the knowledge that does not know. Look into that closed room, the empty chamber where brightness is born! Fortune and blessing gather where there is stillness. But if you do not keep still—this is what is called sitting but racing around. Let your ears and eyes communicate with what is inside and put mind and knowledge on the outside. Then even gods and spirits will come to dwell, not to speak of men! (In the World of Men [Zhuangzi 2013, 25])

Qoheleth judges himself to be a wise man and seems to be able to distinguish between good and evil, even though he does not offer any concrete examples. However, knowing the difference between good and evil is not enough because in many situations the world does not reward virtue and punish vice. That is, evildoers who should be punished flourish instead, whereas the righteous decline and perish unjustly (Eccl 7:15; 9:1–2). We cannot help but witness this absurdity repeatedly. As mortals, it is impractical to judge all the wicked and correct what is unfair—only God can do that. In the midst of uncertainty, Qoheleth has strong faith that God will judge people at some time, even though he does not know when that will happen.[6]

---

[6] Seow (1997, 175) argues that the expression "God will judge" in verse 17 does not need to be an eschatological judgment. According to Seow, Qoheleth is not certain about the time of God's judgment, although he is convinced that the future of humans belongs to God.

Chuang-tzu's notion of judgment starts with the basic issue that humans cannot even distinguish right and wrong. First, he says, it is impossible to judge each other. It is unfair to decide who is right and who is wrong because every individual has a different standard of judgment. If we bring a third person to decide between two persons, will it be correct and just? Chuang-tzu suspects the third person's ruling will not be correct and just because it is hard to be perfectly objective in judging between two persons, so the third person might be biased and decide in favor of one person over the other. It is intriguing that Chuang-tzu mentions that heaven (天) is omnipotent and can never be cheated by humans. That is, it is impossible to deceive heaven, and even though we try, our dishonesty will surely be revealed in the future. Human judgment, however, is not always trustworthy.

## Death

Qoheleth and Chuang-tzu are very comfortable bringing up the issue of death. Actually, they speak favorably about the end of life.

> All go to one place. All are from the dust, and to dust all return. (Eccl 3:20)

> Again I saw all the oppressions that are done under the sun. And behold, the tears of the oppressed, and they had no one to comfort them! On the side of their oppressors there was power, and there was no one to comfort them. And I thought the dead who are already dead more fortunate than the living who are still alive. But better than both is he who has not yet been and has not seen the evil deeds that are done under the sun. (Eccl 4:1–3)

> A good name is better than precious ointment, and the day of death than the day of birth. It is better to go to the house of mourning than to go to the house of feasting, for this is the end of all mankind, and the living will lay it to heart. Sorrow is better than laughter, for by sadness of face the heart is made glad. The heart of the wise is in the house of mourning, but the heart of fools is in the house of mirth. (Eccl 7:1–4)

> Zhuangzi's wife died. When Huizi went to convey his condolences, he found Zhuangzi sitting with his legs sprawled out, pounding on a tub and singing. "You lived with her, she brought up your children and grew old," said Huizi. "It should be enough simply not to weep at her death. But pounding on a tub and singing—this is going too far, isn't it?" Zhuangzi said, "You're wrong. When she first died, do you think I didn't grieve like anyone else? But I looked back to her beginning and the time before she was born. Not only the time before she was born, but the time before she had a body. Not only the time before she had a body, but the time before she had a spirit. In the midst of the jumble of wonder and mystery, a change took place and she had a spirit. Another change and she had a body. Another change and she was born. Now there's been another change and she's dead. It's just like the progression of the four seasons: spring, summer, fall, winter.

Now she's going to lie down peacefully in a vast room. If I were to follow after her bawling and sobbing, it would show that I don't understand anything about fate. So I stopped. (Supreme Happiness [Zhuangzi 2013, 140])

"Such men as they," said Confucius, "wander beyond the realm; men like me wander within it. Beyond and within can never meet. It was stupid of me to send you to offer condolences. Even now they have joined with the creator as men to wander in the single breath of heaven and earth. They look on life as a swelling tumor, a protruding wen [boil], and on death as the draining of a sore or the bursting of a boil." (The Great and Venerable Teacher [Zhuangzi 2013, 50])

Regarding the end of life, Qoheleth takes a submissive attitude toward God. Death comes at the time God appoints for each person—death is just one of the countless appointed times for the human, and we have no choice but to admit this (3:1–8). Some people have shorter lives and others have longer lives—it is a matter of our life span, and we all die at some point. In Qoheleth's teachings about death, he does not use words describing the emotions of fear, anxiety, sorrow, solitude, grief, or mourning. Death is the one of the rare things that happens to all humans equally—people eventually die no matter how much effort they put into defying it.

Chuang-tzu even praises death. He sings a song at his wife's funeral; this sort of attitude is far from the traditional manner of those suffering from the death of loved ones. The reason he does so, he explains, is that his wife's death is as natural as the coming and going of the seasons, so he does not need to feel sorrow. Everything in the universe has Tao, and it can be "sublime and humble, minute and titanic" (Höchsmann 2001, 21). As Eske Møllgaard (2007, 22) puts it, "Things complete and destruct, but the Way, which is the movement of this completion and destruction, does not itself complete and destruct. Like Heaven, the Way is the transcendental life that gives life to the living but does not itself live and die." Therefore, the end of one's life does not mean the end of one's Tao—Chuang-tzu's wife, who also contains Tao, can be transformed into another form in the flow of Tao, as she was when she was born as a human being.

## Implications: Possible Meanings of Meaninglessness

In the end, Qoheleth concludes with the motto of his teachings once again: "Vanity of vanities, says the Preacher; all is vanity" (Eccl 12:8). As we have seen above, *hebel* connotes a wide range of meanings that originate in neutral points and expand to negative meanings. It connotes sighs, mourning, and complaints in regard to all kinds of issues that we face in our daily lives. It has become a versatile concept for Qoheleth to express not only his philosophy but also his emotions regarding various matters and their consequences.

Qoheleth's *hebel* can be compared to the concept of 無 (*wú*) in the philosophy of Chuang-tzu. This is a similar concept to *hebel* in that its primary meaning is the neutral concept of nothing, but it can be developed to incorporate negative meanings. The main motto of Chuang-tzu's philosophy is 無爲自然, which means "to do nothing and to follow the way of nature." This is not to be interpreted literally—it is more like an ideal conception of living one's life in the way of nature without the artificial interventions of human beings.

Both of these great philosophers are skeptical about the meaning of worldly affairs, but they admit that it is hard to be indifferent to all the issues going on around them. Their skepticism toward life is the base point, the essential attitude, and the device that connects the alpha and the omega in their philosophies. Qoheleth and Chuang-tzu do not stop when they find out that everything we do or do not do might be meaningless. Rather, they start searching for the meaning of meaninglessness through the realization that we are merely human beings and hence should be humble to our God and to mother nature.

## Works Cited

Anderson, William H. U. 1997. *Qoheleth and Its Pessimistic Theology: Hermeneutical Struggles in Wisdom Literature.* Lewiston, NY: Mellen Biblical.

Christianson, Eric S. 1998. *A Time to Tell.* Malden, Sheffield: Sheffield Academic.

Chuang Tzu. 1998. *Wandering on the Way: Early Taoist Tales and Parables of Chuang Tzu.* Translated by Victor H. Mair. Honolulu: University of Hawai'i Press.

Chuang-tzu. 1989. *Chuang-tzu: A New Selected Translation with an Exposition of the Philosophy of Kuo Hsiang.* Translated by Yu-lan Fung. Beijing: Foreign Languages Press.

Fox, Michael V. 1998. "The Inner Structure of Qohelet's Thought." Pages 225–38 in *Qohelet in the Context of Wisdom.* Edited by A. Schoors. Leuven, Belgium: Leuven University Press

———. 1999. *A Time to Tear Down and a Time to Build Up: A Rereading of Ecclesiastes.* Grand Rapids, MI: Eerdmans.

Höchsmann, Hyun. 2001. *On Chuang Tzu.* Belmont, CA: Wadsworth.

———. 2007. *Zhuangzi.* New York: Pearson Longman.

Krüger, Thomas. 2004. *Qoheleth: A Commentary.* Edited by Klaus Baltzer. Translated by O. C. Dean Jr. Minneapolis: Fortress.

Kynes, Will. 2018. "The 'Wisdom Literature' Category: An Obituary." *JTS* 69:1–24.

Machinist, Peter. 2004. "Ecclesiastes: Introduction." Pages 1603–6 in *The Jewish Study Bible.* Oxford: Oxford University Press.

Møllgaard, Eske. 2007. *An Introduction to Daoist Thought: Action, Language, and Ethics in Zhuangzi.* London: Routledge.

Seow, Choon-Leong. 1997. *Ecclesiastes: A New Translation with Introduction and Commentary*. New York: Doubleday.

Sneed, Mark R. 2012. *The Politics of Pessimism in Ecclesiastes: A Social-Science Perspective*. Atlanta: Society of Biblical Literature.

Sorajjakool, Siroj. 2009. *Do Nothing: Inner Peace for Everyday Living: Reflections on Chuang Tzu's Philosophy*. West Conshohocken, PA: Templeton Foundation.

Thompson, Kirill Ole. 1998. "'What Is the Reason of Failure or Success? The Fisherman's Song Goes Deep into the River' in Fishermen in the Zhuangzi." Pages 15–34 in *Wandering at Ease in the Zhuangzi*. Edited by Roger T. Ames. Albany: State University of New York Press.

Whitley, Charles Francis. 1979. *Koheleth: His Language and Thought*. Berlin; New York: de Gruyter.

Zhuangzi. 1998. *The Essential Chuang Tzu*. Translated by Sam Hamill and J. P. Seaton. Boston: Shambhala.

———. 2013. *The Complete Works of Zhuangzi*. Translated by Burton Watson. New York: Columbia University Press.

———. 2015. *Zhaungzi*. Translated by Hakjoo Kim. Goyang-si, South Korea: Yeonamseoga.

# CONTRIBUTORS

Tauʻalofa Angaʻaelangi
United Theological College, North Parramatta (Australia)
School of Theology, Charles Sturt University (Australia)

Sarah W. Ayub
Forman Christian College, Lahore (Pakistan)
Naulakha Presbyterian Church, Lahore (Pakistan)

Anton Deik
Bethlehem Bible College, Bethlehem (Palestine)

D. Gnanaraj
Torch Trinity Graduate University (Korea)

Elaine W. F. Goh
Seminari Theoloji Malaysia (Malaysia)

Jione Havea
Trinity Methodist Theological College (Aotearoa / New Zealand)
Public and Contextual Theology (PaCT) research centre, Charles Sturt University (Australia)

Sehee Kim
School of Theology, Boston University (USA)

Brian Fiu Kolia
Malua Theological College (Samoa)
University of Divinity (Australia)

Peter H. W. Lau
Seminari Theoloji Malaysia (Malaysia)
University of Sydney (Australia)

M. Alroy Mascrenghe
Department of Religious Studies, University of Cape Town (South Africa)
Methodist Church (Sri Lanka)

Clement Tsz Ming Tong
Carey Theological College, Vancouver (Canada)
Department of Asian Studies, University of British Columbia (Canada)

Laila Vijayan
United Theological College, Bangalore (India)
Senate of Serampore College, University (India)

Mariana Waqa
Vunilagi Community Reading Project (Fiji)
School of Theology, Charles Sturt University (Australia)

# Scripture Index

*Hebrew Scriptures/Old Testament*

Genesis
| | |
|---|---:|
| 1:11 | 59 |
| 1:11–12 | 59 |
| 1:12 | 59 |
| 1:27 | 20 |
| 2:7 | 35, 60 |
| 2–3 | 59–60, 64 |
| 2:5 | 59 |
| 2:6 | 59, 91 |
| 2:8–9 | 59 |
| 2:10–14 | 59 |
| 3 | 54 |
| 3:14–19 | 59 |
| 3:17–19 | 60 |
| 3:18 | 59 |
| 3:19b | 60 |
| 4 | 59 |
| 12:1–3 | 63 |
| 12:6–7 | 63 |
| 30:4 | 182 |
| 30:9 | 182 |
| 37–50 | 135 |

Exodus
| | |
|---|---:|
| 3:8 | 63 |
| 13:25 | 46 |
| 24:7 | 90 |
| 30:34–36 | 92 |
| 33:3 | 92 |

Leviticus
| | |
|---|---:|
| 11:45 | 182 |

Numbers
| | |
|---|---:|
| 6:25 | 121, 129 |
| 23:21 | 30 |

Deuteronomy
| | |
|---|---:|
| 22:22 | 182 |
| 28:50 | 129 |

Judges
| | |
|---|---:|
| 5:25 | 46 |

1 Samuel
| | |
|---|---:|
| 25:43 | 182 |

2 Samuel
| | |
|---|---:|
| 13:5 | 99 |
| 20:16 | 46 |

1 Kings
| | |
|---|---:|
| 2:43 | 130 |

2 Kings
| | |
|---|---:|
| 18:36 | 130 |

Isaiah
| | |
|---|---:|
| 6:1 | 94 |
| 52:14 | 109 |

## Scripture Index

| | | | |
|---|---|---|---|
| 57:13 | 35, 87 | 7:6–27 | 118 |
| 59:16 | 109 | 7:27 | 118 |
| 63:5 | 109 | 8 | 18, 85 |
| | | 8:1–21 | 189 |
| Jeremiah | | 8:1–36 | 122 |
| 9:16 | 46 | 8:8 | 117 |
| 20:18 | 30, 159 | 8:18 | 117 |
| 29:7 | 18 | 8:22 | 46 |
| | | 8:35 | 117 |
| Psalms | | 9:1–12 | 85 |
| 19:4–6 | 178 | 9:1–18 | 122 |
| 23:1 | 80 | 9:10 | 17, 45 |
| 31:18 | 129 | 9:13–18 | 118 |
| 37 | 189 | 10:2 | 99 |
| 39:6 | 49 | 10:17 | 46 |
| 39:12 | 49 | 10:19 | 46 |
| 47:8 | 94 | 10:27 | 99 |
| 49 | 189 | 11:4 | 99 |
| 67:2 | 129 | 11:12 | 46 |
| 80:1 | 80 | 11:21 | 99 |
| 80:4 | 129 | 12:4 | 46 |
| 80:8 | 129 | 12:21 | 99 |
| 80:20 | 129 | 13:13 | 46 |
| 111 | 189 | 13:22 | 46 |
| 111:10 | 96 | 13:24 | 46 |
| 119:135 | 129 | 14:1 | 46 |
| 143:4 | 109 | 14:23 | 30 |
| | | 16:26 | 30 |
| Proverbs | | 18:9 | 30 |
| 1 | 85 | 18:22 | 117 |
| 1–9 | 115, 122, 123 | 19:8 | 117 |
| 1:2–6 | 117 | 19:14 | 46 |
| 1:7 | 45, 96 | 21:6 | 35 |
| 1:20–33 | 118, 122 | 21:9 | 175 |
| 2:4–5 | 117 | 22:6 | 46 |
| 3:13 | 117 | 22:14 | 119 |
| 3:13–18 | 118, 189 | 22:29 | 30 |
| 3:13–20 | 122 | 24:21–22 | 130 |
| 4:6–9 | 118 | 26:4–5 | 130 |
| 5:1–6 | 118 | 27:15 | 175 |
| 5:1–14 | 46 | 31 | 124 |
| 5:3–5 | 124 | 31:10 | 175 |
| 5:5 | 118 | 31:10–31 | 124 |

Scripture Index

| | | | |
|---|---|---|---|
| 31:10–33 | 46, 117 | 2:1–11 | 189 |
| 31:13 | 30 | 2:3 | 179, 191 |
| | | 2:5 | 186 |
| Job | | 2:7 | 176, 178 |
| 1:21 | 176 | 2:8 | 179 |
| 3:3–5 | 159 | 2:11 | 94 |
| 3:11 | 95 | 2:13 | 104 |
| 7:16 | 49 | 2:14 | 104 |
| 28 | 189 | 2:15 | 72 |
| 28:28 | 96 | 2:16 | 105 |
| | | 2:16–17 | 106, 107 |
| Song of Songs | | 2:17 | 72, 80 |
| 4 | 175 | 2:18 | 176 |
| | | 2:18–19 | 190 |
| Ecclesiastes | | 2:18–23 | 29–39 |
| 1:1 | 176, 178 | 2:21 | 72 |
| 1:1–2 | 69 | 2:22 | 47 |
| 1:1–2:9 | 192 | 2:24 | 39 |
| 1:2 | 22, 87, 88, 119, 120 | 2:25–26 | 43–52 |
| 1:2–12:8 | 127 | 2:26 | 18, 49, 119, 182 |
| 1:3 | 30 | 3:1 | 2, 191 |
| 1:3–11 | 24 | 3:1–8 | 6, 131, 158, 196 |
| 1:3–12:7 | 69 | 3:1–15 | 5 |
| 1:4–7 | 1 | 3:9 | 1, 47 |
| 1:4–8 | 175 | 3:9–10 | 190 |
| 1:4–11 | 39 | 3:9–13 | 10, 53–66 |
| 1:5 | 178 | 3:10–12 | 39 |
| 1:7 | 88, 90 | 3:11 | 20, 131, 182 |
| 1:8 | 1, 106, 123 | 3:13 | 182, 191 |
| 1:9 | 1 | 3:14 | 131, 182 |
| 1:9–10 | 175 | 3:16 | 89, 160 |
| 1:11 | 89 | 3:16–17 | 5, 107, 108, 137, 138, 158, 160, 193 |
| 1:12 | 176, 178 | 3:16–4:3 | 69–83 |
| 1:13 | 190, 191 | 3:17 | 182 |
| 1:13–18 | 189 | 3:17–18 | 130 |
| 1:14 | 88 | 3:18–20 | 89 |
| 1:14–16 | 188 | 3:20 | 195 |
| 1:16 | 176, 178 | 3:22 | 107 |
| 1:16–17 | 88 | 4:1 | 43, 50, 72, 73, 75, 160, 192, 193 |
| 1:16–18 | 19 | 4:1–3 | 72, 73, 75, 128, 137, 158, 160, 195 |
| 1:17–18 | 13–25 | | |
| 1:18 | 88, 89, 189 | | |
| 2:1 | 117 | 4:2–3 | 73, 75, 80 |

| | | | |
|---|---|---|---|
| 4:3 | 83, 106 | 7:25 | 128 |
| 4:4 | 123 | 7:26–28 | 43, 50–51, 175 |
| 4:8 | 160, 176 | 7:29 | 138 |
| 4:13 | 192 | 8:1 | 1, 8, 115, 121, 123–125, 189 |
| 4:13–16 | 192 | 8:1–9 | 5, 127–138 |
| 4:16–26 | 128 | 8:1–17 | 141–151 |
| 5:1 | 182 | 8:1–21 | 189 |
| 5:1–6 | 118 | 8:2–9 | 72, 75 |
| 5:1–7 | 160 | 8:7 | 189 |
| 5:2 | 182 | 8:9 | 192 |
| 5:2–6 | 182 | 8:10 | 56 |
| 5:6 | 47 | 8:10–17 | 69–83, 109 |
| 5:7 | 182 | 8:11 | 109, 186 |
| 5:8 | 47, 181, 193 | 8:12–13 | 96, 182 |
| 5:8–9 | 75, 137 | 8:14 | 24, 56, 89, 191 |
| 5:11 | 47, 176 | 8:15 | 131, 182, 191 |
| 5:15 | 176 | 8:17 | 111, 131 |
| 5:17 | 47 | 9:1–2 | 193, 194 |
| 5:18 | 191 | 9:1–10 | 72, 73 |
| 6:2 | 89, 123, 182 | 9:2 | 191 |
| 6:3 | 123 | 9:4–6 | 106–107 |
| 6:3–5 | 89 | 9:5–6 | 181 |
| 6:4 | 95 | 9:7 | 179, 181 |
| 6:8 | 189 | 9:9 | 118, 123, 175, 179, 181, 182 |
| 6:12 | 131 | 9:10 | 121 |
| 7:1 | 106 | 9:11–12 | 72 |
| 7:1–4 | 195 | 9:13–18 | 118 |
| 7:5 | 106, 123 | 9:14 | 123 |
| 7:10–12 | 85–97 | 9:15 | 123 |
| 7:13 | 121, 188 | 10:3 | 129 |
| 7:13–14 | 39 | 10:4 | 129 |
| 7:13–18 | 53–66 | 10:12 | 106 |
| 7:14 | 116 | 10:16 | 193 |
| 7:15 | 193, 194 | 10:19 | 179 |
| 7:15–18 | 72, 99–111 | 10:20 | 129, 166 |
| 7:15–22 | 5 | 11:1 | 3 |
| 7:16 | 117 | 11:1–6 | 5 |
| 7:16–17 | 188 | 11:7–12:7 | 24 |
| 7:19 | 106, 128 | 11:9 | 100, 138, 181, 182 |
| 7:20 | 138 | 12:1–7 | 176 |
| 7:23 | 128 | 12:3 | 123 |
| 7:23–24 | 94 | 12:7 | 24 |
| 7:23–8:1 | 115–125 | 12:8 | 22, 119, 120, 196 |

| | |
|---|---|
| 12:9–11 | 3 |
| 12:9–14 | 24, 186 |
| 12:10 | 80 |
| 12:11 | 71, 81 |
| 12:12 | 9 |
| 12:13–14 | 24, 181, 194 |
| 12:14 | 100, 138, 182 |

Esther
| | |
|---|---|
| 3:3 | 130 |

Daniel
| | |
|---|---|
| 1:18–21 | 136 |
| 3 | 135 |
| 8:27 | 109 |
| 9:17 | 129 |

Nehemiah
| | |
|---|---|
| 11:23 | 130 |

2 Chronicles
| | |
|---|---|
| 8:15 | 130 |
| 9:21 | 109 |

*Deuterocanonical Books*

Sirach
| | |
|---|---|
| 19:20 | 93 |
| 24 | 85–97 |

*Christian Scriptures/New Testament*

Matthew
| | |
|---|---|
| 10:16–24 | 135 |
| 22:2 | 135 |

Luke
| | |
|---|---|
| 24:25–27 | 127 |
| 24:44–45 | 127 |

John
| | |
|---|---|
| 5:39 | 127 |
| 14:16 | 167 |

Acts
| | |
|---|---|
| 5:27–29 | 135 |

Romans
| | |
|---|---|
| 13:1–7 | 135 |

1 Corinthians
| | |
|---|---|
| 10:23 | 100 |

2 Corinthians
| | |
|---|---|
| 1:20 | 127 |

Titus
| | |
|---|---|
| 3:1 | 135 |

1 Peter
| | |
|---|---|
| 2:13–17 | 135 |

Revelation
| | |
|---|---|
| 21:3–4 | 158 |

*Asian Classical Texts*

| | |
|---|---|
| Akaporul Vilakkam | 172 |
| Analects | 6 |
| Bhagavad-gītā | 6 |
| Dao de Jing | 6 |
| The Grand Scribe's Records | 187 |
| Heart Sutra | 6 |
| HY Zhuangzi Yinde | 102–105 |
| I Ching | 6 |

| | |
|---|---|
| Kaliththogai | 179 |
| Mathurai Kanchi | 177 |
| Pathu pattu | 177 |
| Puraporul Venpaa Maalai | 174 |
| Qiushui | 102, 104 |
| Qiwulun | 103–105 |
| Sangam | 171–182 |
| Silapathikaram | 154, 163, 165 |
| Tirukural | 154 |
| Thirupalliyellucchi | 173 |
| Tholkappiyam | 171, 172 |
| Xiaoyiuyao | 103 |
| Xiuyaoyou | 103 |
| Zhuangzi | 99 |

www.ingramcontent.com/pod-product-compliance
Lightning Source LLC
Chambersburg PA
CBHW022019220426
43663CB00007B/1139